Four Acres under Slavnik

FOUR ACRES
UNDER SLAVNIK

A Slovenian Migration Story

AMY FRADEL

Head of Tide Press
Belfast, Maine

Book design by Jay Martsi.
Printed in the United States of America.

ISBN: 979-8-9887532-0-9 (paperback)—979-8-9887532-1-6 (ebook)

Library of Congress Control Number: 2023918745

This book was set in BC Figural, a contemporary digitization of typefaces designed by Oldřich Menhart in the 1940s with forms modeled by spirited marks of the hand-held pen.

Contents

Preface

My interest in genealogy began when my husband, Arch Davis, told me he wished that he had the photo of his Uncle Arch, a New Zealander killed in the Greek islands during World War Two, that had been among his mother's cherished possessions. I promised him that I would find it. Without ever leaving my house in Maine, I talked with his extended family in New Zealand and Australia, chatted with kindred souls, and discovered a family tree going back to Cornwall in the 1700s. Military archives, ships' manifests, old photos, newspaper articles, and books written by distant relatives illuminated details about his ancestors we never imagined. After six months I found the original photo of Uncle Arch in the archives of a New Zealand library and obtained a digital copy. The process of discovery was so engrossing and fun that I did not know what to do with myself when it was done. My husband said, "Why don't you do your own family?"

My father's parents, Janez and Marija Fradel, immigrated to the United States from Slovenia in 1913. The Fradel family is small and my father, aunts, and uncle were dead, so I did not think I would learn much more than what I already knew, but I asked my cousins to share their memories, however small and seemingly insignificant. My mother had already told me every story she knew about

1

her in-laws and I planned to visit her in Maryland for a few days in October 2011 to do more research. Two weeks before my departure she had a heart attack. Death cheated me of my chance to have that long conversation with her about the mysteries of the past and look through family photo albums one more time.

When it was time, I traveled to Maryland to help clean out her house, my childhood home I had left 40 years earlier. To reach the attic of the house, one had to climb a ladder, remove a panel in the ceiling, and hoist oneself through the narrow space. The attic had no floor; instead, loose boards were laid across the joists, and stepping in between them would break through the ceiling, so we seldom ventured up there. For decades my brothers told stories about a German sword and Nazi banners hidden away, but I never saw them.

Alone in the house I decided to confirm that there was nothing of interest up there. That's when I found the cardboard box. It contained my grandparents' naturalization papers, old photos from Slovenia, and dozens of letters written in Slovene to my grandparents between 1913 and 1961. Everything came from my Grandma Fradel's house in Latrobe, Pennsylvania, and had notes from my Aunt Mary and my father on them. I knew I was on to something interesting and mailed the entire box to my home in Maine for more careful inspection.

I found a professional translator willing and able to work with the flowing, old world script and archaic dialect. David Dolenc produced word-for-word translations of 70 letters, explained obscure words and phrases, and provided cultural interpretations.

In 2012 I took a road trip to research my family's story and visit the places associated with my Slovene grandparents. It started in Cass, West Virginia, a lumber town where my grandfather began his new life in America cutting trees on Cheat Mountain. Cass is now a state park where visitors can ride the old logging train up the mountain. I stopped at the church where my grandparents were married, visited historical societies and libraries, drove around, and soaked up the ambiance. I followed my grandparents' steps through

Pennsylvania, to Black Lick and Farrell, and swung by their house in Latrobe. The new owners showed me around and I felt really good about their stewardship of the old place. I met up with second cousins, Jan Brooks and Joe Godina Jr., then I headed to Cleveland to visit Alma Babuder, a "shirt-tail" cousin. She had lots to say, pictures to share, and I enjoyed the visit tremendously. Lastly, I dropped in to see my first cousin, Pat Walker, in Medina, Ohio.

"Amy, you are the first cousin to ever come to my home, and in honor of your visit I am going to open this box." The bankers box sat on her dining room table. "When my mother died 25 years ago my father sent it to me and said the family pictures were in here, but I wasn't in the mood to look at my childhood pictures and I have never actually opened it."

Underneath Pat's baby pictures were more letters to our grandmother, lots more letters—maybe 250 more—along with photographs and memorabilia, including lace pieces that Grandma had made, and bits of traditional Slovene clothing. I marveled at a tiny decorative belt—it might have fit around one of my thighs. There were also hundreds of wartime letters from our Aunt Jane, who had served overseas as a nurse. I left Pat's house with most of the goods, knowing that I needed to get a better job so I could afford to have all these letters translated.

I could guess who some of the people in the photos were, but what could I do with one-hundred-year-old photos of unidentified people? All those people and their children were long dead. I might never know. I decided to contact my cousins in Slovenia, Milenka and Ivan Fabjančič. We had fun together during my visit there in 1977 when I was a footloose young woman wandering through Europe and Asia. We had not been in touch for decades. I changed my profile picture on Facebook to a youthful photo of my cousins and me standing in front of the family home in Povžane, and sent friend requests to the people I thought were likely to be their children. Soon we were communicating again. I scanned and emailed the old letters and photos, along with lots of questions. Ivan's daughter,

Marinka, proved to be an able translator. They told me that the content of the letters was all news to them. In their family people did not talk about the past.

Before long, they invited me to visit and I thought that it would be super to travel to Slovenia for *opasilo*, a village festival held every August my grandmother had talked about. I wanted to go in 2013, because it would have marked one hundred years since my grandmother's departure, but the timing did not work for us. I selected two weeks in August 2014, and told my husband that we were going to Slovenia.

"I don't want to go to Slovenia," was his exact response. I told him that this was a family trip, and I had to have family with me. I also needed someone to protect me from any overzealous hospitality.

"Aren't you going to learn some Slovene?" I asked in the lead-up to the trip. Arch is usually quite interested in learning new languages. He told me I could teach him some words on the plane.

The family picked us up at the Trieste airport, and we stayed at Biščevi, the 500-year-old stone house where my grandmother had lived. Among the family who assembled were some excellent young English speakers. My relatives were attentive, hospitable, intelligent, and lively hosts who, despite my preconceived notions, did not over-feed us. They took us on a tour of my family's ancestral homeland, focusing on important sites, and our passion for music and history. My husband fell in love with Slovenia.

Milenka's husband, Alojz Grahor, turned out to be an intrepid sleuth in the quest for family history. He and Milenka had already visited the church where the status animarum—the book that records baptisms, marriages, and deaths—was kept (it has since been moved to the Koper diocesan archives) and assembled a fabulous family tree on a green poster board showing the connecting relationships. Whenever I pose a question to Alojz, he finds the answer. Ivan Fabjančič is also a treasure. He took those old photos, drove off to visit the most ancient denizens of the region and came back a few hours later with the identities of most of the people in the pictures.

Our relationship with my cousins—and with Slovenia—has strengthened over the years. In January 2015 we received a wedding invitation for that July. Archie declared that if he was going back to Slovenia, he needed to learn Slovene to be able to converse with Ivan over slivovic and a few beers, and has been studying Slovene every day since then. In 2018 and again, the following year, we attended language classes at the University of Primorska, stayed at Airbnbs in Koper, just steps from the university, and rented a car to get around. We have yet to tire of Slovenia. We hoped to make this an annual event, but a global coronavirus pandemic prevented us from returning for two years. I now depend on Archie's language ability for translation and communication, although when I am there, I am able to get by with a few Slovene words, gestures, some goodwill, and the excellent English spoken by the younger generation.

My 12 years of research has traced the Fradel line back to the early 1600s, when record-keeping began in rural Primorska. This project has turned into something bigger than names and dates. My office and laptop are filled with letters, photos, scraps of papers, notes on conversations, and memorabilia. My head is full of stories, memories and dotted lines connecting everything together. I've heard the tinkling of the bells as the cows come home from pasture in Povžane. I have been to Trieste and Ellis Island. I am full of the who, what, when, where, and why of the immigration experience of my Slovenian ancestors.

My grandparents and their extended families were participants in the upheavals and cataclysmic changes Europe underwent from 1913 to 1961. I am privileged to know about their lives. I feel compelled to gather all that I have learned and write their story, for once I am gone, who else will do it? Even if nobody ever reads this book, I will write it anyway.

Amy Fradel
18 January 2022

Introduction

This work of non-fiction shares historical accounts of a Slovene immigrant family in America, and the family that remained in Slovenia. The guts of the narrative come from letters that were written to my grandmother in America by her brother and sister back home. I heard these stories growing up, some written by my Aunt Mary who had her own interest in preserving the family's history. My cousins in Slovenia have supplied a wealth of information that often filled in missing pieces and enriched the content of the letters. Additionally, I have searched the excellent digital libraries of Slovenia, studied the history of the region, and visited these places myself. I've used internet-based and published resources to support my knowledge of my grandparents' lives in America, European politics as it played out through the decades, and the World Wars. My knowledge as a nurse practitioner helps me understand the medical conditions described in the letters and the health issues of the period.

My people come from Primorska, the coastal region of Slovenia. Specifically, they lived in the valley between the Brkini Hills and the Čičarija plateau of southwestern Primorska. This book relates the unique history of Primorska as my relatives experienced it, from 1913 to 1961.

I always thought migration to America was a one-way trip. I imagined how frightening it would have been to board a ship knowing that you were never coming back. As my research progressed, I was surprised to find out that it did not always happen that way. Nearly everybody from Brkini and Čičarija who got on a transatlantic ship planned to return in a few years, and a majority did return. Statistics put the pre-1914 return rate for Slovenes and Croatians at over 50 percent, but as political and economic realities dramatically changed after the Great War, any migrant knew that the voyage to America most likely meant never returning home.

The Slovenes in Brkini and the valley under Slavnik are all connected by blood or marriage somewhere in the foggy reaches of time, but aside from parents and siblings, the most important factor in my grandparents' social relationships was the shared experience of migration. Those of us in countries where our ancestors landed tend to view migration positively, as a fresh start in a new world, but the painful reality of migration is one of loss for both sides. Migrants who traveled to America endured the obvious losses of home, social support, language and culture. On the other side, the departures tore apart the fabric that weaves village communities and families together. Prior to 1890, migrations to America had not occurred on such a monumental scale.

Transforming a story told in handwritten letters in an archaic Slovene dialect to something that modern English readers can appreciate requires the explanation of three key concepts that I present here, rather than trying to explain them within the story. The first is knowing how the language sounds, as this will demystify names and places, and enhance the reader's comprehension and satisfaction. Next is understanding that every house in rural Slovenia has a name. At the time of these events, people were still identified by the name of the house they lived in, although they also had official surnames. Relationships were built around these house names, and you cannot simply change the name to the official surname and get on with the story. I have included a family tree built on house names to show how the main characters are related. The third factor to appreciate is the repetitive use of first names.

SLOVENIAN PRONUNCIATION

In Slovene, every letter is pronounced separately and every word is spelled as it is pronounced. Some sounds are tricky for English speakers. My observation is that many of the sounds unique to Slovene are formed in the front of the mouth, while English sounds come from the back of the mouth. Think about using your lips and cheeks more when you try these Slovene sounds.

These are the hardest:

c always "ts" sound, as in bits.

h never silent, always fully pronounced from the back of the mouth, as in home or hell.

r always rolled. Press the tip of your tongue to the roof of your mouth just behind your teeth, then begin the word "red" in the middle of the mouth and let it roll forward across the top of your tongue. Feel the tip of your tongue vibrate.

š "sh" as in shoes

ž similar to the "s" in leisure or pleasure. It is a little harder sound than sh or š.

č "ch" as in church. It is even harder than ž

šč often appear together. Practice saying "sh-ch" and then speed it up!

Here are some simple sound differences:

a "aw" as in artist or car.

e "eh" as in pet, or egg.

g always hard as in lag.

i variable as in meet, or bit. Never "eye".

j always pronounced as "y" as in yes. At the end of a word it can soften the "l" sound or be silent. Fradel and Cergol are sometimes written Fradelj and Cergolj.

k replaces a hard "c" sound. Karl rather than Carl.

l in many languages, Slovene included, can have a hard or a soft sound.

o as in hot, or pot.

s purely "s" as in set or sir.

u as in spoon or balloon.

The letters **b, d, f, m, n, p,** and **z** have sounds that are similar to English. The letters **q, w, x,** and **y** are not present in Slovene. If you see them, they are words adopted from another language. **V** has tricky rules. Depending on its location in the word, it is pronounced with a "v" sound as in victory, or as the "u" sound in balloon. Here are some examples that are important to the story.

Slavnik mountain is pronounced *Slaw-oo-nik*. In modern Slovene, my grandparents' village is spelled Povžane and pronounced *Po-oo-zh-aw-ne,* but when spoken the "oo" often sounds like a soft "l", as in *Pol-zh-aw-ne* and in fact, in this archaic dialect people wrote what they heard and it was often spelled Polžane. If the writer wrote it this way, I left it. The word *polž* means snail, and my modern Povžane cousins have taken advantage of this quirk in the language to make the snail the mascot for their village and business. I have kept the Slovenian *Trst* for Trieste as it was written in the letter to give the reader a feel for the sound of the language because language is a treasured part of Slovenian culture.

The words of letters written in the archaic dialect were often run together, without commas or periods, and spelling was not standardized—they spelled what they heard. The first translations came up with names that were inconsistently spelled, with a little Italian thrown in, along with a guesswork of spelling and grammar. I later learned about correct modern Slovenian spelling and grammar, but have kept some archaic forms for sentimentality, flavor, and convenience. The evolution of my surname, Fradel, is an example of dialect, influence of other languages, and literacy. In the status animarum of the 1600s, it was recorded as "Fredeu," but the "u" gradually morphed into "Fredel," and by 1795 became "Fradel." In modern Slovenia it is pronounced with a rolled r, an "aw" sound for the a, and then softened at the end with what some linguists call an Italian l: "Frrraw-delj." My family in America say "Fruh-dell" while my Uncle Rudy's grandchildren in America said "Fray-dle" to rhyme with ladle. The spelling depended on the way the priests—the record keepers at the time—heard it, and whether he recorded it in Latin, German, or Slovene in the status animarum.

HOUSE NAMES

Even today in rural Slovenia each house has its own name and the family that lives there is called by that house name. This custom goes back centuries and the house name is likely that of the person who built it. Nowadays, people know their neighbors' surnames and refer to the house by its number, but in the past, neighbors usually knew each other only by their house name. For example, the house where the Fradel family lived was called Jurkotevi. In modern standard Slovene, a woman of that house is Jurkoteva but in the old days it could have been Jurkotova or Jurkova. A man of that house is Jurko. An easy guide is this: If it ends in "evi" it is the name of the house and all the people living there. If it ends in "eva" or "ova" it is a woman. With a different ending, it is a man.

Names could get tricky when a woman married. Sometimes her house of origin was an important identifier and the name of her husband's house was less important. For example, Margeritha Fradel of Jurkotevi married a man from the house, Liparjevi. By rule of her present abode, she should be Margeritha Liparjova, but the speaker might call her Margeritha Jurkotova, to remind the listener where she came from and how she is related to all the other Fradels of Jurkotevi.

Pepa Babuder was born at Blaževi. She and her husband rented and moved so often that a house name could not give her an identity, so everyone kept calling her Pepa Blaževa. Marija Ban was so clearly identified with the gostilna on Gabrk that Marija of Gabrk superseded all other names she might acquire. A man was clearly identified as the head of the house wherever he resided.

The code surrounding Slovene names and houses and land ownership is difficult to decipher. My family made a map for me of all the residences in Povžane, indicating the house name and the official surname of the family that lived in that house one hundred years ago. They had to guess at some. It has taken me ten years and five trips to Slovenia to get this far in my understanding of the code, and I suspect that there is more to learn.

FIRST NAMES

Children received a saint's name and nearly every family had a Josef, a Janez, and a Marija before they used other names. My own family in America (circa 1950) had Joseph Emil, then John Anthony, and I was Mary Anne. As soon as parents did their duty to the saints, they start using nicknames. My parents never called me anything other than Amy.

Names were used over and over again within the same set of siblings. When a child died, a later sibling would receive the same name. Among Valentin and Ivana Fradel's 12 children, three were named Marija, and two were Ivana. To add to the confusion, male and female versions of a name were used in the same family: Josef and Josefa, Ivan and Ivana, Marjan and Marija, Frane and Franca, Anton and Antonija, Stefan and Stefanija, Emil and Emilia.

Variations on Josef were abundant: Jože, Jožef, Josip, and for girls, Jozefa and Josepina. Every Josef and Josefa were at one time or another nick-named Pepe, if a boy, and Pepa, Pepina, Pepka or Pepca if a girl. It was often difficult to know which Pepe or Pepa a letter-writer was talking about. For example, Tona had a husband, a brother, and a son all named Josef. She called her husband Pepe, while her brother was Pepe and her son was Jože.

Variations on John were equally plentiful. Janez or Ivan were used interchangeably, while standard variations include Johan, Joannes and Milan, and nicknames included Janko and Nane. For girls, there was Ivana, Ivanka and Johana. Diminutives were added: A Franca could become Fani, Fanika, Fanica, Francka or Franciska. Antonija almost universally became Tona and Anton could become Tonči. The point is that children were given time-honored names and then lavished with nicknames. Later, names became Italianized or Americanized. To relieve the confusion in this book, I have selected a nickname or variant for each character and stuck with it.

I've used the house name for every man, as he would have been called by his neighbors, and inserted his surname in parentheses when I think a reminder will be helpful to the reader. I selected a spelling variation of each woman's house name whether or not it is modern standard Slovene, and I apologize in advance to any Slovene readers who think that I do not know how to spell. It's dialect? (That's always a good excuse in language arguments.)

The views presented in *Four Acres Under Slavnik* are my views, based on the letters, my research, and my conclusions. As I continue to study the migration experience and the history of Slovenia, I reserve the privilege of changing my views at any time.

U.S   Marija Fabjančič ✚
1890-1982

Biščevi ▭   Jožef
1887-1949

Bazletevi ⬉   Tona
1886-1936

Bilkotevi ⬉   Rezina
1883-1963

Frane Fabjančič
1901-1979

Frane Fabjančič
1874-1959

Helena
1886

Francisca
1884

Josefa
1879

Terezija
1873

Ivana
1867-1911 ✚

Marija
1872-1895 ✚

Rocol
⬉

Terezija   Marija ⬉ ✚
1861 Twins

Josef
1849-1922

Ivan
1845-1885
Fell off wagon

Stefan Cergolj
1832-1916

Stefan Fabjančič
1808-1884

Biščevi

Košančevi

✚ *Marriage*   ⬉ *Residence Change*

Family Tree

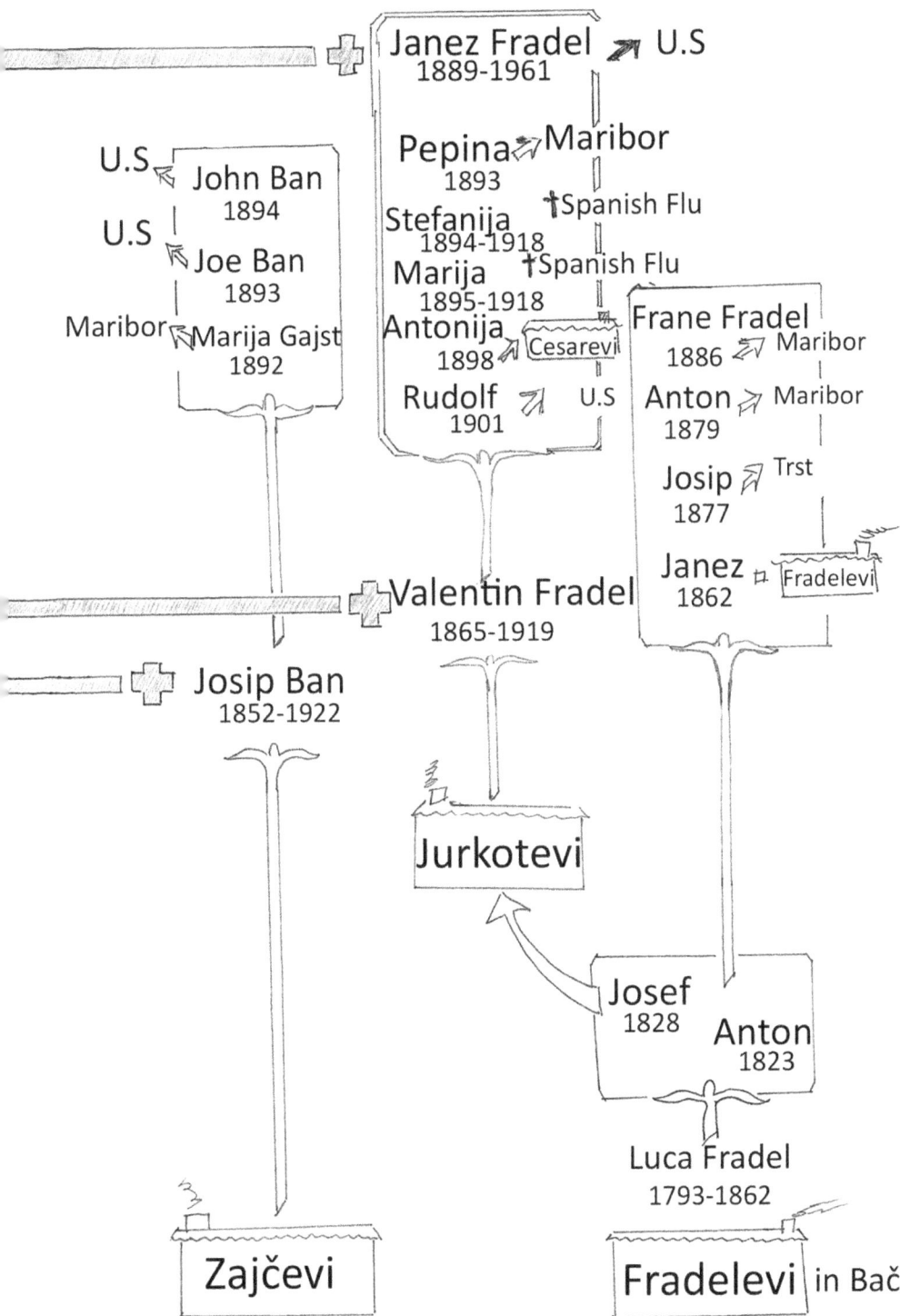

Janez Fradel
1889-1961 ↗ U.S

✝

Pepina ↗ Maribor
1893

†Spanish Flu

Stefanija
1894-1918

†Spanish Flu

Marija
1895-1918

Antonija
1898 ↗ Cesarevi

Frane Fradel
1886 ↗ Maribor

Rudolf ↗ U.S
1901

Anton ↗ Maribor
1879

Josip ↗ Trst
1877

Janez ⚷ Fradelevi
1862

U.S ↖ John Ban
1894

U.S ↗ Joe Ban
1893

Maribor ↖ Marija Gajst
1892

Valentin Fradel
1865-1919

✝

Josip Ban
1852-1922

Jurkotevi

Josef
1828

Anton
1823

Luca Fradel
1793-1862

Zajčevi

Fradelevi in Bač

By House Name

map by Amy Fradel graphics by Grace Davis

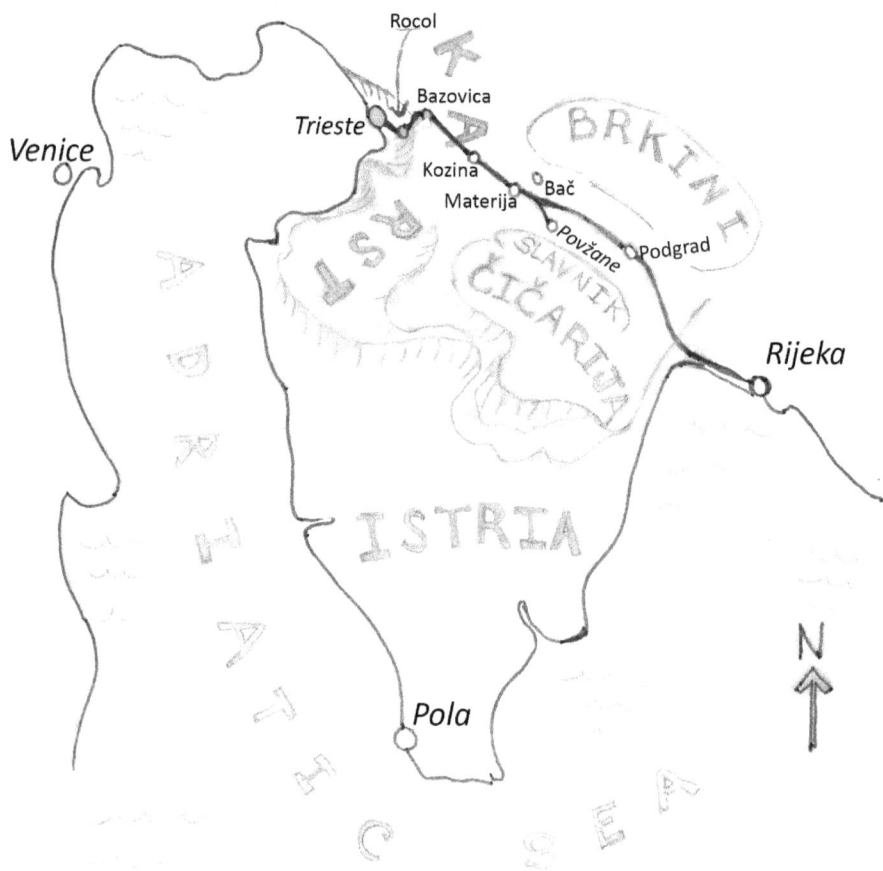

The Road from Trieste to Rijeka
in the Austro-Hungarian Empire

Gorica

Rocol

Bazovica

Trieste

Venice

Kozina

Bač

Materija

Povžane

Podgrad

KRAS

BRKINI

SLAVNIK

ČIČARIJA

Rijeka

ADRIATIC

ISTRIA

N

Pola

SEA

map by Amy Frudel graphics by Grace Davis

CHAPTER ONE

1913: Leaving Home

The port cities of Trieste and Koper are tucked into the northeast coast of the Adriatic Sea. Towering behind them is a thousand-foot-high escarpment, the edge of the Karst plateau of Slovenia. The Karst is formed of porous limestone and is full of caves and underground rivers. To the south, the Istrian peninsula juts into the Adriatic Sea. A road cuts across the base of the triangular peninsula connecting Trieste to the port of Rijeka on the other side. From Trieste, the old road winds steeply to the town of Kozina at the top of the escarpment, then traverses a wide valley for twelve miles to the town of Podgrad. The north side of the valley is a ridge called Brkini. On the south side of the valley is a mountain ridge called Slavnik which is part of the Čičarija plateau. After Podgrad, the road climbs upward and winds through the forests of the Čičarija plateau before descending to the southern coast of the Istrian peninsula and Rijeka.

The Čičarija plateau is limestone. The Brkini ridge is an impermeable flysch rock. The two types of bedrock form a visual line about a half mile on the Brkini side of the valley road. Most of Čičarija lies within Croatia. The Slovene people who live along the valley road on the Čičarijan limestone side of the line cannot truthfully say that they are from Brkini despite their intimate social and cultural ties to it, but neither will they say that they are from Čičarija which might suggest that they are Croatian. They say *"nismo Čiči ne Brčini, smo juštu na konfini"* (we are not Čičarijan and not Brkini, we come from the border) or they might say "the valley", or more specifically describe that they live "under Slavnik." These are my people.

Slavnik mountain is forested and sparsely populated. From its peak one can look out over all the valley and Brkini, which is dotted with dozens of villages of tightly clustered two-storied homes and barns built of stone, and roofed with orange tiles. Brkini is known for its abundance of fruit and nut trees—apples, pears, plums, cherries, walnuts, and chestnuts. Its soil is impermeable and it lacks rivers and streams therefore it has never had enough water to reliably support agriculture. Until modern times, crops, animals, and people relied on a few shallow wells, cisterns, hand-dug ponds, and rain; in times of drought, hunger was real.

Four miles from Kozina on the valley road, under Slavnik mountain, three villages abut one another. Materija is the first and largest one, with houses on either side of the road, a post office, a store, and several places to eat and drink called *gostilnas*. On the north side of the road, Bač nestles on a slight hill. A few hundred feet beyond Materija a street cuts off to the south at a 45-degree angle into a cluster of 30 houses. This is Povžane, the village of my grandparents.

The houses of Povžane, built from hand hewn wood beams and stones dug out of the local fields, were patched, and rebuilt as time demanded. All the windows of the houses face Slavnik, and on warm mornings families would throw open the wooden shutters to greet the mountain that defined who they were. Those shutters were the only thing that held off the rain and cold on other days. Buildings for storage and animals adjoined the residences, making for a maze of paths and archways between the homes.

In the center of this maze sat a prosperous house called Košančevi in which the Fabjančič family had lived for centuries, even before the 1630s when the local church was built and the priest began a status animarum recording all baptisms, marriages, and deaths in

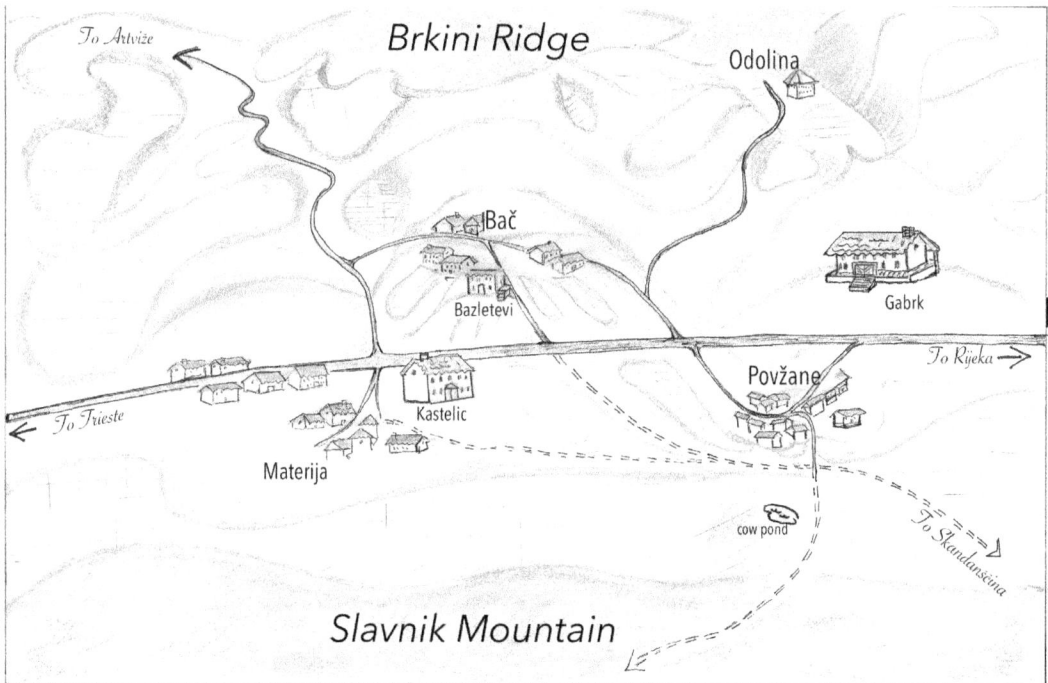

To Artviže

Brkini Ridge

Odolina

Bač

Bazletevi

Gabrk

To Rijeka

Povžane

To Trieste

Kastelic

Materija

cow pond

To Skandanščina

Slavnik Mountain

The Valley under Slavnik

map by Amy Fradel graphics by Grace Davis

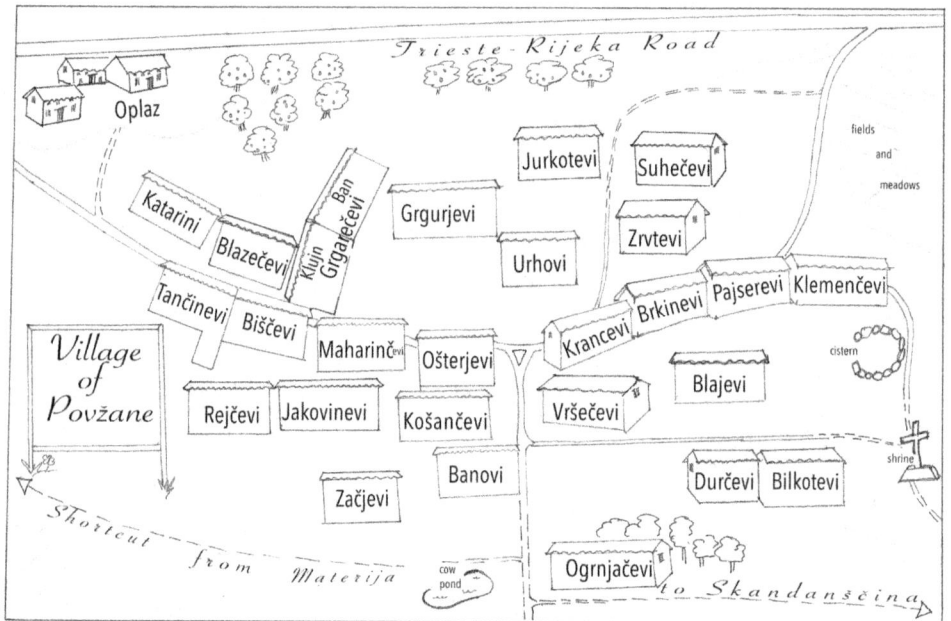

Trieste-Rijeka Road

Oplaz

fields
and
meadows

Katarini

Ban
Grgazečevi

Kluji

Jurkotevi

Suhečevi

Grgurjevi

Zrvtevi

Blazečevi

Urhovi

Tančinevi

Biščevi

Maharinčevi

Ošterjevi

Krancevi

Brkinevi

Pajserevi

Klemenčevi

cistern

Village
of
Povžane

Rejčevi

Jakovinevi

Košančevi

Vršečevi

Blajevi

shrine

Banovi

Durčevi

Bilkotevi

Začjevi

Shortcut from Materija

cow
pond

Ogrnjačevi

to Skandanščina

map by Amy Fradel graphics by Grace Davis

Houses of Požane

the region. In 1845 a son, Ivan Fabjančič, was born and in 1849 there was another son, Josef. Like most of the men of Brkini and the valley, the brothers were short and strong with smiling eyes in their youth. As they aged they became stout and their broad, round faces grew leathered and red after years of cutting trees, digging rocks, making lime, and tilling their few acres. As the eldest son, Ivan inherited Košančevi, and local custom determined he would always be called by his house name, Ivan Košanc. He married a Dekleva girl from Bač, and their household grew to include six daughters and a son. Josef faced the usual dilemma of a younger son. Should he go elsewhere, perhaps to work in the big city of Trieste, to earn money to purchase some land? Could he rent and hope to buy land gradually with the proceeds of his surplus produce in the Trieste market?

Josef was fortunate. The house called Biščevi was just a few minutes uphill stroll to the main road that cut through the village. The Cergolj family who lived there had two sons and twin daughters, but they lost their sons to early childhood plagues. The first twin, Terezija, married a man in Rocol in Trieste. The other twin, Marija Cergolj, would inherit Biščevi. In 1877, Josef Fabjančič of Košančevi was deemed to be a suitable match for Marija and ultimately he became the master known by all as Josef Biščev. He and his wife would have eight children but only four lived beyond their third birthday. The survivors were daughters, Rezina and Tona, and a son, Jožef. Their youngest was Marija, born on 23 November 1890. She was my grandmother.

The Košančevi and Biščevi cousins were the best of friends despite their age difference. For example, Ivana, the eldest daughter of Ivan Košanc was twenty years older than Marija, the youngest daughter of Josef Biščev. Tragedy struck the family when Ivan Košanc fell off a wagon in 1885. Wagon accidents were not an unusual cause of death; they were akin to the frequency of fatal car accidents today. He was only forty and his wife was pregnant with their sixth daughter. A woman with young children could not afford to be widowed for long, and his wife, Marija Dekleva, quickly remarried. This marriage produced no children so little Frane, only nine when his father died, eventually became master of Košančevi.

Located on the other side of the Trieste-Rijeka road was the village of Bač, perched on a small hill. The main street that curved through the village was lined with free standing homes, unlike the duplexes and rowhomes of Povžane. At number three stood the prosperous house called Fradelevi, and the family name remained that of the builder. A little piece of family lore said that the Fradels came from France but that had to be in the foggy reaches of time because the Fradels were living at Fradelevi when the priests began keeping records in the 1630s. Anton Fradel was born in 1823 and his brother, Josef, was born in 1828. Josef Fradel solved his younger son dilemma by purchasing a small house on the east side of Povžane at number eleven. The house name was Jurkotevi and Josef Fradel became known as Josef Jurko. He and his wife had three daughters and one son who survived the perils of childhood. Possibly because Josef Jurko started out with very little and had such a small family, Jurkotevi struggled financially. Their son, Valentin, was born in 1865 and despite his lack of affluence, a man with his own home and four acres was a desirable husband. In 1887 a match was made between 22-year-old Valentin and 20-year-old Ivana Fabjančič of Košančevi. Life was not easy for them. Their first born died at age two, and their first son, Janez Fradel, was born on 23 February 1889. He was to be my grandfather. Ivana bore eleven more children but only four girls, Pepina, Stefanija, Marija, and Antonija and one son, Rudolf, survived beyond three years.

The marriage of Valentin and Ivana drew the houses of Jurkotevi, Košančevi and Biščevi closer together. The marriage of Ivana's sister Marija Košančeva to Josip Ban, second son of the house of Zajčevi, drew them and their three sons into a tight kinship circle in Povžane. All the cousins were among the children who attended the newly built school in Materija, established by the Austro-Hungarian government. According to my grandmother, it was a five-minute walk from Povžane. It was one simple room with only desks and a slate board. A male teacher instructed in Slovene and discipline was maintained with a wooden ruler across the knuckles, and fear of a whipping upon returning home. Gathered close to a wood stove in winter, they learned reading, writing, arithmetic, geography, religion, and national songs. The girls were taught to sew and crochet by the teacher's wife and the boys also learned some practical skills. Classes were held six days a week, and the students were dismissed early enough to take coffee and bread to workers in the fields in the afternoon, and to help with chores at home.

The Biščevi children attended school every day and were encouraged by their family to do well. A few students whose family had a little money, such as Božidar Kastelic and Josef Dekleva, would go on to secondary school in Ljubljana, but most everyone was destined to continue farming. The Jurkotevi household struggled and the children stayed home to help with sick brothers and sisters, farming, and tending the livestock. As time went on it became apparent that their mother, Ivana, was not well. She suffered from tuberculosis.

Farmers grew what they needed for their families. The sale of their surplus produce: cheese, eggs, sheep, goats, chickens, pigs, milk, firewood, foraged mushrooms, and *brin* (juniper berries used to flavor gin) in the Trieste market—a twelve-mile walk along a gravel road— was vital to their meager economy. The more prosperous families owned a wagon with oxen to carry their goods to market. There was a train from Kozina to Trieste but it was not a practical way to get produce to the market. My grandmother recalled going to Trieste during the peaceful years before the Great War. Her daughter, my aunt Mary Hrebar, recorded her words:

> Mother first visited Trieste with her mother when she was six or seven. Then she joined her older brother and sisters in taking produce to the market by carrying their best produce on top of their heads in a basket with handles on it made from woven sticks called a *plenir*. It was supported on their heads with a roll made of old cloths or wool called a *svitek*.

Mother carried milk, eggs, homemade butter, cheese, cottage cheese, green beans, peas, carrots, dried beans, potatoes, cabbage, and fruit such as strawberries and cherries. Homemade *pršut*, *klobase*, and live chickens also went. When whole lambs or calves, hay, or bundles of wood and twigs were taken to market, the wagon with iron wheels, pulled by oxen, was used.

They would start to Trieste at 11 at night for the 12-mile walk. The road was winding and steep. They had to rest five times because of the heavy load on their heads. They walked to Kozina, then to Nasirec, Krvavi Potok. and Bazovica before they descended the Karst bluff to Rocol where her aunt lived, and into Trieste. In the villages along the way there were places to water oxen or hire additional animals for a particularly steep part of the road when needed. They would get there at five in the morning. After selling everything, they used the money to buy staples such as sugar, coffee, rice, and macaroni. Mother always bought tobacco for her father.

One bad experience Mother vividly remembers is the time there was an abundance of mushrooms around Povžane, so she picked quite a few, took them to market and found that there had been a bumper crop everywhere, as the marketplace was flooded with them, so much so that all the peddlers had to dump their mushrooms into the Adriatic Sea. That day she made only 17 cents, which she placed in her pocket. She bought a lemonade for two cents, had 15 cents left, and while drinking her lemonade a pickpocket stole her money. She had to borrow from her aunt in Rocol to bring home the coffee, sugar, etc. her mother expected. Mother had steady customers for the milk she brought in to market because her family never diluted it, as some did. After selling it to these people, who were actually wholesalers, they diluted it and re-sold it.

Aunt Mary tells another story that when Janez Fradel of Jurkotevi was 12 years old and in Trieste for market day, he sent a postcard to Marija Fabjančič of Biščevi. Getting anything in the mail was exciting, even if it was from your grown-up cousin's son whom you saw nearly every day. Aunt Mary told this story as evidence that they had been destined for one another from an early age but as the true story unfolds, I'm not so sure about destiny. Nevertheless, there was no stigma associated with marrying a first cousin, or in their case, a first cousin once removed.

Opasilo, a festival to honor the patron saint of the village, was the highlight of every year. Povžane is dedicated to St. George, whose feast day is 23 April, but since farmers are busy with planting in April, opasilo was and still is held on the second Sunday in August when the harvest is underway. After morning Mass, there was singing, dancing, and a picnic at the church, then a big feast at home, and more outdoor dancing to the sounds of accordions, guitar, and flute at night. Every village had, and still has, its own opasilo. One can stay quite busy throughout the summer attending the numerous festivities throughout Brkini and the valley. Traveling to other villages for their opasilos gave young men the opportunity to meet young women. Marija loved the excitement of opasilo; it was her chance to wear her best clothes, dance, flirt, and shine.

Marija finished school at age 14. She had been an excellent student and knew how to read and write Slovene well. She was admired by Božidar Kastelic, a smart and funny boy a few years older than her, but he disappeared to Ljubljana for a few years to study, something that a girl like Marija could not even consider. She worked in the fields with her parents and brother, Jožef. Sometimes they joined a crew of other young people to work for someone else for pay. One of the more pleasant tasks was walking in the evening to the grassy valley at the base of Slavnik where the cows grazed and drank from a hand dug pond, to lead them home. Her best friend and neighbor, Pepa Blaževa, would sometimes go with her. The task took little effort because the cows knew where to go. The sounds of the bells around their necks tinkled through the valley as the girls giggled and gossiped on the stroll home. As did her two older sisters, Tona and Rezina, before they married and had families of their own, she helped her mother around the house with cooking and housekeeping. Tona's little girl, Fani, lived at Biščevi and was like a little sister to Marija. Long walks to Mass at St. George in Tublje or St. Stephen in Brezovica in the evening and on Sundays provided additional opportunities to chat with her girlfriends. Marija's best friend was her brother Jožef who was two years older than her. They did the outdoor tasks together, went to Trieste, and opasilos together, and shared confidences. He looked out for her as a loving big brother would.

Jožef was a strong yet quiet and humble young man who dutifully and proudly knew his place in the world. He was Jožef Biščev, the only son and heir of his father. He lived in the most beautiful spot in the world and learned from his ancestors how to till its soil, respect its trees, and care for the animals. He embraced his duties to care for his parents. He was a Slovenian with a love for his language and culture. He loved to read and learn about the rest of the world. He was a citizen of Austria with respect for the Emperor Franz Josef, and when he was called to military service, he went. From 1907 men were allowed to vote and he appreciated the patriarchal order that the Empire brought to his corner of the world.

Marija was a beauty. (photo 1) She had a perfectly oval face, framed by wavy light brown hair, and soft brown eyes, with just a slightly Slavic look about her. She was somewhat vain and took great care about her clothes. By village standards, all the Biščevi girls dressed well, and they drew the eyes of the young men of the village. Marija had numerous admirers but her willful tendencies caused her to chase after the ones who did not win her parents' approval. She could marry after she turned 16 but there was no great hurry. Naturally, there was a lot for parents to consider, and although it was the father's duty to choose his daughter's husband, he would make the decision only after consulting with the elders of the extended family. A husband should come from a family that they liked, he should be hardworking and sober, and preferably be a firstborn son who would provide a home and land for his wife. Less desirable was a man with a trade who might take her to live in

Kozina or Trieste. The worst was a younger son with neither land nor trade. Further, the choice of a husband should promote peace and harmony in the village.

In 1909 Jožef Biščev was 22, and his sister Marija was 19. At Jurkotevi, Janez Fradel, their friend and son of their cousin Ivana Košančevi, was 20. He had become a sharp-looking young man of medium height and sturdy build. Janez had dark blonde hair, blue eyes, a strong angular jaw with a cleft chin. He carried himself with confidence and pride. As the eldest son, it was his duty to help his father on the farm. Valentin needed help; his wife was unwell, his daughters Antonia, Marija, Stefanija, and Pepina were between the ages of 11 and 16, and Rudolf was only eight. Other men in their village were going to West Virginia to cut trees. Janez yearned to see the world and convinced his parents that a few years in America would help them financially. He made his first voyage to America in December 1909.

*

Rural Primorskan men, especially younger sons, commonly went elsewhere to earn money for a year or two to help their families or buy land. Usually, they went no further than Trieste, but between 1890 and 1914, America offered opportunities many times more lucrative than any in Trieste. In 1899, the Chesapeake & Ohio Railroad began work on a new rail line that would run alongside the Greenbrier River in West Virginia. For the West Virginia Pulp and Paper Company and its subsidiary, the West Virginia Spruce Lumber Company, the new rail line provided an opportunity to harvest the previously inaccessible virgin red spruce forests in the high plateaus, ridges, and valleys of Cheat Mountain in the Allegheny Range. The lumber company began construction of their own narrow-gauge railroad that would enable them to cut trees and deliver them to the new C&O rail line. Work was proceeding rapidly and the railroad was in desperate need of workers to lay ties and rails and build switchbacks that would enable the short, powerful, coal-fired steam locomotives to ascend the steep grades leading to the untouched mountain forests. When one area was cut completely, the rails were torn up and re-used in a new area. The railroads delivered West Virginia spruce boards of the highest quality, as well as paper products and chemicals, to the rapidly growing industries and cities of America, and to its ports, to be shipped worldwide. The trains returned to Cass with a steady supply of workers recruited from Italy, Austria, Hungary, and Poland who had just arrived at a bustling Ellis Island in New York Harbor.

Josip Ban was the first from the valley under Slavnik to work in Cass, West Virginia. He was the second son of Zajčevi, and part of the tight kinship circle with Jurkotevi, Biščevi, and Košančevi because of his marriage to Marija Košančeva one of the six daughters left fatherless when Ivan Košanc fell off the wagon. Poor Marija died at age 26, leaving at least three sons, and Josip quickly remarried. Four years later he was widowed again. Probably feeling quite cursed, at 48 years old he responded to a 1906 advertisement in Trieste that enticed laborers to work at the West Virginia Spruce Lumber Company, with a package deal that included transportation. He went by train to Le Havre, France, traveled on the steamship *Latouraine* to New York, and then by rail to Cass. He ultimately recruited several dozen men from Brkini and the valley to work for the company, including his nephew, Janez Fradel, my grandfather. Janez borrowed money for his passage on the steamship *Laura* that departed from Trieste. The voyage across the Atlantic Ocean to Ellis Island took about two weeks and he arrived 17 December 1909, then traveled onward by train to West Virginia. The 1910 U.S. census records indicate he was living in a big lumber camp in Davis, with Josip Ban, other men that he knew from Brkini and the valley, and a crew from Poland.

Circumstances forced Janez to return home in 1912. His 44-year-old mother had succumbed to tuberculosis while he was away and his father was struggling. Unfortunately, whatever money Janez brought home did not really improve his family's life. Janez had an air about him when he returned home, and was now quite the worldly man in Povžane. Strong and handsome, with the allure of the returned adventurer and the promise of America written all over him, he began (or resumed, perhaps) his relationship with his mother's cousin, Marija Fabjančič. Because he was over 21, compulsory military service in the Austro-Hungarian Army awaited him and he was drafted into the 97th regiment stationed at Karlovec, just across the border in what is now Croatia. (photo 3) The 97th was comprised of Austrian citizens from Primorska, Istria, and Italy and had a reputation for being lackadaisical with a high desertion rate. Janez managed to return to Povžane frequently to see Marija, but after five months of service, for reasons unknown, he deserted the military. He secured passage on the ship *Polonia* in late March of 1913, and returned to West Virginia.

Not until after he left did Marija Fabjančič realize that she was two months pregnant and the ensuing gossip spread through the village like wildfire. When her mother found out she screamed things at Marija that she would later come to regret, and both her parents said scandalous, hateful things about cousin Janez and the entire Jurkotevi clan. Valentin Fradel had little defense to offer for his son since he was already unhappy about the way he left. Marija's eldest sister, Rezina, was furious and embarrassed. To resolve the situation and quell all the turmoil, Marija's father told her she must go to Janez in America, despite the anger and pain his desertion caused her.

Janez borrowed money for her passage and since Francka Ban, a niece of Josip Ban, was ready to leave for Cass to marry her betrothed, she and my grandmother traveled together. Marija's brother, Jožef, took them by wagon to Trieste on 13 July 1913. He had made Marija a wooden suitcase, the kind that workers and soldiers used called a *baul*, which could be stood on its end and doubled as a wardrobe. Marija packed three dresses, a coat, and hand-knitted stockings. She had been told not to bring much because American styles were different, and the plan was that she and Janez would be home again in two or three years. She took a lot of cheese because she was worried about being hungry on the passage. Jožef stood on the shore and waved until they were out of sight. Sixty years later in a letter to a friend my grandmother recalled, "It was a beautiful evening and the sun was setting in the Adriatic Sea as the *Kaiser Franz* Josef I left Trieste at six o'clock and the band was playing beautifully on our ship."

At six months pregnant, the ride in steerage could not have been comfortable for Marija. Stories about transatlantic steerage crossings describe the lack of privacy, how passengers preyed on one another, and the dangers for women traveling alone. But Marija and Francka had each other and they were graciously watched over by Mr. and Mrs. Dablok, a couple from Kozina who traveled with them. The eleven-day passage included stops in Patras, Palermo, Naples, and Algiers to take on more passengers. In telling the story of her passage in her later years, my grandmother never mentioned any discomforts, not even the big event on the ship that was reported in the *New York Times* on 27 July 1913. At the moment the *Kaiser Franz Josef I* passed over the final resting place of the *Titanic*, reports state that the liner "lurched upward as if lifted by a tidal wave and the ship shook from stem to stern." The upper-deck passengers—the wealthy and aristocratic—crowded the top deck and took pictures. After about five minutes a whale at least 70 feet long floated out from under the ship with a great gash in the middle of its back. Confined to steerage, perhaps clinging to her baul and nibbling on her generous supply of cheese, my grandmother never knew what happened.

The ship arrived without further incident at Ellis Island on 25 July 1913. Marija and Francka each had sewn into their clothes the minimum twenty-five dollars that was required for entry, and the processing at immigration took just a couple of hours. They were transported to Pennsylvania Station, where they bought a box of food for one dollar that contained one large salami, a loaf of bread, an apple pie, and some biscuits, to sustain them for two days of

travel. Grandmother said that Mrs. Dablok offered her a banana and
she didn't know what to do with it. The two young women arrived
in Ronceverte, West Virginia, at half past one in the morning and
spent the rest of the night on the platform. In the morning, the C&O
passenger train took them the last 83 miles to Cass.

Although Cass had three churches, none were Catholic. The closest one was in Elkins, 50 miles away, so ten days after Marija's arrival,
she and Janez took the train to Elkins to be married. The Elkins
Station was a handsome, newly built brick building surrounded by
an open area that was weedy and undeveloped. Across the muddy
road, the Hotel Del Monte offered lodging for railway workers and
travelers and it was there that Janez and Marija stayed the night
before the wedding. On Thursday 7 August 1913 they acquired their
marriage certificate at city hall and walked the three blocks to St.
Brendan's Catholic Church, a modest wooden structure with a front
steeple. Father Daly, a priest from Ireland, performed the marriage
rite. They went to a studio to have a formal photograph done, one
that they would send to the family in Povžane before taking the
train back to Cass.

In 2012, I made an appointment to view the church archives and
was welcomed to an office at the back of a modern St. Brendan, an
impressive modern structure of local spruce beams, fieldstones, and
glass that commands a majestic view of the hills and valley below
Elkins. The archive was a thick, cloth-bound book into which all
the marriages for over a century were recorded. The old book on the
shelf looked so out of place in the contemporary church. I carefully
turned the yellowed pages near the front and found Janez and Marija's wedding entry. Francka Ban and Janez Tomazič were married
there on 1 September.

A curious note about the marriage entry involves the names of
the parents of the bride and groom. The names on the original
certificate, written out by Father Daly, puzzled my Aunt Mary. As
previously mentioned, Janez's mother's maiden name was Ivana
Fabjančič, and she was a first cousin of the bride but Janez said that

his mother's name was Ivana Kosancich (actually a bad spelling of
Košančeva, her house name). Was this deliberate, to avoid questions
about their cousin relationship? Marriages between cousins were
common and acceptable in the culture of Slovenia and under Austrian law—and, as a matter of fact, in West Virginia. Perhaps they
had heard that Americans frowned on cousin marriages and sought
to avoid scrutiny. The truth is that some embarrassment about their
kinship persisted in later years. My father, my aunts and my uncle,
would admit to my generation that grandfather's mother was a
Fabjančič and my grandmother was a Fabjančič, but they always
followed it with an emphatic "But they were NOT cousins!"

The peak years of prosperity in the lumber town of Cass ran
from 1909 to the onset of the Great Depression in 1929. In 1913,
when Janez and Marija arrived, Cass was booming, with a general
store, a butcher shop, clothing stores, a barbershop, school, hotel,
restaurants, a movie theater, and a baseball team. There were two
trains daily to Ronceverte.

The ethnically-diverse population of 1,700 people who lived
there operated within a rigidly stratified society and the new couple found their place in it. On the west side of the Greenbriar River,
the West Virginia Spruce Lumber Company had built homes for its
employees who did not live in the male-only lumber camps. The
managers resided in neat, two-story white clapboard houses on
Big Bug Hill (it was the equivalent of today's gated community;
there were no gates but everyone knew not to enter without invitation), while another area of town offered more modest homes for
the white American mill workers and mechanics. All homes were
supplied with running water and electricity. Planked sidewalks
enabled the residents to walk around without getting their feet
muddy. Out of sight of these neighborhoods was Bohunk Hill where
immigrants lived segregated lives. *Bohunk,* derived from "Bohemian
and Hungarian," was American slang; a derogatory word for low
class laborers from anywhere in Eastern Europe. Over time, the

immigrant men might gain recognition from their fellow American workers and their children might get to know their schoolmates, but the immigrant women never mixed with other women.

Janez and Marija shared a boarding house on Bohunk Hill with twelve Slovenes, including Josip Ban and his sons, and Andy Sis-kovič, the brother of her sister Rezina's husband. Marija was paid to do the cooking, and her salary covered their rent and board. A dollar a week was withheld from the workers' paychecks for medical expenses, which included the services of the company doctor and a midwife. "Granny" Bird attended Marjia when she gave birth at home on 21 October. The couple named their daughter Ivanka, but soon they all Americanized their names to John, Mary, and Jennie (who later changed her name to Jane).

East Cass, the land across the Greenbriar River not owned by the company, was accessed by a wire suspension footbridge and decent people knew not to go there. For many men who lived in the mountain camps East Cass was their destination for time off, and they headed to "Dirty Street" for its saloons, poolrooms, gambling joints, boarding houses, hotels, and restaurants. The establishments served copious amounts of whisky, wine, beer, and even cocaine was available. Brawls were regular events and murders were frequent and for these reasons East Cass kept two or three policemen employed full-time. A Black section of town, located beyond East Cass, had its own school and church. The town of Cass is now part of a state park. There is a museum and visitors can ride the train, tour a reconstructed lumber camp, the general store and a few of the American quarters that have been refurbished. All of East Cass is gone, and nothing but a big green lawn remains of Bohunk Hill.

John and his Slovene friends faced danger from every aspect of work and life on the mountain. Death from falling trees, getting crushed between rail cars, or loss of limbs in the sawmill were the most frequent accidents. Suicides and domestic murders were regular events. Drunkenness exacerbated all the dangers. It was common for a worker to get loaded on Dirty Street and buy additional whisky to drink on his walk back to camp following the rails. Many a drunk would pass out on the tracks during the night and be run over by the first morning train. The Greenbriar River and its tributaries regularly flooded the town. Fires on the mountain, in the train sheds, in the mill, and in the wood heated homes were regular perils. Diphtheria swept through every fall and typhoid appeared sporadically. A smallpox outbreak, which affected twelve people and killed two, was cut short when the company responded swiftly with door-to-door mass vaccinations.

Although West Virginia was as mountainous as their home in Brkini and the valley, the environment was dramatically different for the Slovene workers on the mountain. The huge canopy of virgin trees did not admit sunlight. Flying ash from steam engines posed a continual risk of fire, requiring that someone walk the tracks, putting out the sparks. Rolling logs, horses spooked by trains, shifting weights on the flat cars, and brake failures threatened life and limb. Yet the work went on through rain, snow, and ice, with the short, robust Shay locomotives pushing their loads up steep grades switching in a giant "Z" from one ridge to another. The clanging and grinding of mighty gears, the great hissing as steam was released, and the billowing steam and smoke made for a very noisy and powerful display of industrial might. It was inspiring and fearsome, especially when compared to the quiet pace of Brkini where the wagons were pulled by oxen, and life was dominated by the reaping of wheat and storing of root vegetables, the constant fear of war and poverty, and long winters without enough food.

The West Virginia Spruce Lumber Company employed over a thousand men. A continuous polyglot stream of workers arrived and departed daily, with very few women amongst them. Italian workers were favored for maintaining the rails, watching for washouts after a rain that might weaken the tracks and cause cars to derail. Austrians were preferred in the pulpwood operations for "their hearty,

cheerful and contented natures."* Attempts were made to group
men in the camps according to nationality, none of which ensured
harmony. The term "Hungarian" might actually embrace Slovaks,
Serbs, and Bulgarians. "Polish" might include Russians and Ukrai-
nians, and "Austrian" could mean Slovenes, Croats, and Czechs. The
company could not be bothered to keep records of all the foreigners
with difficult-sounding names so they were identified by an aluminum or a brass scrip token—"Austrian number 256" and the like.
When one was killed it was recorded as, "Italian #142 killed today."

Average pay in the camps was $1.50 per day plus room and
board. The food was plentiful and good and included daily meat, an
unimaginable luxury in Brkini and the valley. Immigrants were paid
much the same as Americans, although grievances about money or
language barriers would explode into fights among the different
ethnic groups and the Americans. Unions did not thrive amongst
the independent-minded lumbermen. When they were dissatisfied,
they were more likely to move on to something better. Occasionally
there was a strike, but the strikers never won. Once eight Italians
were dynamited as they slept in their mountain camp, an act pinned
to resentment of foreigners taking American jobs, but no one was
held accountable.

During his first sojourn in West Virginia, my grandfather lived in
the lumber camps and managed cutting, clearing, and hauling with
a horse, according to Aunt Mary. As each section of the mountain
was cleared, the camps were moved to the next area to be logged.
After his marriage, he moved into the sawmill, pulp operations, or
the extract plant that derived tannins and dyes from the discarded
bark. This work enabled him to live in town and be home every
night with his wife, rather than in a camp. John, Mary, and baby
Jenny moved to the town of Spruce, high on Cheat Mountain, and
then to Richwood, to follow the work. In these new environs they

*Clarkson, R. *On Beyond the Leatherbark: The Cass Saga*, p. 123.

were forced into mixed company, no longer living with just Slovenes. The company boarding houses and their occupants were rough, and it became an increasingly difficult and lonely time for Mary. She began writing to friends and family back home. Her brother Jožef corresponded regularly, with a letter every one to two weeks. When John and Mary moved, she might have missed some letters. Others were lost and the mail halted altogether during the war years. But the letters that my grandmother managed to save give a good account of life back in Povžane through the decades.

CHAPTER TWO

Early Letters

Mary was thrust into a rowdy, demanding new world at a vulnerable stage of her pregnancy, much against her will. She ached for the companionship of her mother and sister, who could have helped to prepare her for motherhood. Her friend, Francka Ban, had moved to other work sites with her husband and Mary had no other Slovene women around her. It had not been her ambition to seek wealth or adventure on another continent, and she yearned to be part of the only community she had ever known. She hung onto every bit of news from home, every bit of gossip, and every connection to Brkini and her valley people who had come to America. She longed to hear every detail about who had arrived and who was leaving. In her mind, she was returning home in two or three years and wanted to make the best of their time in America so she and John and their child would return with money and success and build a good life in Povžane among their own people.

Mary threw herself into making their lives sound good to the people back home. She wrote to her brother about the wedding, and relied on him to share her positive news with everyone at Biščevi. She told him about the camaraderie of their friends and relatives at the boarding house and painted a rosy picture of her job as the cook; when Jožef wrote back, he nicely referred to them as her "guests." Jožef read and wrote letters for, "Mama and Ata," (their parents), and for "Nono," (their grandfather Stefan Cergolj) because they were not literate, and conveyed news of Fanika, their little niece living at Biščevi who Mary loved and missed terribly. Jožef also wrote about the house of Rejčevi neighbors who had men in America, the Blaževi women who still gossiped about Marija's unplanned pregnancy despite scandals of their own, and their sisters, Tona Bazletova and Rezina Bilkotova.

The festivities of opasilo in Povžane took place a few days after Mary's wedding in West Virginia. Suppressing her homesickness was hard as she imagined what it was like without her. Jožef wrote about opasilo and his upcoming *šalcerat*, which were the military exercises required of Austrian citizens after completion of their period of conscription.

> *18 August 1913*
>
> Dear Sister, Before I give you our news, let me send my best regards to all of you and tell you that your letter finally arrived after eight days of waiting. Mama, Ata, and Nono had been unwell for seven days but on Monday they started to feel better. The oxen have been sick since opasilo, just like they were last year at this time, so we cannot go anywhere with them. I must go *šalcerat* on the 22nd and will be away for 14 days, which is difficult when there is so much work to be done with the harvest.
>
> Piro Rejčo is still working in America but his brother, Jože Rejčo, came home on the return voyage on the very same ship that you took to America. Blažovka has been gossiping about how you went to America in a bad manner, but her daughter, Tona, left the village for two days, came back, then ran off with that Poklukar boy. That silenced the old hags who said bad things about you! Franca left Zidarc, she rightly parted from him, and now she is a tame Godmother [a bartender]. Riko finished šalcerat, and now spends a lot of time with Kata. Our sister Tona Bazletova is healthy, just like you left her, and our Rezina Bilkotova and her family are the same. Everything else

is as usual, except that we worry about the harvest because it rains every day.

Opasilo was great, except that we all missed you. I am sure that you miss your home, and that the house you were born in is closer to your heart than the largest one in America. But a man gets used to everything, and I will get used to living without you, and you without me. But I will never forget you.

Janez's father came to see us and asked if we received any letters from you. Mama told him about the letters that have come, and his father is upset and afraid that Janez will not write to him again. I am telling Janez, and you, that he should treat his father the right way, and write to him often. He should also send him a few *kroners* [crowns] now and then, because he needs them.

We send our best regards, Fanika also sends regards. She often sings "Aunty is sailing across the sea, searching for the port of love, and the band is playing music, and she is dancing beautifully."* Give my best regards to Josip Ban, and Drej Bilko, and to all your guests. I hope that we will see each other again, and I wish for your happiness. Z Bogom Z Bogom [With God]

After Mary read her letters, she sat back and closed her eyes to envision her village again, as she used to see it from her upstairs window when the shutters were wide open, and recall the voices of people back home. Povžane was built on a slope and neighbors lived so close you could often overhear them talking. Rejčevi, home of the Granduč family, was down the slope from Biščevi, the house of Mary's family, and they had an intimate view into their dooryard even without trying. Jože Rejčo was home again, just as she and John would be one day. The Blažečevi household, the home of Mary's childhood friend, Pepa Blaževa, was located behind them across the street. Pepa's grandmother, Blažovka, was always a loud woman,

---

*Barčica po morju plava—The boat is sailing across the sea—is a still popular children's folk song. You can hear it on YouTube.

and she led the gossip about Mary's pregnancy and abandonment by
John until gossip about the daughters of her own house took over.
Tona scandalously left her husband and child to run off with "that
Poklukar boy" to Zagreb, and Franca left her spouse, Zidarc, to work
as a "tame godmother," or bartender. Her eldest sister Rezina did
not respond to her letter. Mary imagined she was still angry about
the shame Mary had brought to the family. She was sure that her
middle sister Tona would write soon.

Antonija, called Tona, wrote often, signing her letters with a big
A. She lived with her husband Josef Godina, the eldest son of the
house called Bazletevi, about a quarter of a mile away in Bač, with
her mean mother-in-law and two of her three children. Her eldest,
Fanika, stayed at Biščevi so Tona had reason to visit often. Within
days of reading the first letter that Mary had sent to the rest of the
family, Tona sat with pen and paper in hand at the kitchen table of
Biščevi with Nono, Ata, Mama, and Fanika. Jožef was still at šalcerat so
Tona assumed the responsibility and honor of writing one of the first
replies to America. After a hard day of harvesting, the long light of the
warm Saturday evening in August drew neighbors into the kitchen
to hear about the letter and send their greetings to John and Mary.

23 August 1913
Dear Sister, We all wish you a happy start to your marriage. I
am writing from Biščevi with Mama and Ata and everyone else
gathered around me. It was hard to wait for your letter, dear
sister. Your departure is hard for all of us and we feel like you
died. It is particularly hard for Mama; she is never at peace. Ata
is doing fairly well, although last week he was deathly ill. Nono
is weak, and brother Pepe had to go šalcerat yesterday for 14
days; this was not good since there is so much work to do this
month. All of our cattle have been sick for the entire month;
therefore, we cannot work at all. Fanika prays a lot, and sings
you will come home soon, and bring her candy as you used to
do when you went to Trst. We used to have nine in Biščevi, now
there only three left and it feels empty and desolate.

My dearly beloved sister, Mama asks you to forgive her for taunting and cursing you. Now she only wants to see you again. She is longing for you and crying "my poor child" anywhere she goes. For four days Mama went to the post office to look for your letter, and she was crying every time. Now I am here to read the letter for her, and to write to you for her since brother is away.

For opasilo, people came from Trst and from Brezovica, but it was so cheerless and empty without you. Although it was sad, it was even worse for the *Marijino vnebovzetje*. [The Assumption of the Virgin Mary's body to heaven on 15 August is one of the most important religious and public holidays in Slovenia].

Rezina Bilkotova has not been back here since the evening when you last saw them. They do not even let their children visit, but you have seen them act like this before. Blažovka was barking so much about you that it is good that you left. Then on 14 August Tona left her husband and her daughter from Trst and went to live with Poklukar. When she wanted to take money out of the bank, her husband took her depositor's book away. Now we have peace, because the old hags have nothing to talk about anymore.

Mama, Ata, Nono, and Fanika send you regards. Valentin also sends you his best regards, write to him and help him a little, you know he does not have it easy with all the children. Write to Mekovka from Maharinčevi, she is right here, sitting next to me, and wishes you all the best. We all send regards to you, and Drej Bilko, Josip, Franc, and Jože Ban. Z Bogom Z Bogom **A**

Terezija, called Rezina, also had three children. Her husband, Josef Šiškovič, was the eldest son of Bilkotevi. The house was part of a duplex that sat off by itself at the west end of the village with a panoramic view of the open fields and orchards in the lowlands at the foot of Slavnik. The second son of Bilkotevi was Andrej, he was called Drej Bilko, and was living in Mary's guesthouse in Cass.

There he was known as Andy and simplified the spelling of his surname to Siskovič.

Both of Mary's sisters had married first sons of a household, and Slovene tradition maintained that when the bride joined the household she was to be under the rule of her mother-in-law, the *stara tašča*. Depending on the fairness of the stara tašča and the patience of the bride this could be a difficult relationship. Tona had a bitter relationship with her stara tašča at Bazletevi, while Rezina faired better at Bilkotevi.

Mail was not delivered to the home so walking to the post office in Materija was a part of daily life for families waiting for news from America. The prosperous house of Kastelic that was also a popular store and gostilna was near the post office and was an obvious place to stop and chat. The arrival of a letter or package was never a private affair. Everyone in the village soon knew of it. On her way to the post office, Rezina had to pass by her childhood home, but she seldom stopped to see her parents. Tona's home was just a stone's throw out of her way, but Rezina didn't stop there either. She occasionally bumped into a family member on the road, and exchanged a few chilly words.

The walk from John Fradel's family home at Jurkotevi to Biščevi took only five minutes. Although his relationship with the Biščevi household was strained, John's father, Valentin Jurko, stopped by the house frequently, looking for news of the newlyweds. Like most of his generation, Jurko depended on his daughters to read and write for him. While any letter from Jožef or Tona was formatted with a date, ornate greetings, and beautiful penmanship, the letters written by Jurko's daughters lacked these niceties, and were filled with misspelled words.

Valentin dictated the next letter to one of his daughters soon after he had visited Biščevi. The letter was undated, but his description makes it sound like August. "You are asking about the harvest. We'll have a little bit of everything" indicates that he already knew that the harvest would be good because most things were close to being ripe and ready for picking. The folk name for August was *Veliki srpan* which translates to "large reaping-hook month."

> O my Dear Son,
>   Before I write anything else, I am sending best regards to you and Marija, from myself and from sisters and brother. Let me tell you that we are all healthy and I hope that you are as well. Thank you for your letter and for the photograph that you sent.
>   I am catching my breath; you know how there is always something to take care of and worry about. Things around here are pretty bad, even if we wanted to sell one of the oxen it would not be possible, and money is tight. You are asking about the harvest. We'll have a little bit of everything, thank God. But these days everyone wants to have food at home that you cannot get.
>   But what is not right is that Marija wrote three letters home and you wrote none in over three months. What are you thinking? That your home and business is now with them? You should be ashamed of yourself, if not for all of us, then for your father. I and brother and sisters are sending you our best regards. Z Bogom
>   Valentin Fradel

On the back of the letter Valentin sarcastically dictated: "write back again in a year or two." He was angry that John wrote so seldom. He had not communicated much during his first sojourn in America, either.

Mary was in her final weeks of pregnancy, as frightened as any woman about to give birth for the first time, and feeling so alone. She could not pour her heart out to her mother because she knew how upset her mother would become. Mama was best when she had only herself to worry about. Instead, Mary whined to her brother in her recent letters, asking for reassurance that she was still loved, and that her place in Povžane was waiting

for her. Ivanka (Jennie) was born by the time this letter arrived
from Jožef.

28 October 1913

Dear Sister and Janez, You write that you have been expecting my letter for a long time. I could not write because I was
away from home helping others make lime, and Mama did not
want to ask somebody else to write a letter because you know
how people talk. Poor Tona is sick, she has been in the hospital
in Trst since the 20th. Just now Mama went to see her, and I am
writing because the others have not yet awakened.

You ask if we ever remember you. Of course, we cannot forget
you! Not a day passes that we do not think about you. Fanika
asks when you will come home. When Mama is sick, she is
sad for you, but when she recovers, she is pleased that you are
there because nothing would be here for you. She treats Tona
badly, you know how she is, and she also treats Rezina badly.
We do not miss you just because there is now so much more
work to do; we have Blaj's boy to help us take the cows out for
pasture, so we complete every task on time. But I do miss you
often, especially when I read your letters. As I write to you,
tears flow from my eyes, and I do not want to read the letter
aloud in front of Mama.

Regarding the livestock illness, I do use the oxen for short
periods with the wagon, but the illness has now spread to
Pivka. Nothing goes as planned. We had 11 pigs, and Bazletevi
had 12, but it was hard to sell them at the fair. Nonetheless we
took 77 guldinar [$23] for them and we still have three at home.
Now we are picking brin and we should get some 200 kroner
[$30] for them so that we can pay our taxes. Pepa Blaževa has
not changed; she is walking around and checking when Janez
Ogrnjač's wife will die. Zajčevi's Nane got well, he was sick
for about 20 days; Drej Ogrnjač returned from the hospital,
he was in for 70 days with typhus. Mekovka often asks about
you, Kastelic, and brother-in-law Bazle send regards, Marica

Bilkoteva [Rezina's oldest daughter] always worries about you, but the other Bilkotevi think of you, or us, as much as they think about the last year's snow. We do not care because they have not done anything good for anyone and I have no hopes that they ever will. Ata misses you a lot. I wish that we can all be happy and healthy until you return home safely, and then we will drink half a liter together.

In the new year, Tona was visiting at Biščevi and wrote for Mama and Ata and everyone else who gathered as soon as they knew she was writing to America.

17 February 1914

Dearly beloved Sister, We expected to receive many letters after you had your baby girl, but you have not written! Mama would like to know who her Godfather is? She wants to know if you have enough food and supplies, if she is eating well or crying, and if you take care of everything yourself, or if you have a woman to help you? Mama is very sad, and cries night and day, longing to hear from you. She had a beautiful chest made for you so you will not have to keep your things in some old box; she will send it to you. Grgarečevi are worried since they have heard that things are bad in America. Francka Ban wrote that work is scarce and that her husband works only three days a week.

The winter was so cold you could hear things crack, and the snow was as high as the Grgarečevi and Blažečevi. Aunt Mekovka sends her best regards, and complains that you do not write. Kastelova sends greetings and is hoping to hear from you; her husband was badly injured in a cave next to Divča and broke his leg and arm. Mama and Ata, Pepe, Fanika and Nono all send you warm regards. Mama begs you to write to her. Z Bogom Z Bogom

Tona added a personal note:

My dearly beloved Sister, you were offended I did not write
when I came home from the hospital, but I did write, and
then I waited for your answer, but nothing came. Mama and I
worried that something was wrong. Please forgive me. I do not
feel very well, although I am not sick. But anyway, write to me
and tell me how you are, and how things were when you had
your girl. Z bogom **A**

Contrary to Francka Ban's message about the shortage of work,
the West Virginia Spruce Lumber Company was expanding operations in 1914. A few months after Jennie was born, John and
Mary Fradel were on the move from Cass to other company work
sites, so many letters did not reach them and there were lags in
communication. Mama was right in recognizing that Mary needed
help with the baby and John knew that womanly and family companionship would be good for his lonely wife. He wrote to his
younger sister, Marija Jurkoteva (Fradel), to propose that she join
them in America.

News of Jožef's pending wedding plans was revealed in a letter
from Josef Bazle (Godina), Tona's husband. In a pleasant and con-
cerned tone, he wrote that Mary should "be taken care of by her
family," meaning that there should still be a dowry, a payment, and
gifts from the bride's family to the groom as custom dictated. Given
the circumstances, Mary's wedding had taken place without one.
Josef Bazle, like a growing number of people, resented the influence
the Roman Catholic priest exercised over families, especially the
ones who had privileged lives and did not share the hardships of
their parishioners, even in times of drought and hunger. While "Z
Bogom" means with God, "Zbogom" means goodbye and the closing
in Josef's letter was a deliberate snub to religious sentiment.

16 April 1914
   Dear Marija and Janez, We are glad you are healthy and
content, unlike those who say life is not good in America. On

Nationalism was a growing sentiment throughout Europe. In 1848, starting in Sicily and advancing to France, Germany, Italy, Hungary, and Austria, there were nationalist revolutions against all the European monarchs. Historians call it the "Springtime of Nations," but it ended in failure and increased repression. In the midst of this political unrest, Austria and Hungary, often adversaries, formed a compromise they hoped would strengthen their kingdoms and keep their ethnic minorities subjugated. In 1867 they joined together to become the Austro-Hungarian Empire. It was called the "Dual Monarchy," because the Austrian Emperor would also assume the title, King of Hungary. They merged their military forces, while maintaining separate governing bodies for internal affairs and the governance of their respective minorities.

The Austrian Imperial Council recognized that a lack of autonomy of their Slavic people was a potential source of revolt. In efforts to prevent this they invested in roads, railroads, and other infrastructure in Slavic lands. They established village schools where lessons were conducted in the local languages, and in 1907 gave voting rights to every male citizen. In general, these concessions helped Slovenes remain loyal to the emperor.

Slovene is an ancient Slavic language with complicated structures and many dialects. Slovenes never had their own nation but their language tied them together as a people. It was considered a peasant language, not capable of poetry and literature, or higher education. Franc Prešeren—an influential and revered Slovenian writer—showed in the first half of the 19th century that the Slovene language was capable of deep expression. He remains a national hero to this day, and one of his poems set to music is the Slovenian national anthem. Under such influence, Slovenian demands within the empire focused on promotion of the language and education more than political autonomy. The later years of the 19th century saw an increase in Slovene language books, cultural societies, and local reading rooms. Ordinary Slovenians, such as my family under Slavnik, benefited from Austrian progressiveness. For example,

our end, Tona is still weak, but I think she is improving. Jožek
healthy and doing well in school; we could not wish for bette
Fanika is not the healthiest, but Zorka is very well. I wish we
were all that well, but it is not too bad, although we have quite
a lot of expenses with these illnesses. At your home in Polžane,
your mother is healthy, although she will never admit it. Your
father is a little weaker, and your Nono Štefan looks smaller
and smaller with age, but things are going fairly well because
they always help each other. Therefore, do not be afraid.

The girl [your brother] Pepe will marry is from Maganjatevi
in Vareje. She is similar to you Marija, only slightly taller. The
family is very nice, Kljun sister's daughter works there. They
would have already been married, but her father cut his leg
and she is needed at home. The wedding might happen after
the holidays, maybe in Vareje. Later today we plan to see the
priest and check if it could be done on St. Stephen's Day, the
day after Christmas. You know how people talk about this
and that around here, so we'll do our best to take care of the
wedding plans soon.

I have already told them your family should leave something
for you when the wedding is over, and they put this in writing,
so they do not forget. You can rest assured things will be done
as if you were at home. I will take care of this for you. So, my
dear Janez and Marija, I am warning you not to forget your
home, and to take care of your father Valentin. You know he is
quite hurt. The poor man is sad because you have not written
to him for so long, and because you never send him anything.
Send our best regards to Josip Ban and to all your friends. If
anything changes, we will write to you about it. We'll look
forward to your answer.

Best regards, Godina Family
Zbogom and be well.

*

Mary's father, Josef Biščev, born in 1849, his wife, born in 1861, and Valentin Jurko born in 1865 never attended school. Josef Biščev was sufficiently self-taught that he could read a little, at least enough to read Mary's letters, but they were all essentially illiterate. Their children born after 1880 attended government schools. Jožef, Tona, and Mary of Biščevi had beautiful penmanship and wrote long eloquent letters. Jožef loved to read newspapers and books. Mary exchanged poetry with her friend Božidar Kastelic who went to a secondary school in Ljubljana.

The Austrian Imperial Council continued to float ideas to quell Slavic unrest. The Archduke Franz Ferdinand, heir to the Dual Monarchy, was a proponent of plans that would increase Slavic autonomy such as a triple monarchy of Austria, Hungary and the Slavs, or a federal system, such as a "United States of Central Europe" but not many were on board with such a plan.

The Hungarian National Assembly was comprised of Magyar nobles who considered themselves superior to all Slavs. They continued to rule their Slavic subjects, especially the Croatians, who were always stirring for independence, with an iron hand. On Hungary's southern border, an independent Kingdom of Serbia sought to establish control of all the southern Slavic people formerly ruled by the Ottomans.

In 1908, the Dual Monarchy annexed Bosnia, tightening control in a territory it had loosely administered since 1878. Bosnia was an especially vital part of what Serbia felt was their entitlement. The idea that Slovenia and Croatia could become part of an independent nation of all southern Slavs resonated among politically minded people. Tensions grew and Hungary dealt aggressively with Serbia by imposing severe trade restrictions that strangled its economy. All the players were part of mutual aid treaties that created delicate balances among the great powers of Europe. Thus, when the Archduke Franz Ferdinand was shot while visiting Bosnia, the world was rocked.

CHAPTER THREE

1914–1918: The Great War

The assassination of Archduke Franz Ferdinand and his wife on 28 June 1914 in Sarajevo by a Serbian nationalist, put in motion a chain of events that would lead to World War I. The people of Brkini and the valley knew that all their men would soon be summoned into battle for the Austro-Hungarian Empire. Jožef's wedding to Josefa Rožanc could not wait for St. Stephen's Day and was hastily arranged for 7 July. Pepa, as she was called, became the *nevesta*, the bride of the eldest son of Biščevi, and when she moved in, she became the servant of his parents.

In the first letter to her sister Mary after the assassination, Tona wrote only of ordinary news of their friends and family, almost as if not talking about the imminent war would keep it from happening. Tona announced her big news: "I am in a different stage," she wrote— a direct translation of the Slovenian phrase used to announce a pregnancy. From the village gossip the letter contains, it seems that Tona knew more about Francka Ban in West Virginia than Mary did. Francka was also pregnant; only much later they would learn that the baby did not survive.

July 1914

My dearly beloved Sister, Thank you for the photograph. [photo 2] Your little girl is such a nice and sweet child, but you look too slim. You say that you have a lot of work to do. Francka from Gabrk writes that all she does is cook for her husband. She will also have a small one soon.

I can tell you that Biščevi got a nevesta. She looks like you, she is the same height, has the same posture, and does her hair the same way as you. Many are saying that we lost one Marija, and gained another. The wedding in Vareje was truly beautiful. They had 36 guests and we were there for three days. I missed you all the time.

My dearly beloved sister, thank you so much for remembering that I am poor. Thank you for everything that you sent. May God give you everything that is good, and grant that you will be able to earn a lot, just as you were hoping. Thank God that I have recovered and I am feeling very well. I can tell you that I am also in a different stage. I am expecting in November, if God makes everything happen. We are both happy about it, just as if it was the first time. Fanika says that this will be her baby, that she will change its diapers, and take care of it. She is a good child, and so is Jože. He does well in school and has all the top grades. This year he will receive Holy Communion and Confirmation. Give my regards to Drej Bilko [Andy Siskovič]. He wrote that some from Polžane will come home, and Grgurjeva thought that he would come home as well. Z Bogom **A**

Those who planned to return home from America could no longer do so after transatlantic passenger service promptly ceased at the end of June. The Emperor's wagons arrived in Materija on 27 July to muster the men into the 97th Regiment, the same unit from which John had deserted a year earlier. Jožef described the scene that day in a letter he wrote from a hospital in Hungary, four months later.

I would like to write to you about our departure from home, but it is not possible to describe everything. It was in the morning on the 27th of July and it was raining when we gathered. Everyone from the village came. Two carts were ready for the men, and we climbed onto them. We were 45 altogether. The women and children followed us to Materija. Everyone from the village that was alive came along, and there was a lot of screaming and crying. Once in Materija, children and women returned home, and the boys and men were taken to Kozina. My wife and her mother came along to Trst. Just imagine how sad our departure was.

The very next day, Austria and Hungary declared war on Serbia. Russia, Serbia's ally, declared war on Austria and Hungary. In a December letter, Tona replied to Mary's queries for more details:

Dearly beloved Sister, You asked if official summons had been served. Nobody received any. The order came one day announcing which ages needed to report, and the very next day they came to the municipality, and the men went. Oh, my dear, there were more people in Kastelic than ever before. All the children, women, and everyone that was alive came; there was so much crying, singing, and music that I cannot even describe it to you. God forbid that you would ever see or hear anything like it. The men went to Kozina, and all of us that could not part went with them. Our brother Pepe was married for only 20 days before he had to leave home, before they even had a chance to get used to living together.

My dear, you are worried who else had to go—Frane Ban, Toni Ban, Pepe Maharinc, Jože Zajc, Jože Rejčo, Jože Slogar, Toni Blaj, Toni Zvrt, Toni from Gabrk, Jože Ogrnjač, Drega Štefak, Jože Žnjidar, Janez Škrk, and so many more that I cannot write all of them. Now in this twelfth month, the draft is for everyone up to 36 years of age. Jože Grgarec, Jernej Kranc, and the new judge, Mrčelj, from Podgrad were taken. Sometime afterwards, the army asked Jurko about you, and he told them that they should ask me, but they never did.

The war sparked inflation in Europe and those who had financed
John and Mary's travels were anxious to get back the money John
owed them. His father advised him that John's debt to him alone
was over 1,000 kroner ($155). Pressure was on him to pay up, and
conflicts arose as to who would be repaid first. Consider that John
earned $1.50 a day plus room and board, and worked six days a week
at the West Virginia Spruce Lumber Company, for a total of $9 a
week, with a dollar held back for health care. (A dollar was worth
6.5 kroner, so he brought home 52 kroner per week). A passage to
America averaged $70—or 455 kroner.

A few months into the war, Ata wanted to write to John, so Tona
sat with him to write down his words. Ata wanted to advise John
on how to resolve a conflict about money that had arisen between
his father, Valentin Jurko and his uncle, Frane Košanc. Ata disliked
both men and did not take sides. John had sent fifteen dollars (100
kroner) to his father, and Frane Košanc demanded that the money
be given to him. Valentin was angry because he believed that John
was encouraging Frane to do this.

Frane, now 40 years old, was responsible for the interests of his
six sisters, primarily the dowries paid to their respective husbands.
Ivana, Valentin's deceased wife, was one of those sisters. Frane
claimed that Ivana's dowry gave him the obligation to look after
his sister's children and to have a say in what happened at Jurkotevi.
Valentin had acquired the property through his own inheritance,
not through the dowry, so he did not agree that Frane's status as
his deceased wife's brother gave him any rights at Jurkotevi. This is
what Ata had to say about it:

> *1 Nov 1914*
>
> My dearest daughter Marija, We are healthy, thank God, and
> hope that God gives health and happiness to you as well. Plan
> to save as much money as you can, you will need it. Košančevi
> and Bilkotevi are doing well. Antonija Jurkotova is courting.
> Janez's father is his usual self; we do not talk much, and it is
> best this way. We are doing fairly well as the nevesta is helping

us. After brother Pepe left, he wrote frequently to tell us that he was alive and well but we have not heard from him since 19 September. We know that he is in a foreign land. Now they are enlisting ages 24 to 36. Jože, and Jože Zlogar, and Jože Ogrnjač, all three of them went in the army on 26 October.

Frane Košanc told us that Valentin is angry because he is ignored. But the real reason that Valentin is angry is because Frane wanted to steal the 100 kroner that you sent, and you said that Frane should do it. But you should still write to him because he is your father.

As Ata's dictation continued, it failed to make any sense, and Tona gave up trying to write for him. She finished the letter in her own voice, trying to smooth things over.

And now, my dear sister, do not take everything Ata wrote seriously, do not worry about it. Janez's father is sad because you never write to him. You know what he told you when you left, and what he would do, and that he would not write to you. But when you write to others, you could also write to him.

Life here is getting to be very expensive. White flour is 34 krajcar [10¢], coffee is 40 [2¢], and corn flour is 20 [6¢]. But we thank God that the harvest was good, and we have a little bit of everything. Mama, Ata, Pepa, Nono, and I, and my children, send regards, and Pepe, my husband, also said to send you his best regards. Mekovka, Grgarečevi, and Liparjevi also send you regards. Z Bogom Your loving sister **A**

Valentin was still angry about the 100 kroner, and needed to explain to John what he had done with it. Marija Fradel, Valentin's 19-year-old daughter, wrote down her father's words a few days later.

4 November 1914

Dear Son, Before I write you more, I am sending you my best regards. Thank you for the 100 kroner, I received it and used it to pay off the bank in Podgrad and Mikolj, and supplied

Klemenka a little. You asked how much of the loan remains.
You know well that an additional 1,000 kroner would not be
too much, and then everything would be clean. If you can send
it, then we can pay it off.

Dear Family, you ordered me to buy land. I will take care of
this when possible. Right now, there is nothing available. We
still have supplies, and two young bulls, and one cow, and one
young heifer, and 18 sheep. If we do not go to Štajerska, and
if you pay the debt, you will find everything here when you
come home.

Štajerska is a region in northeastern Slovenia and Maribor is its
major city. At the turn of the century, workers were needed in its
growing industries. That Valentin was considering the move suggests how financially insecure he felt. His Fradelevi cousins were in
Maribor, sending reports of early success, which might have been an
enticement to him, but in the end Valentin's thoughts of moving to
Štajerska were fleeting. Little sister Marija added her own thoughts
and responded affirmatively to John's proposal that she join them.
It is clear that she was expecting the war to end quickly, and that
she would soon be on a ship to America.

Dear Brother and Marija, It is especially hard for the girls from
our village because nobody knows what will happen until the
moment that the men are called; then all of a sudden, they just
have to go. But we hope that there will be no further need to go.
Our father was at salčerat, from 27 May to 26 June. When they
open the sea, I will go to America immediately. You write that
you have a lot of work, and that it would be nice if I could help.
I will be happy to come because here is not for me anymore.

Grgurjeva is worried because Drej Bilko does not write to
her. Do you know anything about him? Rumors are that he will
come home for her. Father sends his regards to Gašper, and tell
him that he received the money. We send warm regards from
our hearts, and to the little one we send many kisses. Z Bogom
Marija Fradel

In November 1914 Jožef wrote to his sister in America from the military hospital in Hungary and his letter gives the perspective of an ordinary Slovenian farmer sucked into the start of the Great War. He said that he had spent time with the 97th, a big understatement considering what actually happened in that regiment. Jožef skipped over the sorry details because he might have presumed that Slovenes in America were well informed about the progress of the war, or he might have been aware that information about this matter would not get past an army censor. There is a modern re-enactment group for the Austro-Hungarian 97th Regiment in Trieste. They have a website that tells in colorful detail the twisted history of what happened.

When war was declared on Serbia on 28 July, Russia was already mobilized and ready to invade the Austro-Hungarian Empire. The 97th Regiment was comprised of Austrian citizens which included ethnic Italians, Slovenes and Croatians of the Littoral, or coastal area. The 97th which now included the standing army, the reserves (like Jožef), and new recruits, was mobilized in August 1914 and sent to Lemberg (Lviv) in Galicia (the border area of the Ukraine and Poland today) to resist the Russian invasion. They marched with outdated arms, accompanied by a musical band, as if they were going to meet the Turks in another era. On the very first day, confronted with the reality of modern battle, the commander had a nervous breakdown and had to be carried off the field. Instruments were thrown into ditches, men panicked, and deserted. The 97th was rounded up and plans were made to execute them all. Eight were shot before Emperor Franz Josef intervened and the men were dispersed to other units where they served through the war.*

Ogrsko, 29 November 1914
    Dear Sister and Brother-In-Law, Let me tell you that many things have happened to me since I last wrote to you. As you

---

*http://www.kuk-ir97.com/indexing.html or Austro-Hungarian 97th Regiment.

already know, 20 days after the wedding, I was called to serve
in the army. On 11 August we left Trst for Galicija, and here we
are fighting for our home and for the Emperor. I do not have
to write more about this, as you have probably heard, or read,
how things are in the time of war, but I can tell you that what
I had to go through, I would not wish this even on my enemy. I
am praying to God, and to the Holy Virgin, to protect me, and
give me solace. I believe that you know how things are going
with the 97th Regiment with which I also spent some time.

On 20 October, I was wounded in my leg, but it was not bad,
and I have already recovered. The bullet went through my foot,
just behind my toes. I have been in the hospital for 38 days,
and I asked for time off. They promised me two weeks off, but
it is not yet clear what will happen after that time. Will I serve
as support, or will I have to go back to Galicija? My dear sister,
please ask for peace and pray for me.

Jožef also wrote to John to tell him of the last time he saw his father,
Valentin Jurko. The poor man was frantic as the war fell upon them,
his eldest son and heir stranded in America, and fear that he himself
might even be called to serve. He could not write and he needed
Jožef to write his will and communicate to John.

Dear Janez, On the very morning of mobilization your father,
Jurko, came to our house, like many times before. We started
talking about you, and he wanted me to write down some
things. He wanted me to come along with him immediately, but
within an hour I was summoned, and I had to go, and everything was in a state of madness. As often before, Jurko was
thinking about all kinds of things, and he said that he had now
decided, once and for all, what to do with all of you. He said
that he would write down in his Will that he would give 600
guldinar to each of his children, and that if you plan to return
home, that he would put Jurkotevi aside for you. If you are not
satisfied with this, he will give it to Dolfi [Rudolf]. Now I do
not know what he actually did, as I was away for four months,

and was worrying about bullets that were flying around my head like rain. But while he was talking about this, and after he left, Mama was crying. I was consoling her, and told her that I could not read your mind to know if you would come home, but that I would like to see you again.

Dear Sister, I do not know how things would be for you because of the army. Maybe you know? Dear sister, I would write more but I almost cannot, as memories from our youth are coming back, how we lived together, and how things are now. I know that you will also be sad when you will read this, but Courage! God foresees everything, as much sadness, so much happiness.

Once again, I am sending my best regards to you and to all your friends from Polžane. Please mail your answer to my home. Z Bogom

Fabjančič Jožef

Mail service in wartime Austria must have been very good, because the absence of a letter from Jožef for only 20 days caused the family a great deal of anxiety. As the war advanced, only Tona's letters reached Mary.

9 December 1914

My dearly beloved sister, Things are very sad here. My Pepe has been in the army for eight weeks. He is nearby in Kozina, but I worry all the time that he will be transferred. Our brother was wounded in Galicija, and you can imagine that this is hard for us. Brother had not written in 20 days, and we were worried that something bad had happened. We were afraid that Mama and Ata would lose their minds, but now that Jurkotevi has received a letter from brother, they are consoled. All the men are away, and not many are left to work. My time is coming fast. I am so afraid that I will die when I will have to go to bed because I have no one to help me, and you know how hateful my stara tašča is. I wish that my husband could be home.

Dear Brother-In-Law, Valentin always worries whether you
will write to him at all. He would like you to return home, and
then says that he knows that you will not come. It would be
best that you decide on your own, and do whatever you think
is best. Jože Urh [Josip Ban] always says something good about
you when he writes to us from America. He says that you are
doing well, and that you earn up to 60 guldinars per day. But
we know that you do not want him to lie like this! [18 dollars a day was a fantastic lie]. Everything here has become so
expensive. Please write to me, and tell me how things are, and
how your girl is. Is she still gaining weight like she did before,
and is she still so sweet? A

Tona expected to give birth in November, but it did not happen
until 14 December. The baby was a boy they named Karel. Kastelova,
matron of Kastelic, kindly stopped in to see Tona in her postpartum
time, as did Margeritha Liparjeva, her next-door neighbor, who
was also Valentin Fradel's sister. So, Tona was not alone in her
childbirth after all.

Modern obstetrical practices do not let a baby go more than two
weeks beyond its due date because placental deterioration causes
hypoxia and brain damage. Karel's appearance was unremarkable
at birth and it was likely his intellectual disability was caused by a
genetic metabolic disorder, or autism. Either problem would only
gradually reveal itself.

Mary included a dollar in the envelope with her letters to Tona
when she could afford to do so and, as usual, Tona thanked her pro-
fusely. In the first seven months of the war, prices had risen about
60 percent. Flour had risen from 30 to 50 krajcar [9 to 15¢]—that
is if one could find it. Corn flour was up from 20 to 36 krajcar [6
to 11¢]. Mary's dollar was worth 325 krajcar and one can imagine
what a treasure it was.

16 December 1914
I have to thank you for being so generous to me. You would
like to know how things are here, but I cannot describe

everything. I received your letter, but I could not write back since I was in bed. On the 14th of this month, God gave me a boy. Many married men are now in the army, and every woman is pregnant. My husband is near Pula but after the New Year they will transfer him. Our beloved brother was moved to a Ljubljana hospital, but this will not hurt him, as he will not be sent back. You asked what happened to Pepe Bilko. [Rezina's 12-year-old son died from an illness during the early years of the war] I was his Godmother and he was a good boy. Fanika is never very healthy, Mama is well although she often cries, as you know. Nono is still doing well and Ata, as you know, likes to pour it a lot. Kastelova sends regards, she was so nice when you went to say goodbye to them. She always asks about you. You should write to her sometime. Liparjeva also sends you regards. **A**

After his release from Ljubljana Hospital, Jožef was home for two or three months convalescing at the beginning of 1915. He went to Trieste in his uniform to have his photo taken and sent a copy to his sister, Mary. (photo 4) On 8 March, he returned to active duty in Galicia. There, the Austro-Hungarian forces were decimated in battle with the Russians because their weapons and strategies were not suited to the advances of trench warfare. One survivor stated that "the Galician plains were soaked in blood." To the south, the Austro-Hungarians had tried to invade Serbia three times in the fall of 1914 but were forced to retreat. In October 1915, joined by the Germans and Bulgarians, they attacked again and simultaneous attacks from three sides were sufficient to overrun Serbia, driving its army and a large civilian population to retreat over the mountains during the winter, to the Albanian coast. As they passed, the Albanians picked them off in revenge for past Serbian atrocities. Hundreds of thousands of Serbs died in the "Great Retreat." The remnants were taken by French ships to Corfu, where thousands more died from exposure and illness. They regrouped and joined Allied forces in Greece for a comeback in 1917.

On 6 May 1915, Tona wrote:

> There are rumors that you might come home, but you should
> thank God that you are in America. We cannot get flour, even
> for the holidays, nobody had it. People are eating polenta that
> was made from corn meant for the chickens. Rezina has a baby
> boy, born in March, whom they will name Frane. I'm doing fine,
> although I worry too much, and I'm always sad. Many from
> around here are dead. There has been no letter from Riko in
> six months. My husband is still near Pula. Our beloved brother
> in Galicija is in great danger. Of 38 men, 36 were dead imme-
> diately and one was taken by the Russians; our brother was the
> only one who survived. He writes that he is healthy, and he is
> consoling everybody else whenever he writes.

The letter continued with a message from Ata:

> My dearest daughter Marija, only a few of us are left to work.
> Nono cannot do anything anymore. It was only Pepe and me,
> but he went back to Galicija on 8 March. We received your
> letter and the photograph on 25th of March. Pepe wrote to us
> on 27 March that he is healthy, and that we should not feel
> sorry for him, and that we should be strong. You should be
> thankful that you have meat; here we cannot even make grits,
> as one cannot get flour. You should stay there until things here
> get better and maybe you will even save enough so you can
> buy some land and a house when you return. I'm telling you
> to stay there until this unrest settles and shortages end. I send
> you regards from my heart. Stay with God.
>   Your Father.

*

Italy had been a unified kingdom only since 1870, and it had ambi-
tions to expand into Austrian territory. In the London Agreement
signed on 26 April 1915, France, England, and Russia promised Italy

that they could have Tyrol, much of Slovenia and Croatia, Dalmatia, and certain Adriatic Islands if they would break their treaty with Germany and enter the war on the Allied side within one month. On 23 May 1915, Italy invaded Austria through the Julian Alps—a mountain range so close to Brkini that they can be seen on a clear day. For the next two years, the Italians fired uphill and the Austrians fired down upon them. Neither side advanced nor retreated more than ten yards in what the Italians called the Isonzo Front and the Austrians called the Soča Front, named for the river that ran through it. Both sides dug themselves deep into trenches and caves in the mountains and the snow. In addition to fire power, gas attacks, and avalanches, the soldiers starved, and suffered thirst, fell ill, and froze to death. In our age of global warming, and melting glaciers, their bodies are still emerging.

The Austro-Hungarians set their Russian prisoners to work expanding an existing cow path through the Vršič Pass from the eastern side of the Julian Alps to supply the entrapped Austro-Hungarian soldiers holding off the Italians from the west. Most of the Russian prisoners perished in a hellish ordeal of starvation, exposure to freezing temperatures, and disease. After hundreds of them were killed in an avalanche, the survivors built a wooden Russian-style chapel on the eastern side of the pass to commemorate them. Representatives of the Russian and Yugoslavian governments, and after 1991 the Slovenian government, gathered there annually in a gesture of solidarity and peace—this gathering was suspended when Russia invaded Ukraine in 2022.

As Russia withdrew from the war following the Bolshevik revolution, the Germans turned their efforts to the west. In October 1917 the German Army came to the aid of the beleaguered Austrians in the Julian Alps. With air power and troops, they attacked from the north and helped drive the Italians out of Austria. The Italian retreat is famously described by Ernest Hemingway in A Farewell to Arms.

This sweet letter from Pepa, Jožef's eighteen-year-old bride, was written to "dear little family" in America a month after the Italian invasion. The center of the fighting in Kobarid, or Caporetto as the Italians called it, was only 47 miles away. Could she actually hear the thunder of the guns? She said that she was not allowed to write more because of censors, then went on to express her fear in euphemisms. Sometime between 27 March and 6 May 1915, her new husband fought in a battle in which he was the only one to escape death or capture. Lightly wounded for a second time, he was convalescing in hospital when he wrote, unsure if he would be sent back to Galicia or to the Soča Front. Later letters imply that Jožef participated in the fight in Serbia. Pepa speaks of a photo of Ata, Mama, Fanika, and herself done in a studio in Trieste. The photograph was mailed to West Virginia, but John and Mary had moved, and it was returned. They sent it again, but it would not reach Mary until after the war.

Polžane, 28 June 1915

Dear Little Family! I want to write you a few lines, but let me first send you warm regards from our hearts, from me, and Mama, and Ata, and Nono, and Fanika. We are all healthy, thank God, and we wish the same for you. Today we will send you our photograph, but let me tell you that we have sent it already on 6 May but it came back because you have moved. We received your letter from 17 May. We are glad that you are healthy, and that everything is well. Let me tell you that my dear husband came back, he was slightly injured, but now he is fine again. Otherwise, he is always healthy, thank God. Now we fear that he will have to go back where he has already been twice, that he will have to go for the third time. It is sad, I am telling you, and he always writes that he believes in God who will make this War end, and that he will return home safely. God and the Holy Virgin, have mercy on us here, and on him over there, and protect him from evil. I would write you more, but I am not allowed. But I can tell you that your father Jurko also came home from šalcerat, thank God.

My Dear! Let me tell you that here we have a truly beautiful morning and everything looks good. And we are happy with this. God have mercy, and give us kind-hearted peace. Let me tell you also that we hear thunder almost every day, but we never get the rain. But we have hope and believe in God that he will not bring us that rain. Here we are still all local people, and our work gets done well. Thank God that until now, all of us are always healthy, and we hope that this will stay true in the future as well.

Let me tell you that Pepe also wrote to you from the hospital, but I think that you will not get the letter as he sent it to your old address. He always writes that he never receives anything from you, that now for two months he has not received anything. I write to him almost every second or third day and now we also gave him your new address.

Now I'll finish this writing of mine and I'll send you warm regards from my heart and from all of us. Trina Mekovka and Grgarečevi are also sending you best regards.

Z Bogom Z Bogom.

Stay who you are. God. God.

Pepa

John and Mary moved to Pennsylvania sometime in 1916 or 1917 and much correspondence was missed. Tona complained bitterly that she missed Mary's letters, but some letters from America still reached their destination. Marija Fradel, John's little sister, was an ecstatic recipient of one, and she responded in turn like a happy 21-year-old looking forward to a life-changing adventure. A photograph of her taken in Trieste shows an attractive blonde woman who looks a lot like her brother. (photo 5) Her optimism for the imminent success of the journey suggests that she was oblivious to the reality of events around her. She only knew that she had received a letter from her brother, who was offering to help her come to America. Had she read a newspaper, or had a frank conversation with anyone about her plans, she would have known that the war was far from over.

17th of February 1916.

Dear Brother and Marija, You ask if I really plan to come there, if I really have the will. You bet I do! But it will not be cheap. With some money now, I could get ready. Marija, write to me how you prepared, what I should take, and at which station you will be waiting for me. If you cannot send the money, tell me, maybe Dad could give it to me, but I will need money for the fare. I am counting on you. The first pay that I earn will be for you. I am asking you to please take care of everything, and respond as soon as you get this, as I am waiting eagerly.

We were lucky that we had very little snow so far. We already have ten tiny lambs; others are not ready yet. The only bit of news is that the Nono of Biščevi [Stefan Cergolj] died on the 12 February. When I arrive, I will tell you more about everything that is going on here. Biščevi has written to you many times, and they sent their photograph. They are writing today as well. Especially to the little one, many greetings and kisses, until the day we see each other, from your devoted sister, Z Bogom.

Marija

Looking Forward to Seeing You!

She wrote "please answer" upside down at the top of the last page as if she was bursting with impatience and excitement. After young Marija Fradel's letter, no mail arrived from Slovenia until the spring of 1919.

CHAPTER FOUR

1919: The Old Austria Is Dead

After the assassination of Archduke Franz Ferdinand, Austria had declared war on Serbia, so Russia attacked Austria ... Germany was Austria's ally, so it invaded Belgium ... the British jumped in to defend Belgium and Britain and France squared off against Germany.... World War I was complicated; few ordinary people understood what it was about then, and even today its causes are difficult to grasp.

John and Mary had not had mail from Europe for at least three years. John was required to register for the American draft but was not called up, possibly because he was still an Austrian citizen and America was at war with Austria. Additionally, his work at the Marshall Foundry in Black Lick, Pennsylvania, produced materials that were critical to the war effort. Biščevi and Jurkotevi knew only that Austria was allied with Germany and they were fighting Serbia, Russia, and Italy, but they knew nothing of the widespread European destruction. Worrying and waiting for letters from the front, they struggled with hunger as their crops failed, and their desperately-won harvests were requisitioned by the army.

Before 1914, the British and the Ottomans had been allies. The British failed to deliver two warships it had promised to build for the Ottomans, so they changed their alliance when Germany provided the ships. Italy had a pre-war alliance with Germany and Austria and was enticed away by the British and French with the promise of war spoils. After the Russian Empire collapsed in the wake of the 1917 Revolution, its army was withdrawn from the war. The Americans were latecomers to the fighting in defense of France and England. Thus, when the end of World War I came in November 1918, the Serbs, French, British, Italians, and Americans ended up defeating the Ottomans, Germans, Austrians, and Hungarians. The victors set about dismembering and vanquishing the conquered in a manner destined to bring about another war.

The defeated Ottoman Empire, which had once stretched from North Africa to the Middle East, was broken into little bits by the French, English, and Italians to fit their colonial agendas. The Balkan regions of the former Ottoman Empire—Montenegro, Macedonia, and Kosovo—joined the Kingdom of Serbia and this expansion sent political tremors that could be felt in Croatia and Slovenia. A federation of all southern Slavs was a controversial idea.

Germany had its borderlands chipped away by the victors. A non-militarized buffer zone in the German Rhineland kept France and Germany apart, while reparations demanded of them strangled the German economy and led to the rise of fascism.

The Austro-Hungarian Empire dissolved into its ethnic parts as the ideal of self-determination of nationalities was promoted at the Paris Peace Conference. The new nation of Austria sought to bite off chunks of Slovene-majority areas as the southern border of Austria was being defined. In the north central borderlands, the Slovenes successfully fought back to salvage Maribor, but lost part of Carinthia to Austria. The new nation of Hungary unsuccessfully tried to claim Prekmurje in the east. Italy had lost its battle against Austria, but their side won the war. They regrouped and prepared to claim the spoils promised to them in the London Agreement.

Months before the war's end, the National Council for Slovenian Lands was established to seize the opportunity for Slovene independence, but it did not have the army nor the political experience to resist Italy on its own. They hastily joined their southern neighbors to establish the Kingdom of Serbs, Croats, and Slovenes (the Slavic name for Croatia is Hrvaška, hence it was called the Kingdom of S.H.S.). When Austro-Hungary and Italy signed the armistice of Villa Giusta on 3 November 1918, which was to go into force the next day, the Italians did not wait for the ink to dry. They took possession of Trieste that same day and in the next two days helped themselves to all of Primorska in Slovenia, and Istria and a small part of Dalmatia in Croatia. The British and French did not fulfill all the territorial promises they made to Italy in the London Agreement. Parts of Croatia were handed to the Kingdom of S.H.S. and Rijeka, the port of the former Hungarian Empire, remained independent. The Italians were enraged and cried, "*Vittoria mutilata*"! (Mutilated victory!)

The Treaty of Rapallo on 12 November 1920, formalized the line of Italian occupation. The eastern border of Italy was defined as the mountainous watershed that channels the flow of water west to the Adriatic or east to the Black Sea. The line of occupation passed over the peak of Mount Triglav, the highest point in the Julian Alps, and a cultural symbol to Slovenes. Around Postojna in the south, the line pushed eastward to appropriate the forests around Javornik and Snežnik. Still, Italy wanted more.

"The Adriatic Sea, which is our bay, must change, if we are to realize our Mediterranean dreams, from the hands of the low barbarian Slavic race into our hand," Benito Mussolini pronounced on a visit to Pula in Croatia.

The Kingdom of S.H.S., soon to become the Kingdom of Southern Slavs, or Yugoslavia, risked further invasion by Italy. In 1924, the Italians appropriated Rijeka, which had aspired to be an independent city-state. Altogether, one-third of Slovenian lands and one quarter of its population became part of Italy.

At the time of the armistice, the world was in the grip of the second, and deadliest, wave of the Spanish flu pandemic. The first wave in the spring of 1918 was relatively mild. Soldiers throughout

Europe were affected, but none of the combatants wanted to admit their losses. Neutral Spain was the first to report massive deaths, thus it was mistakenly believed that the flu originated there, and it was dubbed the Spanish flu. In fact, it had gripped American soldiers in Kansas as early as March. Transports of American soldiers to Europe were underway at that time so President Woodrow Wilson's War Department downplayed the illness, and newspapers went along with the official policy believing that honesty would impede the war effort.

The epidemic went quiet during the summer months of 1918, then returned with a vengeance in October and November. Healthy young adults were unexpectedly hard hit. The disease was a terrifying spectacle: High fever and cough appeared suddenly. The lungs filled rapidly with fluid, suffocating the victim, and causing the skin of the chest and neck to turn blue, then black. It was said that a person could be well in the morning, and dead by afternoon.

Jožef was among the tired, defeated, walking-wounded, and coughing Austro-Hungarian soldiers who were transported from their battle stations to Trieste by train. The streets of his beloved city were patrolled by Italian soldiers who made sure that repatriated Slovene soldiers did not linger. Under the grey sky of early winter with a cold drizzle of rain, Jožef followed the road out of Trieste that he knew so well, climbing eight miles up the Karst escarpment to Kozina, and another four miles along the valley road to Povžane. The locals had been hungry during the war. The harvests were poor and whatever gleanings they made had been taken by the army. The fields were bare, the trees held not even a shriveled apple and the cattle were lean. People only watched from their windows as they passed. Many were nursing their own who had fever, cough, and shortness of breath, and those who were well feared contagion from the soldiers. As Jožef approached Biščevi on 9 November, he had tangible proof of God's mercy to find his parents alive, and his resilient wife and their little girl waiting for him. He quickly learned that the murderous influenza was visiting many homes in the villages under Slavnik.

The restoration of international mail service was slow. The lack of family news for nine months after the armistice was painful for Mary. She hoped to return home now that the war was over, while her husband pushed harder than ever to earn a living. He never had the warm attachment to his family that Mary had to hers, and he did not share her strong emotional pull homeward. Their little family was living in an apartment above the Kokas General Store in Black Lick in 1917 when Mary learned that she was pregnant again. More than fifty years later my grandmother shared with me how upset she was about it. Going home with one small child in tow would be easy enough, but additional children would complicate the journey. She heard of a potion to end a pregnancy that she could get by asking quietly at the pharmacy, but after consideration , she did not have the courage to speak about it. John Francis was born on 9 October 1917 and soon the family was on the move to another foundry job in West Middlesex, Pennsylvania where Joseph Emil, my father, was born on 21 November 1918 during the worst of the pandemic.

Mary wrote repeatedly to Jožef. A letter she wrote on 13 February 1919 was the first to arrive. It came in May and he replied promptly. His letter would not reach America until July 18.

15 May 1919

Dear Sister and Janez, After long anticipation we received your letter. It was so hard to wait for your letter. Dear Sister, I have a lot to tell you. For three years we could not write, and we have not heard anything from you. Ata was so sick that he lost vision in one of his eyes, but now he is recovered. I believe that you knew that Nono died in 1916. I returned home on 9 November 1918. The good news is that we have a daughter, she is two and a half years old. Her name is Marija.

Dear Sister, you ask about the rest of the family. In Bilkotevi, their oldest son died when he was 12 years old; the rest of the family is healthy. They have a new son, Frane, who is four years old, and they have three girls, Marija, Tona, and Francka. In Bazletevi, they are well. Our entire family is not getting along with Bazle. We have not spoken since my wedding. Fanika is still with us, but she is not as sharp as she used to be; she is leaning towards Bazle, her father.

Dear Janez, you also send regards to your father Valentin and sisters, but God! There is nobody to send regards to. Father and Marija and Stefanija have been covered with black soil for half a year. Within two months, all three of them died. Marija died in the last days of October, Stefanija died on Christmas and Father eight days after Christmas. Your sister, Pepina, married exactly a year ago to Jože Babič from Štefaktevi. Rudolf and Antonija are left alone at home. It was hard to look forward to your letter, as you can imagine how things are in a home if the master and the housewife are not there. I will write in more detail some other time.

Marija Fradel, John's 23-year-old sister, who had been so excited for the sea lanes to open would never see America. She died suddenly just three days before the armistice. Her sister, Stefanija, aged 24, perished on 22 December. Valentin seemed to be recovered from the flu, but when he got out of bed on the morning of 2 January 1919, he dropped dead. He was 54. Pepina, now married to Jože Babič, already had a nearly two-year-old son named after his father.

Jožef's letter continued with the serious details of Valentin's Will written hastily when the war began and amended after Pepina's marriage.

Your father's last Will states that if you, Janez, come home, then you will be master of the house, Rudolf and Antonija will each get 600 guldinar [$180] for dowry, and Pepina will get an additional 200 guldinar [$60] since she recently had a dowry. The money has changed to lire and the numbers are smaller. If you do not come home, you are to get 600 guldinar for your dowry, and Rudolf will become the master of the house. But, when the judge was here to administer the Will, he made you the master of the house and all three, sisters and brother, are to get the same dowry. I visited the judge that same day, and mentioned the 1200 guldinar [$360] that you sent for the land. The judge wrote everything down but did nothing more, as I do not have proof of the money you sent. The procedure is not complete, and everything will be done again. Therefore, dear Janez, come home as soon as possible. If you do not have anything more than your good salary to go on, you will lose more at home than what you earn there. Z bogom

After this letter arrived in July 1919 letters began to flow with detailed reports of others. Janez Maharinc, their neighbor at #5, had been killed in the war. Their friend, Riko, the one who "had been playing around with Kata after šalcerat" in 1913, had been missing since the early war. His death was now confirmed. Jože Zlogar was missing. His brother, Pepe Zlogar, and Janez Blaj suffered broken legs. Jože Rejčo (Granduč) had returned from America in 1913 at the time of Mary's departure, he was conscripted, but it was the Spanish flu that killed him. His brother, Piro, stayed safe in America and he would be among those who hurried home after the war. Ivan and Frane Fradel, the cousins at Fradelevi in Bač, were among the wounded. Ivan was deployed to the Soča Front. In March 1916, he saved his team in an avalanche for which he was awarded the Silver Cross; the following August, he was wounded. Frane Fradel, a member of the 97th infantry 11th company, was seriously injured in an early battle, 5 November 1914, on the bloody plains of Galicia "with both legs broken so that he would never be the same." It's hard to know if Jožef meant that they were amputated or that he walked with a limp. Jožef went on to write:

> Thank God that I am fine, my wounds have healed well, and I did not have any bones broken. We have to thank God that most of us here in Povžane who carried arms are doing well. I cannot say that we are the same as we used to be, because we had to suffer a lot for 52 months, and I am sure that at some

point this will catch up with us. I cannot describe to you how
hard it was, but thank God, everything is behind us.

My wife is always healthy. I do not want to brag about it,
but if you ever come home, you will see that I could not have
gotten a better wife, even if I searched for one with a halo. She
is hardworking, understanding, and patient. Our daughter is
a very kind child; she just turned three today. Greetings from
my heart. Z Bogom.

In the first two to three years after the war, many Brkini people
returned home from America. Francka Ban returned to Bač with her
husband and two daughters, and so did her uncle Josip Ban. John
and Mary seriously considered returning and wrote to Jožef about
plans to build a house and buy more land. They moved from Black
Lick, to Sharon, and to Pittsburgh where John found work at Nesta
Machine, gaining experience in pouring molds in steel foundries.
They returned to Black Lick where John had intermittent work. Mary
stayed alone with the children in Black Lick while John returned
to Sharon because it was hard to find housing suitable for a family. The frequent moves and the uncertainty of steady employment
contributed to their deliberations. Mary yearned to come home,
but the enormity and risks of moving their young family back to
the economic and physical hardships of rural Slovenia presented a
difficult choice. Her brother alternated between encouraging them
to come home, and warning them to stay away.

Valentin Jurko had come to Biščevi on that morning of 27 July
1914 to talk to Jožef about his will, just as the men were leaving with
the army. He had worried through the night, and needed Jožef's help
to put his plan on paper, but time ran out. That Valentin turned
to Jožef for help tells something of his character. The younger man
was a natural leader: competent, literate, and ready to engage with
other people and their problems. Jožef and Valentin continued to
discuss the will through letters and when Jožef was home on medical leave. Jeroft, a clerk at the municipal office wrote the will and

The Austro-Hungarian Empire used a silver standard until 1892. The *guldinar* had been the standard unit and *krajcar* were the subunits; not considered to be worth much at all; just a *soldov*, an old Slovene word for a coin. In 1892 they switched to a gold standard and the *krone* (crown) became the standard unit. Both units continued in circulation.

Silver standard pre-1892   Gold standard 1892–1919
1 guldin = 100 krajcar   1 guldin = 2 kroner

USD exchange rate in 1914
1 krone = 15 cents or 6.5 kroner = 1 USD
1 guldin = 30 cents or 3.25 guldinar = 1 USD

Postwar Italy in 1918
(1 lire = 2.5 kroner)
6.25 lire = 1 USD

Italy in 1920
25 lire = 1 USD

it was updated after Pepina's marriage in May 1918. Pepina's dowry had been 400 guldinar, so she was to get only another 200 from the estate. Valentin was trying to be fair so that one of his sons would get the land and each of his other children would get 600 guldinar.

Valentin specified payment in guldinar in his will, although guldinar had been replaced by kroner as the official Austro-Hungarian currency in 1892. Both currencies had continued in circulation before the war, and continued to do so for several years after the war, while the new governments grappled with currency decisions.

Inflation skyrocketed so it is hard to give a good estimate of the value of Valentin's 600 guldinar in 1920. It was still enough money to fight about. As the value of Italian currency declined and the strength of the U.S. dollar increased it became very easy for John to repay his debt incurred from travel to America. Consider the 1,000 kroner (2,000 guldinar) debt that John had in 1914. At that time John owed 155 dollars, a third of his annual income. By 1920 he could repay it with 16 dollars, and paying off 600 guldinar to each of his siblings as specified in the will required little effort from him.

And so, the thorny issue of the family farm arises, one that is central to this story. I had heard about the farm in Slovenia when I was little and I imagined it as I would imagine an American farm, with a house and a red barn surrounded by green fields. But farms do not look that way in the valley under Slavnik. All the stone houses with their attached buildings for animals and storage are tightly clustered in the village, just as they were in medieval times for protection against invaders, and management of precious water supplies. A farm consisted of parcels of varying sizes that were spread all over the place—a big meadow here, a little garden patch there, a root field someplace else. Jurkotevi encompassed 13 different parcels ranging in size from 2,700 to 24,800 square feet. The total land area was a little under four acres.

Valentin's will stated that John would inherit the farm, as an eldest son should, if he came home. Otherwise, he would get 600 guldinar, and Rudolf would get the farm. That seemed simple enough and truly what Valentin wanted, but the will gave no deadline for John's return, and the judge did not set one. The judge was in a hurry and, for him, matters were simplified if he assumed that John would return. By making this decision, he did not leave an easy option for Rudolf and he avoided a counter suit from Jožef Fabjančič, who was determined to fight for John's ownership. Jožef always fought for John because he hoped, expected, and prayed that his sister and her young family would eventually return to take their rightful place in Povžane. The judge took what seemed to be the easy way out when he executed the will on the assumption of John's imminent return. This sly little twist, contrary to the spirit of the will, would have repercussions for decades, even into the next century.

Pepina did not want to wait around for John to show up to get her money. The age for inheritance was 24 and she was 26 years old and about to leave for Maribor. She wanted the farm to be auctioned so that she could have her inheritance in cash right away. With depreciating land values and inflation, quick cash may have been more useful to her than waiting for the 200 guldinar promised to her in the judge's decision. Antonija was about to be married and she and her husband wanted to farm at Jurkotevi. Over the ensuing years she would make several attempts to get it. No one knew what 17-year-old Rudolf wanted, nor did he. His uncle, Frane Košanc, and a few others in the village tried to promote his interests, without much help from Rudolf.

John and Mary in America heard the news of the deaths of Valentin, Marija and Stefanija on 18 July. John was faced with the shocking realization that his father had been dead for six months already, a long time to leave a farm unattended in the middle of the growing season. One can imagine the conversations that my grandparents had. Mary would have made the case for their return and John would have been full of conflicting feelings. John made a proposal to Jožef that he take care of Jurkotevi until he could come home. With urgency, he had Mary write again with the proposal to her trusted brother. Jožef was thoroughly frustrated with the situation and the slow communication. He wrote back on 14 August 1919:

> Let me tell you that I received four of your letters at one time, one from February, one from May, one from 15 July, and one from 18 July. Thank you from my heart for all your greetings. Dear Janez, you want to assign me as the custodian of your property. As you know, I do not have time to take care of your things, as I can hardly take care of my own. We have only a few people here that can work. I would make the extra effort

for you, even if my work had to wait, but the situation with
your family is difficult. They will blame me if your farm goes
bankrupt. My wife nags me that we will not be able to reap
our own fields if we have to manage Jurko's farm, and we will
quickly burn through your 600 guldinar.

You want to pay your sisters and brother everything that
is due to them in the Will. You do not understand that it is
not possible to pay them off until the official procedure of
the Will is finished. Further, you can't pay them off until they
are 24 years old. If you send the money now, you would need
to open an account with a lawyer, who would meet with the
judge when he comes. The judge will put the money in the
vault until they are of full age. The judge should have been
here already, but he has not come. Another choice is for me to
hold your account.

Meanwhile, devilish people are instigating trouble. Since
she cannot get the land, Pepina is often against what the others want. If the land were to be auctioned, she will get ⅛ of
the farm's value. The worst troublemaker is Jože Vurk who
represents Pepina, Antonija, and Rudolf. I do not know why,
but he is angry with you. Your family is teasing, and asking
why should they do the work for you? If they actually did the
work, they will not do it well, and the value of the farm will go
down. Rudolf, at this time, is generous to work for you, but he
sold one piece of livestock without telling anyone, took some
firewood, and had one tree taken down in the valley. But do not
mention this to him, because he will know that I was the one
to tell you. I do not know what you have written to Antonija,
but she is crying, cursing us, and asking for all kinds of bad
things to happen here.

Therefore, dear Janez, do this: Send your account to me with
detailed instructions of what needs to be done, in particular
with the livestock. Write to Rudolf about your plans, so that
you and I will act in the same way. I would like to see you
back home, though it might be better that you are in America.
Here you would suffer, and quarrel with everyone, until Pepina

sends everyone away with 300 guldinar. You always ask us to take care of Ata and Mama, and, of course, they are well cared for. They worry about things that they see wrong at Jurkotevi, and it hurts their hearts. Tona and Rezina always look forward for news from your letters. I tell them that they should write to you themselves if they want to know more, and that if they cannot afford the stamps for a letter, I will give them the money.

Greetings from my heart and from all our family. God has given us a son, on 8 August, his name is Jože. Z Bogom, Z Bogom

John had already written to discuss the details of returning home, purchasing more land, and building a new house. Jožef responded as soon as he got that letter, on 21 August 1919.

I received your letter from 21 July, thank you from my heart for your greetings. Dear Janez, you write that you have sent me the authorization and the money, but I have not received anything. As you asked, I spoke to Pajser about the garden. He does not want to sell all of it, so I offered a little something for one or two meters. You asked me to talk to Bazle about digging out stones, but when he needed about 15 carts of stones for his own project, he bought them, rather than digging them out himself. He has not changed a bit. Therefore, do not count on Bazle and Rudolf to do anything.

I know that you wish to build a new house, and it is true that the old one is not good to live in anymore. But these days you can expect to pay eight times as much as you did 10 years ago. If you come home everything will need to be done, there is as much work in the house as there is outside. So, if you get this letter, you will know how things are, and decide if you will dare to do this.

All the preparations are made for Antonija Fradel to be married to Cesarevi in Artviže. In your absence, her uncle Frane Košanc will send her off. I told him that he should write to you to ask if you want to give Antonija a dowry out of the farm. He disagreed with me, so on his own he went to Podgrad to speak to the judge, and as I predicted, the judge said that she cannot get more money than what was left for her.

Therefore, Dear Janez, I do not know what will happen at Jurkotevi after Antonija leaves and Rudolf is there alone. Things are already going badly; he is giving things away and there will be nothing left. I told Frane to sell those two goats and lend the sheep to others. The oxen should stay because you will need them if you come home in the spring; if you are not coming, it would be better to sell them. One is getting old and Rudolf pushes the other one too hard. He only worries whether he has enough to drink.

In the following three weeks there was a flurry of letters and money was sent to pay his siblings off, but John still had not addressed Jožef's concerns. People blamed John for the farm's decline and demanded that the Will be annulled so that everyone could receive an equal share. Jožef was put in the middle of the drama but had not been given the power to do what he thought needed to be done. It was harvesting time, Biščevi had its own harvest to get in, there was work at Jurkotevi to get done and decisions to be made before winter. Jožef was exasperated with Rudolf and compared him to the village n'er-do-well, Janez Durc, whose house was always a mess, and whose clothes were in rags.

Jožef finally got angry with John. His usual cheery greeting was gone, his salutations and wishes of good health were curt. He signed his full name, last name first, in official Slovenian style. Jožef repeated with greater force and in more detail what he had said in previous letters.

8 September 1919
Dear Janez and Sister, Today I received the 1,015 lire [about $40—the exchange rate was very favorable to John] that you sent. I've already told you that until the legal process is finished, the money cannot be used to pay off your sisters and brother. If the legal process is not finished soon, I'll put it in a bank.

I also received your authorization to be caretaker, but I will not accept the responsibility. The way it was written, nothing can be sold and that is why I do not accept it. If you want to protect your property, the first step is to sell some things. It is like taking things out of the fire so that they will not burn; this needs to be done fast because things are not going well. If Rudolf has somewhere to go for a day, he stays away for the entire week. That is why there is not enough hay and why most of the grass still needs to be mowed. Two goats will soon die of hunger because nobody is taking care of them. If nothing else, the goats need to be sold. There is not enough hay for even one of the oxen to survive the winter, so I would sell the one in poorer condition. I cannot sell the sheep even though they are about to die. I already asked you what to do with the cattle, and until I have your permission in writing, I cannot do anything.

Dear Janez, it is a sad view for someone that comes to your home. The oxen no longer have the hay-rack, the cart is broken, everything is in disarray. I came one day and everything was standing open, but nobody was home. It hurts me as if it were my own. It may seem harsh to drive your own family out of the house, but Antonija is getting married and Rudolf should go and work elsewhere. It is not hard to imagine that Rudolf will sell all the animals and run away to be like Janez Durc. I am chasing away Frane Košanc who is siding with Rudolf. I would do anything for you if this authorization would allow me to sell what needs to be sold, store the rest, and lock the house. It is hard to wait for your reply; the sooner I could do this, the less would go to ruin. Warm regards, Z Bogom

Fabijančič Jožef

After Jožef's angry letter, three months passed without another one. Either he quit writing or, more likely, the letters were filled with business details so Mary set them aside for John to deal with. A letter from January 1920 is saved, then letters are weeks or only days apart. John gave Jožef full power of attorney, a court date was set, and John had introduced the idea of sponsoring Rudolf to come to America. The cheerful exclamation points were back, despite the fact that Jožef was suffering from sciatica so severely that he couldn't leave the house for at least six weeks, the usual duration of an acute sciatica.

Jožef lamented the way things had changed since the days of the empire. Kaiser Franz Josef had been Emperor for 68 years before his death during the Great War. Ordinary Slovenes viewed him as a father figure; a metaphor for order and tradition and the days when the infrastructure was maintained, children were educated in Slovene village schools, literacy was rising, and the rural economy, though poor, was stable. *The Radetzky March* by Joseph Roth is an insightful novel that gives a feel for Slovenia in the empire, as well as Jožef's sentimentality for the old days. In the difficult years that were to follow, Jožef would often sigh with a variable mixture of anger and sadness about the loss of "the gratefulness of old Austria."

3 January 1920

Dear Sister and Janez!!! Let me tell you that my family is healthy, thank God. My daughter, Marija, is now three and a half years old and she is a very kind child. My little Jožek is five months old, he is very brave, as if he were one year old. I am very pleased with my family. My wife and Mama get along well, even better than you and Rezina did. Every now and then Mama rebukes her, but my wife never says anything back, she suffers for a few minutes, and then everything is well. That is how we live a peaceful life.

I have not been able to work for the past month. First, I had pain in my back, and then in my leg, so that I cannot walk or do anything. I have improved so that I can walk a little inside the house using a cane. You know how hard it is for me to live without working. Life is also hard because of the business with your estate. I would like to see the end of this, but I cannot go anywhere to get things done. Once I am able go to Podgrad, things should move forward. I will write more after I talk to the judge. You write that you are doing well. I believe you. Everyone that comes home regrets it, and plans to go back to America. Frane Martin came home recently and he says that he will go back.

Tona Bazle has another son, named Ivan. She is just as poor as ever and Bazle is still the same. He did not want the child to be baptized, but the baby was weak, so my wife took him to the church. I did not come along because of my back, but I would not have gone if I were well. I have not been in their house for three years and I will not go now.

Dear Sister, you asked how is it possible that nobody asks about you. Well, you do not know that the gratefulness of the old Austria has died of hunger. The way things are here, if one helps another, he is sometimes remembered, but once you go away, or get sick, or old, nobody remembers you. This is how it is today.

CHAPTER FIVE

1920: Rudy

The Jurkotevi household was in chaos with Valentin dead and John away, and Jožef Biščev squabbling with Frane Košanc about leaving Rudolf in charge. John found out about the mess in mid-July 1919 and it wasn't long before it was suggested that Rudolf should come to him. Perhaps he thought that this was a kindness to bring his little brother to join him in America, but Rudolf was not enthusiastic about the proposal. Jožef Biščev had no patience with the boy. He wrote:

6 January 1920

Dear Janez, Rudolf wrote to you that he is ready to come to America because it was fall and getting cold, and he had nowhere else to go. I am sure that he will not go anywhere. He is full of excuses for whatever is wrong; others are to blame or others wrongly influenced him. In fact, it is his head that is to blame. He thinks that he will be able to live a good life without working. To be honest with you, it is hard for me to imagine him in America, unless another brain comes into his head.

Now, as I read in the Trst newspapers, and as you explained in your letter, it is unlikely that the new immigration rules in

America will allow him to go. Even if he suddenly changed his mind, it would be difficult to get everything ready by March.

I can see that you do not have any plans to come home. If you are going to stay in America, then you have made a mistake by sending money here. What I have received so far, I will put in a bank in Podgrad, just to have some peace of mind.

*

Prior to 1880, most immigrants to the U.S. were Protestants from western and northern Europe who came to farm and open the western frontier. The two million Irish Catholics who arrived during the potato famine of 1845-1855 faced hostility for their perceived laziness, poor manners, public drinking, their religion, proclivity for criminality, being inherently dirty and spreading disease. Rapid industrialization between 1890 and 1914 created a huge demand for workers which triggered a "Great Wave of Migration." An estimated twenty million people poured into the country—mostly Jews and Catholics from eastern, central, and southern Europe. The U.S. population was only 75 million, so nearly one in four Americans was a new immigrant.

From Trieste alone, steamships embarked once or twice a week, stopping in Rijeka and ports in Greece and Italy to gather a thousand or more passengers for the two-week trip to New York. Other immigrants traveled by train to Bremen and Le Havre, the other major ports of exit, where there were facilities to house them while they waited to leave. A new immigration center was opened on Ellis Island in 1892 to process the arrivals, and few laws restricted who could come. The Immigration Act of 1903 excluded only anarchists, epileptics, beggars, and importers of prostitutes. At the port of departure, the shipping company recorded a passenger's name, age, marital status, place of origin, destination, and contact information. At Ellis Island, officials checked the information on the ship's manifest. Immigrants were examined for a highly contagious eye disease called trachoma, and obvious tuberculosis. The excluded arrivals were sent back at the expense of the shipping company. The Immigration Act of 1907 raised the entry tax from $2 to $4. Immigrants brought with them the entry requirement of $25 which many had sewn into their clothes.

After the war, the need for workers diminished and anti-immigrant sentiment increased, especially regarding Jews and Italians. Eugenics, a popular junk science in the late 19th and early 20th centuries, was employed to justify this sentiment. Based on skull shapes, people of various regions were placed in categories and ranked on beauty, intellect, and morality. The rankings were used as rationale to exclude certain groups of people. Asians had long been deemed undesirable and the Chinese Exclusion Act of 1882 prohibited the entry of any Chinese. Subsequent laws blocked other Asians. The first effort to slow southern and eastern European immigration began with the Literacy Act of 1917, which required that an immigrant have basic reading ability in their own language, a sponsor, and a visa.

John had sent sponsorship papers which Rudolf needed to present to the American Consulate in Trieste to obtain a visa. He needed to do it urgently so he could leave before Congress passed the expected new law. The Emergency Quota Act, signed on 19 May 1921, limited the number of immigrants admitted to the U.S. annually, then it set a quota for each nationality. To determine that quota, the number of foreign-born people of each nationality present in the U.S. in the 1910 census was counted and the number of immigrants from that group was then limited to three percent. For example, if there were 1,000 people born in Albania in the U.S. in 1910, then only thirty Albanians could be admitted in 1921 until the total limit on new immigrants was reached.

*

In 1920, Mary finally received the photograph of her family taken five years earlier. The picture, now in my possession, shows Mama seated, Ata in a hat, holding a cane; Jožef's young wife, Pepa, and Fani Godina. (photo 6) Jožef wrote at the beginning of 1920:

28 January 1920

My back and leg are better, although I am not completely well. I received your letter in which you thank us for the photograph. You write that you are excited to see a picture of your parents, but you worry if Father really needs a cane. Although he is weaker, he still walks without it. Of course, as he ages, he gets more ornery, but I am happy to have him. You think that Mama looks the same, though with all the bitterness that she experienced since the photo was taken five years ago, she has aged a little. Fanika has grown up; she has changed a lot since she was a little girl. She is rather dense and full of stupidities, which is no surprise since an apple never falls off a hazel-tree. We are not pleased with her; we patiently wait for her to grow up, and finish school, then she will go and taste how good other people's bread is. You also say that my wife is beautiful. We are all beautiful in God's eyes, but I can tell you that she is even more beautiful on the inside. She is a kind, hardworking, and judicious soul. I never imagined that I would get such a good wife. You once wrote and asked in a joking manner, if I would get a wife that would be as beautiful as a flower, as hardworking as a bee and judicious as a judge? Well, she is not as judicious as a judge because she has not been to school, like you and I have been, but as for the other two qualities, I can tell you that I got exactly what you predicted. I am really happy with what has been given to me. But do not think that I am boasting, others can tell you the same thing, and if you come home, you will happily see for yourself that I have not lied.

Dear Sister, you tell me that I sent back one of the letters that you wrote to me. Please do not be offended. There is always something to distract me. I never have peace and quiet. When I was in the army, my head was full of thoughts about home and military matters. I was assigned to be a corporal, and I was forced to do my duty. I promised myself that when I came home, I would live a peaceful life, keep my things organized, not worry about anything. Everything turned out differently. Soon after I came home, I was assigned to be the Village Mayor. I did not want to be, but I had to accept. There is so much happening in these times, and so much to worry about. Just as it was in the army, there is always something that needs to be done, and never enough time. With my own worries, then yours, and then those of the entire community, I often cannot fall asleep. If I concentrate on one thing, I forget about the other. The hardest thing is your business. After we go to the courthouse on 10 February, I hope that everything will be completed.

A few days later, Jožef wrote addressing John directly about his business concerns.

1 February 1920
   Dear Janez!!! I received your letter from 4 January with the money you sent me to buy some land for you. I quietly asked around to see who has intentions to sell. For now, there is nothing. What you have already sent, I put in the bank, but I urge you not to send more until this matter is settled. I will purchase land, if possible, otherwise the money will wait for your return home. I have been to Podgrad, and they came here to go through everything. The estimated worth of your home today is fourteen thousand and 500 lire [perhaps $6,000 at a time when the average U.S. income was $3,269].
   I want to discuss our affairs. As you know, this year Rudolf was in charge of the farm. He would have destroyed everything if I had not watched over him, but I could protect only so much. Four times I was busy in Podgrad dealing with your affairs, and so it was in the last moment that I stopped him. Some say that Rudolf is stupid. Others remark that you may run the farm as you wish after your return, but until you come from America, you are not in charge. Rudolf continues to be baited by devilish people. He sold the pig and one sheep disappeared. He cut down enough trees to fill three carts. He destroyed most of the

tools. He left the crops in the field so long that they went bad and most of what was harvested had to be thrown away. In the end, all he could keep were a few bags of potatoes.

I wanted to sell the oxen earlier, but Frane Košanc objected. He asked me how Rudolf would be able to work without the oxen and accused me of trying to throw him out. The oxen brought 3,250 lire [$1,350] which was one thousand lire less than they should have, since Rudolf was not taking good care of them.

Now, on the 10th we are going to Podgrad to meet with the judge. There are still instigators in Povžane who want the judge to overturn the Will. It is better that you do not know all the details as there is the devil in people, I do not know what you have done to them, that they are so against you. Antonija promises to accept 800 lire according to her father's wishes. She will get an additional 20 lire for every 100 lire because the rates for exchanging kroner and lire were not settled until this year. I paid off Pepina earlier; she still needs to get that additional 20 percent. I have only Rudolf to take care of now. Frane Košanc and some others think that he should get a lot, but I will not let them ask for anything more than the Will permits. I will record the damage that Rudolf has done, and when you come home, we will recalculate everything. It is best to stay away from the lawyers and settle things on our own.

This year we will apply lime to the soil. It is expensive, and hard to find someone to hire for the job. Now is a good time to buy it because if you wait, there will be none left. I estimate that you will need about 20 wagons or more. I have not done anything with your farm, because every time you write, you say something different. Last time you wrote that it would be good to cut grass on half of your meadows. This is not a bad idea. I could cut the grass on at least two of the meadows, and the rest I will split with someone else. I could set potatoes on one or two of your fields and plant oats on another. The rest can stay empty, just as you suggested. You wrote that you wanted to buy another meadow; I was almost certain that I would buy one in Boršt from Drej Vogrnjač, but the deal fell through.

My Dearly Beloved Sister, you ask for news about all the women whose husbands had emperor's jobs. When they returned, they had nothing more than the roof over their heads. You are always curious about the Povžane girls; I never think about this. At the beginning of the war, Tonči's Marija went to serve at a house in Lonjer, in Italy; she earned a child, and now lives as a lost sheep. Pepa from Oplaz married someone in Beka. Marija Rejčeva is now with Jože Grgur. As you would expect, his mother is not happy with her, so he left home about one year ago, and is staying with the Ban family at Grgarečevi. Then you ask about my wife's family in Vareje. Her parents and Nono are well off, they have eight head of cattle, and a large farm. My wife is the oldest of the children. Her brother was in the army for a short period. She has four sisters; the oldest is 20 and the youngest is 10.

Dear Sister!!! Let me tell you about your sister, Tona. You wrote that you sent a few lire to Ata and Mama for the holiday, but they never received it. I just learned at the post office that Tona picked up the lire soon after Christmas and she has spent them. I am ashamed that I have such a sister who denied her own parents what was theirs!

Letters from Tona and Mary's best friend, Pepa Blaževa, were full of rich details about the people in the village that Mary longed to hear so she could feel close to home. Pepa's activities featured prominently in news from others. Jožef often said that Pepa Blaževa behaved in a way that was "not noble," implying some moral judgement, and Mary could count on Tona to provide the juicy details. For example, when Jožef said that Pepa Blaževa's behavior in regard to Ogrnjač was not noble, Tona reported that Pepa hovered around Ogrnjač while his wife was ill, waiting for her to die so that she could take up with him. Pepa had been married before, and was either widowed or divorced.

Mary enjoyed regular news about Rejčevi, the house below Biščevi, where Piro Rejčo had returned from America around 1920 with a lot of money. Employment insecurity and homesickness brought him and others home, but their savings did not last long. Many said that they regretted their decision and declared that they would leave again, but most of them, including Piro Rejčo, were back for good. His sister, Marija Rejčeva, was in a relationship with Jože Grgur, but his mother disapproved—she was not the first girl to be rejected by his mother. Jože rebelled and moved next door with the Ban family at Grgarečevi. Marija Grgareva of this house, a well loved friend of Mary and many others, was married and working in a gostilna in Boršt, one of the towns that Brkini people traversed on their route to Trieste.

John's sister, Pepina Fradel, and her husband Jože Babič, from Štefaktevi in Bač, were living near Koper where his skills as a carpenter enabled him to find work in the port. In 1920, he took part in a strike at St. Anton and when it failed, he became a target of anti-Slovene thugs and Italian police. They fled to Maribor with their toddler, Jože.

Mary suspected that Tona had not written since early February because she was embarrassed about the theft. As a sign of forgiveness, Mary sent her a few dollars, knowing that Tona would then be forced to write a thank you letter and revive their communication.

20 *March 1920*
My dear Sister and Brother-In-Law, Please, do not resent that I haven't written in such a long time. I have not received any money before. Thank you from the bottom of our hearts. May God give you a thousand times more than what you've sent us, and that soon you will remember us again. We had a baby in the new year. We call him Ivan, he is a cute boy, but he cries a lot. We are now rich with five children. Jože is 14, Fanika is 12 and stays at Biščevi, Zora is 10, and Karel is 6. My dear sister,

this winter was hard for me, first the child, and then I was sick, but now we are well, thank God.

Pepa Blaževa is doing well; she works for Štele. She has a son, Ljubo and two girls named Kristina and Zora. Marija Grgarečeva is in Boršt and takes care of the gostilna belonging to Franc Blažev. Your Pepina and her husband are in Maribor. Frane Martin came from America; he lost one of his eyes there. Many others have returned from America. My dear sister, we wish that we would see you once again as well, but we know that it is best that you remain there, so that you will not have to endure the hard work here. Liparjevi and Božidar Kastelic send you regards. Božidar has not yet married, he lives alone with his hired men and girls. Z Bogom **A**

When Jožef wrote, planting time was near and his focus was on the land. He had hoped that John would be there for this second planting after the war and he felt caught in a bind. The unplanted fields and uncut meadows hurt his heart but he couldn't do all the work himself. Frane Košanc and others made his life unpleasant as they accused him of seeking to profit from Jurkotevi. John complicated matters when his plans flip-flopped between buying more land and selling everything. On 21 March, he wrote to John:

> I just received your letter from 24 February. You are disappointed that the estimated value of your estate is only 14,000 lire but you must understand that we wanted to keep it low to reduce the taxes. Your sisters are to blame that the taxes are as high as they are. If you were to sell your farm now it could be worth more than 25,000 lire, if the buyers would purchase each piece individually. But sold in one lot, it would not bring as much.

According to Jožef's accounts of young Rudolf's antics, while he still had the oxen and the cart, he had earned more than 3,000

lire but squandered it in Trieste and returned to Povžane where
no one would hire him. When the oxen were sold, Rudy had been
given money for new clothes but by the summer they were in tat-
ters, prompting Jožef to repeat his comparison to the n'er do well,
Janez Durc. When Rudolf hit the bottom once more, he declared
that he was ready to go to America. John wrote directly to him that
once he had the visa, Jožef would take money from the Jurkotevi
account to pay for his ticket and give him a little extra for expenses
on the voyage. Rudy's interpretation was that he should receive all
the money he wanted from the account to spend as he prepared to
depart. Jožef knew better than to give Rudy any advance, so Frane
Košanc gave him 100 lire in the belief that he would ultimately be
reimbursed from the Jurkotevi account. Rudy went to Trieste for
two days to party, came home empty handed, and was reduced to
begging and borrowing from his friends.

Uncle Frane Košanc had a soft spot for Rudy, a fatherly protec-
tiveness, perhaps. Frane's son was the same age as Rudy. Like the
prodigal son, Rudy was welcomed to stay at Košančevi whenever he
returned to the village empty handed. Every letter that Jožef wrote
in 1920 complained about Rudolf and Frane Košanc.

10 May 1920

If Rudolf is told to do something, he agrees, but he never
follows through, then curses behind your back. Last summer
Ata cut his meadow, sheaved the grass, and let it dry so that he
would have something to give to the oxen in the winter. Then
he went to him and said, "Rudolf, I cut your meadow, gathered
the grass, and had it dried. Get it and take it home." Rudolf
said, "Yes, I'll go." And when Ata turned away, he said in front of
others, "Go and fuck your mother, what do you think, making
sheaves for me." In the end, he left everything in the field to rot.

29 May 1920

Dear Janez, You write that you will send me an invitation
for Rudolf. Taking care of your brother is the right thing to

do and it is possible that he would be a better person there, as he might be afraid of you. I would write to you more often about his behavior, but I do not want to insult you, as I know that it is hard when you hear things like this. But since you are seriously thinking of bringing him to America, I want to warn you, so that you will not curse me someday.

8 September 1920

Dear Janez, I want to tell you more about Rudolf. He works in Odolina for Italians who make charcoal and he earns 300 lire per month. Others have told me that he lost your invitation. The way I see it, he does not have the courage to go to America. Now that he knows I will not give him money, he does not come here anymore. He tells others that I pushed him out of his home. I have asked Frane Košanc many times to send him off to America., but I do not know what Frane tells Rudolf. Frane is hungry for what others have. He believes that he should have something from Jurkotevi. When we were discussing Valentin's Will, he took sides with Rudolf and sisters against you and me. The last time Frane was at my house, he said that if I want him to be on the same side as you and me, that I should take care of him like I take care of my own family. I promised him that I would, just to make sure that things proceeded smoothly. Later, he joined with others to threaten a lawsuit to invalidate the last Will. He says that he was with me before, but that I have not given him what I promised.

Od (of) *dolina* (valley) is part of the valley under Slavnik just short of the line where the bedrock of Brkini begins. A small stream that runs through the village is the only surface water for miles. When cisterns ran low, the women from other villages brought their clothes there to wash. It had a small castle that was the home of Italian nobles, a church dedicated to St. Peter built in 1634, and a few houses that were the home of 20 people in 1920. Its business was making charcoal. The sides of the valley were covered in trees that were cut down and burned to produce charcoal. It was hard, dirty, and backbreaking, poorly paid work, a place where n'er do wells like Rudolf worked as a last resort. Twenty-some years earlier, another wayward cousin, Anton Fradel, notorious for getting busted while partying with the Romani then known as "gypsies" in Trieste and robbing a pasta factory, had also been a charcoal burner in Odolina.

The thought of leaving his own home was unfathomable to Jožef. His sister's wanderings haunted him, and he considered the dilemma of choosing wealth over the security of living on one's own land, poor as it may be. Jožef commented in one letter, "It must not be very pleasant for you to move around like vagabonds, but it is still better to be a vagabond and be well off, than be next to the oven and not have any bread."

29 May 1920

It sounds like you are living like lords, and you are still able to put some money on the side. We live like peasants and have to be careful so that we are able to survive from day to day. But I know that you understand how it is here; you ate bread in Povžane long before you ate bread in America. Dear Sister, you write that you would like to return to the place where you were born. I know that your heart longs to see your loved ones, but I am warning you that a lot of work is waiting for you here, and you could be worse off here than you are there. This year, if God does not give us some rain, we might need to get everything off the fields. Can you imagine that cherries are getting sour in the month of May? We will have no hay, as the tiny grass is all dry.

Dear Janez, you wrote that I should buy as much lime as possible. It is expensive, a *kvintal* costs 15 lire, and you don't have the right pit for storage. I made the pit where you kept your stable manure a little deeper, and raised a small wall around it to hold just 30 kvintals. When you come home, this will provide you enough for building, and a little bit more, and then later you can buy more yourself.

> A kvintal, pronounced *quintal*, is an ancient
> measure equaling 100 kilograms or 220 pounds.

*

As Jožef struggled with the soil and lack of rain, Rudy's lack of direction, the complexities of managing Jurkotevi, and making things
ready for John and Mary's return, while bracing himself for disappointment, bigger things were taking place around him. Trieste,
the largest Slovene city at the time, was the center of commerce for
Jožef and his window to the bigger world. Before the war it had
been a lively, multicultural city, the port of the Austrian Empire,
with a population of 30,000. Slovenes comprised about 40 percent
of that population and had been an integral workforce in the city
for twelve centuries. Many lived in the suburbs, employed as carters,
waterside workers, cooks, maids, masons, laborers and small mer-
chants and as Slovene language, education and culture blossomed
under the Austrian government in the later years of the 19th century,
a Slovene middle class emerged.

Over time, however, Trieste's vibrant multiculturalism had been
systemically eroded by the *Risorgimento* (Resurgence), an Italian
political and social movement that united the various states of the
Italian peninsula into the Kingdom of Italy. The unification process
started with the nationalist revolutions of 1848 and was completed
in 1871 when the Kingdom of Italy took the Papal States, and made
Rome its capital. They declared themselves to be the inheritors
of Ancient Rome, and in a movement called *irredentismo* (redemption) former Roman lands were to be reclaimed by ridding them of
other languages and cultures. After 1870, irredentismo's stronghold
in Trieste gradually turned public opinion, and citizens began to

adopt an Italian sentiment. Irredentists first aimed to destroy the influence of Austrian and German culture, then they turned their attention against the rising Slovene middle class, and often provoked clashes with Triestines of Slovenian descent.

The *Narodni Dom* (Peoples Home) constructed in 1904 in central Trieste, was a Slovene cultural center, a lively place with cafés, meeting rooms, a music school, the Sokol (a sporting organization), *Edinost,* (a political society and newspaper), and a 400-seat theater with a glass roof that opened in warm weather for outdoor performances. It also contained the upscale Hotel Balkan, as well as private apartments. This modern building stood as a symbol of Slovene cultural and economic progress. When the Italians seized control of Trieste after the war, the Narodni Dom became a target of the smoldering hatred of irredentist agitators.

On the afternoon of 13 July 1920, the Narodni Dom, the Yugoslav consulate, and many Slovene businesses in the center of the city were torched and the attackers refused to allow firefighters to extinguish the flames. Irredentists had so far sought the expansion of Italianization mostly in a persuasive manner, but the torching of the Narodni Dom was a turning point. Benito Mussolini, a journalist, and founder of the National Fascist Party, described it as a "Masterpiece of Triestine fascism." On September 20, at a fascist rally in Pula, Croatia, he called for ethnic cleansing:

> When dealing with such a race as Slavic—inferior and barbaric—we must not pursue the carrot but the stick policy. We should not be afraid of new victims. The Italian border should run across the Brenner Pass, Monte Nevoso and the Dinaric Alps. I would say we can easily sacrifice 500,000 barbaric Slavs for 50,000 Italians.

Jožef read about these events in *Edinost* which continued to publish daily even after its offices were burned in the Narodni Dom. The

crop was poor this season and even without mentioning the rise of
fascism and anti-Slovene activities, Jožef's mood darkened.

1 August 1920

There will be nothing to take off the fields this year as everything is burnt from the drought. If you came home to this, you
would definitely go back. Everyone who has returned regrets
it. They earned a few hundred dollars, thought they were rich,
spent money for the ship, and then a little at home, and in five
to six months they have nothing left. Piro Rejčo says that he
will go back in the spring, if not earlier.

8 September 1920

The drought lasted the entire season; we had rain for a day
every two months. Can you imagine that our well has been
dry since our opasilo [8 August]? Thus, the harvest was poor,
with half the hay that we normally have, and no more grass to
cut this year. We have one fourth of the grains, and no turnip.
The few potatoes we harvested are baked by the heat and won't
be worth much. The corn was already ripe at our opasilo. We
are storing it a month earlier than usual. You can see that we
will have only a little of everything, and we have nothing to
sell. God, please, make things better as we will not be able to
live like this.

*

Rudolf was always Uncle Rudy to me. In telling his story we only
get Jožef's version. I have tried to appreciate the problems of young
Rudy from his own unwritten, untold perspective. I imagine Rudy
must have been resentful of caring for the farm since it belonged
to John. He asked himself, "Why should I work the land for my
brother's benefit? He'll return home one day and I will be left with
nothing, no place for my wife and family, and with little thanks from

John. And what does Uncle Frane Košanc want? Does he really want
to save Jurkotevi for me, or is he just using me so he can get a piece
of the land?" Rudy's actions leading up to his departure to America
seem incongruous with the legacy he would build in Pennsylvania
as a dedicated, hard-working family man. We can only assume his
immaturity, coupled with several traumatic losses, may have left him
feeling abandoned and resentful of everyone telling him what to do.
Rudy was only eight when John left Slovenia for West Virginia in
1909, returning briefly before his army conscription, and leaving
again in 1913, so they hardly knew each other. At the age of 10, Rudy's
mother died and at 13, he watched the men of his village leave for
war. He suffered through hard work and wartime privations and
at 17 he lost his father and two sisters to the Spanish flu. His last
two sisters married and moved away soon after that, leaving the
teenaged boy alone in the house he had once shared with seven
other people. What was clear in Jožef's letters was his eagerness
to position Rudy where he would be under the watchful eye of his
older brother. Perhaps then, he would straighten up.

Great Uncle Rudy was 20 years old when my grandfather brought
him to western Pennsylvania. Work was scarce and he moved between
steel factories and coal mines and boarded with other immigrant
families. His granddaughter, Jan Brooks, told me that he learned to
play the tuba, belonged to a community band, and joined a singing
group. Rudy did stone masonry on the side, a skill he remembered
from Slovenia. He remained single until he was 41 years old. He married Ella Zdravecky, whose family he boarded with in Yukon, a small
town in Westmoreland County. Ella had been widowed a few months
after her marriage, even before her son was born. Her son, Lattamere
(Larry) was 16 years old when Rudy and Ella married in 1942. Larry
married Marge, and their children remember Rudy as a sweet, caring
grandfather. When I visited Rudy and Ella in Yukon in their later
years, they kept a large, neat garden on a hillside near the Slovene
Hall and Ella served me thinly sliced pršut with her sweet homemade

bread. In 1969, as my brother was anticipating what he might do if he drew a low number in the Vietnam draft lottery, Uncle Rudy, then 68 years old, spilled the beans about our grandfather being a deserter. To us, at the time, this was scandalous. Uncle Rudy had a better sense of humor than anyone in my family and it was nice to be around him. It is hard to imagine that he was once a difficult teenager.

Jan said that Rudy never spoke of Slovenia. That is no wonder, given his cruel experience. He left and never looked back. My grandparents as well, shared little about life in Slovenia with their children. What my own parents heard from them was passed on in snippets of stories to my generation. These snippets stayed with me and I was eager to find out if they were true. After years of research, I determined that each snippet contained a grain of truth, but most of it was garbled. For example, the fragment of a story my father told me was, "My grandfather, Valentin, was the meanest man in the village, but people respected him, and he was once the mayor." Well, I learned that Valentin was never the mayor and he was actually more pathetic than he was mean. The story was mixed up and the things that my father heard were actually correct about his Uncle Jožef. My Aunt Jane met her Uncle Jožef during her 1937 visit to Povžane; and she had the opinion that he was mean, and shared that with my father. But I view Jožef as a natural leader. Valentin and neighbors sought him out for advice, and he was chosen as the mayor of Povžane and caretaker of Jurkotevi, almost against his will. He suffered the stress that comes from being a wounded war veteran, the loss of his sister who was his confidante and friend, coupled with the responsibilities of caring for his aging parents, his growing family, and John Fradel's property. He was a leader in a village facing growing financial hardships, and an increasingly repressive government. He didn't have too many nice things to say about anybody, especially Rudolf.

*

The son of Frane Košanc, the one who was the same age as Rudy, eventually had three children, the youngest being Emilija, my third cousin. Emilija married Lojze Kljun and they reside at Grgarečevi. In 2014, Archie and I, with some Biščevi cousins, visited them. We sat outdoors and shared the family tree drawn on green poster board with different colored threads to show our connections. Emilija, who was 89 years old, went inside for a few minutes, and returned with a photograph of the young Rudolf Fradel. (photo 7) Soon after his arrival in Pittsburgh, he sent it to Frane Košanc, and, ninety-some years later, his granddaughter, Emilija, gave the photo to me.

CHAPTER SIX

1921–1922: *Italians Not Wanted*

Rudy had his visa ready and boarded the *Belvedere* just a few days after 19 May 1921, the day that the Emergency Quota Act was signed into law. He arrived at Ellis Island on 10 June and took the train to Pittsburgh. Knowing further immigration restrictions were coming, others in Brkini and the valley hastened to leave. The process required an Italian passport, an American sponsor, and a U.S. entry visa before a ticket could be purchased. Many asked John to sponsor them and the couple always had extra people in their home during those years when immigration was still possible. Quarters were tight, however, because they now had four children: Jane, age 7, John, 3, and Joe, 2. Mary was almost one and her birth on 13 July 1920 was an easy date to remember because it was the seventh anniversary of her mother's departure from Trieste, and the very day the Narodni Dom was torched.

Some of the Brkini travelers went to Canada and from there found their way to Cleveland, which was, and still is, the largest Slovenian city outside of Slovenia. Argentina became a popular destination and Brazil seemed promising, although many reported unhappiness there and had difficulty earning enough money for a return passage. Slovenes in America risked being denied re-entry if they left the country without a U.S. passport. Even for those with citizenship, getting visas for a wife and children was not automatic and this led to prolonged family separations.

Rudy was lucky to be among the Italians permitted admission in 1921, since they were considered an "undesirable" population and limited by the Emergency Quota Act. Four million Italians, mostly from southern Italy, had entered the U.S. in the previous two decades and their customs, language and religion stood out, making them special targets for hostility. They were often used as strikebreakers, and accused of stealing American jobs. To make matters worse, the anarchist movement in America was largely Italian, so much so that the word "Italian" became synonymous with "anarchist." In a sensational case in 1921, Nicola Sacco and Bartolomeo Venzetti, two Italian anarchists, were framed in a robbery murder case and later executed. Another well-known event was the lynching of 11 Sicilians in New Orleans in 1891—an act supported by city officials and commended by the newspapers. Lesser-known events were attacks by the Ku Klux Klan and the bombing of eight Italians in their work camp on Cheat Mountain in West Virginia.

The National Origins Quota Act of 1924, better known as the Johnson Reed Act, further strengthened immigration laws with a political goal of promoting a white, Protestant majority in America. The committee that crafted the act cited the incidence of "low intellect, immorality, mental illness, social inadequacy, the likelihood of becoming a public charge, and unsuitability for military service" amongst immigrants from southern and eastern Europe as justification for tightening exclusions. The committee conveniently moved the measuring point for the nationality quota system from the 1910 census back to the 1890 census—a time before the Great Migration brought all those "undesirable" Italians, Hungarians, Greeks, Poles, Slovaks, Czechs, Russian Jews, Serbs, Croats, and Slovenes to America. To calculate the new nationality quotas, the national origin (not just those of foreign birth) of all the people living in the U.S. in 1890 was counted. This gave a wildly disproportionate advantage to those from western and northern Europe where Protestantism prevailed. The quota for every nationality was lowered from three percent to two percent and the total number of arrivals was reduced. Figuring out the national origins of everyone in the 1890 census took years to accomplish, but roughly 85 percent of the immigrants admitted in the following years came from northern and western Europe and 15 percent came from southern and eastern Europe.

*

15 January 1921

   Dear Janez!!! If you want to build your new house at the old place, buying the land behind it from Pajserevi would be useful. But in my mind, this is not the best place for a house, as it is on a slope and it feels oppressive. I suggest you buy the land from Lojze Grgarec that is behind Tanči's house; it is a beautiful spot for a house, it feels natural and it is close to the road. Just let me know what you want so I can tell Lojze. I lent some money to him in anticipation of the day when we might force him into selling something you wanted to buy.

All of the letters from 1921 are neatly missing—perhaps Mary had them organized in a little box that was lost. One can imagine the missives continued to speak of Rudy's departure, John and Mary's plan for coming home, buying land, weather conditions, the quality of the harvest and the comings and goings of people they knew. In January 1922, Jožef Fabjančič, John Fradel, and Frane Košanc were still quarreling about money, debts, and land, while John thought that he should be compensated for the damage that Rudolf had done to his farm.

   John said in his letters that he was still planning to return. It is odd that he had been talking about returning home since 1919 but had never applied for U.S. citizenship and a passport. On 15 September 1921, he finally filed the papers entitled "Intention to Become a U.S. Citizen," a process he knew would be lengthy. He advised Jožef that he would stay in America for a few more years but, for some reason, he did not explain why. Perhaps, for the first time, he was thinking that his return might not be permanent. Jožef responded to this news:

15 January 1922

Let me tell you about our luck in 1921. The harvest was poor, two pigs died, our cow had three calves, but only one was born alive. She was not doing well, so I had to sell her for very little money. Then, God took a milk cow that we hoped would survive the winter.

Dear Janez, you wrote on 21 December that you plan to be in America for a few more years. I agree there is nothing good here, and no indication that things will improve, but I do wish you would come home, and put your things in order, even if you went back again. It is a pity your fields are standing empty, not giving you anything, and getting all weedy. I think they could be rented. Fixing the house is a waste of money unless you are coming home soon. The front side of the roof should hold for a few more years, but the back side should be replaced entirely. The patches I have made over three years do not last long and water in the house causes more damage and looks bad.

Accounting for the damage that Rudolf did with your property will be difficult. Frane will send you an account of all the money he gave me. You cannot complain that Frane sold the sheep. Everyone else in Povžane and I agreed they needed to be sold before they all died of neglect. Rudolf was selling off things from the house and farm cheaply. I suspect most of the things went to your sister, Antonija, in Artviže. Frane Košanc was sometimes abetting Rudolf, and sometimes warning him. Frane was permissive because Rudolf threatened him. He also threatened me. When the oxen had to be sold, Rudolf threatened he would get me with the hayfork if I came close to the barn. Later he said he would burn down my house. I never really believed he would do me harm; nonetheless I took care to be respectful to him.

The burja is the strong wind that blows south from the Alps and funnels through the Vipava Valley to the Adriatic Sea. Residents in the Vipava Valley still put rocks on their roofs to hold their red and orange tiles in place. The burja makes a mighty roar and the few nights I spent in Vipava, I slept poorly due to the din. Since Brkini is below the Vipava Valley, rocks on the roofs are seldom needed but occasionally there is damage. On 5 March 1922, Jožef wrote:

> Dear Janez, I am sorry to hear Rudolf is acting the same way in America as he acted here. It is just like I warned you. Last fall we filled the holes in your house so that water is not running on the hay; we did more repairs in the middle of the winter after the burja tore up a few things. Next fall we will look at the price of straw, and do some more inexpensive repairs. Somebody is renting your home. We agreed he would pay 15 lire per month and I hoped that he would repair the roof. He paid the first month, then nothing more. At first, I thought it was better to have someone in the house, rather than having it empty, even if the rent is late, but now he owes four months. I have warned him that he will have to leave.
>
> As you requested, I will contract the *korenjina* [root field] out so the grass will be cut. If I cannot rent the other fields, we will harvest whatever happens to grow on them. I will not be able to cut your grass, as I cannot even do my own. It annoys me that people are sharpening their tongues about how easy everything is for me because I have two farms! The year before last, we planted a field of potatoes, and sowed a little bit of oats and barley. Rye is still in the box from two years ago. It is all there, waiting for you to come home.
>
> Dear sister, our daughter Franca, [born March 1921] is already walking. Ata is a little better now, although he is aging, just as we are all, slowly. Dear Sister, you ask how other people know what you are writing about. Mama always asks about your letters; I do not tell her everything. When Ata is curious, he reads your letter. Rezina and Tona read two of your letters

when I was away from home. Like all women, they told a little
bit to everyone, and that is how other people know your business. The only news is Božidar Kastelic has a son with Karlina
Vodarn from Brezovica. She works as a maid for Kastelic and
they are not married.

Ata was 73 years old and suffering from weakness, fatigue, diz-
ziness, and heavy breathing, most likely he had congestive heart
failure caused by long term hypertension, a heart attack, or just old
age. Jožef wrote: "He really needs to be saved," believing the only
salvation was the eternal one.

25 May 1922

For the entire winter Ata could not do anything. We thought
he might be better in the summer, but he is getting worse. He
does not have any pain; he just cannot do anything. He eats
very little. He likes a glass of warm wine every now and then,
and will take a little bit of soup and meat. When he stays in
bed, he feels sick, and when he is on his feet, his head feels
drunk. It is difficult for him to stay home, so he follows us to
work, he lies there for a while, he gets sad because he cannot
work, and then goes home. He breathes heavily and comes
home very tired, like he was carrying one kvintal. He says he
would like to see you one more time. Although it's true that
God is almighty, there is little hope the two of you will ever
see each other in this world.

I can see from your letter that times are bad in America as
well. It seems poverty has spread around the world. The grass
grows slowly, and there will be very little hay. Other plants
are only now emerging. Everything a farmer has for sale is
cheap and everything he needs is expensive. But we are happy
with this government and it looks promising. It feels as if one
might be able to advance. This week there will be a draft and
if Rudolf were home, he could go and try the Italian army. We
have been comforting each other that the Italians will be here
only temporarily, but nearly everything is theirs now. Only

the church remains as it was. There is now an Italian teacher in addition to ours. We are happy with him. Our Marija will start school in the fall. Are your children in school? In what language are they learning?

*

The redemption of Ancient Roman territories from the taint of Austrian culture, and the restoration of a glorious and unified Italy, were the goals of irredentismo. The movement had taken hold in Trieste even before the war, and when the formal Italian occupation began, Austrians fled Trieste. Italians who had been educated in Austrian universities rather than Italian ones were denied employment and promotions. Some Slovenes and Croatians embraced Italianization and changed their names and manner of speaking as a means of social promotion. The torching of the Narodni Dom in July 1920 had unleashed violent repression and the forced expatriation of Slovene intellectuals, teachers, and business owners by fascist squads. Five hundred potential dissidents were also imprisoned. Until now, rural Primorska had remained largely unaffected by these events, but in 1922 the irredentists turned their efforts toward the countryside.

The liberal elements of government believed a campaign focused on inclusion and persuasion would achieve the redemption of the rural people from their Slavic ways. Between 1919 and 1922, posters announced in Italian and Slovene that there would be equal rights, more schools, and the opportunity to serve in the military. Jožef read the propaganda and felt optimistic that there was room to prosper under the new regime. In first grade, little Marija would learn both Slovene and Italian, he believed.

The churches of Primorska were ruled by the pope and the government could not control what happened there. Since 1860, every pope had refused to cooperate with any Italian government because they were still angry that the Papal States had been forcibly taken from them. In the latter part of 1922, when Achille Ratti was elected pope and Mussolini became the prime minister, negotiations began between these two authoritarians that would make Catholicism the state religion and promote the Church's bond with fascism.

*

13 August 1922

Dear Sister and Janez!!! What will you do about the requests from Burančevi for sponsorships? In my opinion it would not cost you anything to send the invitations, but tell them you cannot pay for the tickets. What will you do with Jože Bazle? The boy came to see me, and asked that I recommend him to you. He is 16 years old, hardworking, and smart, but you do as you see fit.

Dear sister, you are wrong that Mama does not care about you and your children. She always worries about you. When the photograph of Ivanka arrived, she burst into tears, and she hung it on the wall. She cries every time I read one of your letters to her. She suffers when you write about bad things, and when you write about good things, she becomes nostalgic. Ata also worries about you and he reads every letter you send.

He has not worked for two months. He does not ask anymore what you do or where you are. When he sees me come home tired, tears come into his eyes. He often cries and prays to God to save him, to give him either health or death. He really needs to be saved. It is hard to watch him like this. Please God, save him.

Dear sister, do not resent me because I do not write about everything. If I did, I would write a letter the size of a newspaper every week. Besides, I do not like to write things like this, as I have a soft heart and my eyes fill up with tears. It often happens that I cannot write because of tears.

On 31 August 1922, Jožef wrote with the heartbreaking news that all had expected.

Before I take a pen in my trembling hand, we are all sending
you greetings from our hearts.

   Dearly Beloved Sister!!! It is hard, but I have to share with
you the sad news that we lost our beloved Father. His soul
departed on the 29th at midnight. We buried him this morning, on the 31st, at nine in the morning. He was getting up
and going out until 17 days ago. On 12 August he went to lie
down behind Blažečevi and I had to carry him back home. He
did not leave the house again. He could care for himself until
the last five days, then he could not move; we had to turn him
over every now and then. In his last moments we were with
him, I and my wife, and Mama and Rezina Bilkotova. It was
an easy death. We buried him in the same spot as his parents
are buried. Dearly beloved sister, I know this news will break
your heart, but do not cry, take comfort, and pray for his soul.
We are all devastated we lost such a hardworking and gentle
father. But we thank God that He saved him. We have seen his
life and we know he used it well until the end, and we find
solace in this. He was not for this world anymore.

Slavica, whom John and Mary soon called Sylvia, was born into
the world in Black Lick, Pennsylvania on 17 August 1922, just days
before Ata's death. John was frequently working in Sharpsville or
Farrell near Youngstown, Ohio and Rudy or Andy Siskovič were
often with him. John sent hundreds of lire to Povžane to help people
come to America and due to European inflation a few American
dollars could do a lot of good.

8 September 1922
   It is fall again, and as I've already written, the roof on the
backside of your house has been damaged by the rain and the
cattle, and should be replaced. The son of Janez Ogrnjač bought
Ogrnjačevi when he was a secretary at the municipality, but
now he has left for Gorica, and wants to sell; you might consider it. I was angry that Bubnič Ban secretly sold his fields
for 2,800 lire to Bilko. When he asked me if you would like

to buy his garden, I told him that whomever he gave the meat to eat, should also get the bones. Gašper Grgarec plans to sell the land he has behind our house. I'm just telling you all this, and you decide as you see fit. Grgarec also plans to send his daughter to America.

The invitation that you sent for Burančevi has arrived. The money you sent for the others is also here. I wished you had sent me a statement with the cost per person, so in case one of them does not go, he can repay here. Tenel would have paid me immediately, if I could have told him how much it was. Skominčič is all set to go. Jože Bazle will go to Trst this week to buy a ticket. All the ships are booked so it is not clear when they will be able to leave. They might be able to go with the English line. Tenel says he will go in the spring.

I know it is hard for you to be bothered by everybody, but Berhan from Gradišica has written to you for an invitation for his younger son who is married in Markovščina. The Old Berhan asked me to write to you and it is difficult for me to say no, because my wife's sister is the bride at Berhan. They will complain that I wrote for Burančevi, but not for them. Please do this if you can, I guarantee that you will get it back.

Jožef sent Christmas greetings and news on 20 December 1922. "The Noble Ones" is a name that Jožef sarcastically gives to Slovenia's new rulers.

More and more people are thinking of going to America, but right now no one can leave. They hope the permission will come after the New Year. Perhaps you know more about this than we do. Bazle tried hard, but he could not send his Jože off. I would not have given him the money you sent, except that you cannot catch the snake with a bare hand. Bazle used the money to get Jože ready, and what was left he used to buy one cow. He plans to keep the cow until immigration to America is open, then he will sell it to get the money to cover the expenses.

I was unable to sell the sheep anywhere in Brkini or Čičarija. I offered them at every fair, to either sell or lend out. We have harvested less than half the hay that we had last year. The rye harvest was reasonable, but hail destroyed the barley and the oats. We have only enough beans for seeds. We got three baskets of potatoes. Other people ate all their potatoes from the field. Our storage space is emptier now at Christmas than it usually is on St. George [23 April]. But the Noble Ones do not see our troubles and taxes are rising every year.

I would like to make an arrangement for your farm; you may do it with me or you could lease it to the cooperative. The arrangement would commit to paying all the taxes, do everything, take care of the house, and then give you whatever amount you would agree to every year. Think about it and write to me.

*

The populist sentiments of irredentism were a fertile field for the growth of fascism. Mussolini was a charismatic newspaper editor who promised that under his forceful leadership, the Italian economy would prosper and the Italian "race" would be great again. On 22 October 1922, 30,000 fascists marched on Rome. Two days later—before a crowd of 60,000 people at the Fascist Congress in Naples—Mussolini declared, "Our program is simple: we want to rule Italy," and he demanded the resignation of the Prime Minister. At the same time, the para-military of the Fascist Party, known as the Blackshirts, occupied strategic points in the country, and some 25,000 strong began to move on the capital. Fearing a civil war, King Victor Emmanuelle III acquiesced to Mussolini. He and others did not think that fascism was a threat to the establishment, and many business and financial leaders believed it would be possible to manipulate Mussolini, whose early speeches and policies emphasized free market and *laissez-faire* economics. On 29 October, Mussolini was asked to form a cabinet.

"The March on Rome," as historians have called it, was not a military conquest, it was a tactic to force the transfer of power within the framework of the Italian constitution. It was only possible because public authorities surrendered in the face of fascist intimidation. After this bloodless coup, the liberal forms of irredentism, the persuasion to Italianize, ended. Fascist irredentism became a euphemism for what we now call ethnic cleansing. Taxation was one method "the Noble Ones" used to drive Slovenes out of Primorska.

Even as Jožef assisted in the securing of sponsorships and handling of money for travel, he felt sadness and loss, knowing that this time the departures would be permanent. Prior to the war, before the American exclusion laws, Trieste to America had been a two-way street. Travelers went with the intention of returning in two or three years, and most did return. But everyone who left after 1920, did so permanently. Slovenes in America began to lose contact with the old country and the financial aid they sent home slowed with the worsening of the American economy.

CHAPTER SEVEN

1923: *Staying Connected*

By 1923 my grandparents had been in America for ten years, living on the edge, always on the verge of returning home. They waited for the war to end, then for the world to settle down, for the right moment to go, but life was somehow even more unsettled. Mary longed for the easy familiarity of her family and girlfriends who understood her and spoke her language and dialect. She lived amongst other Slavic and Italian immigrants, but they were not her people from the valley under Slavnik. She stayed in touch through letters and travelers—those returning home who carried messages and gossip from America and those arriving in America with gifts and news from loved ones. Mary's migration experience had transformed her. She was no longer just Marija Biščeva, the smart and pretty girl from Povžane, surrounded by her family and cousins. She was a world traveler separated from her past, afloat in a strange world, and she yearned for the sense of belonging she once had. She developed strong connections to others who shared her emotional circumstances—the Slovenes from her valley who migrated to America, to Maribor, and to Australia; those who migrated yet chose to return home, and families who experienced loss when one of their own left and felt the same yearnings as Mary did to stay connected. Central to her life were Biščevi (Mary's family), Jurkotevi

(John's sisters), and Košančevi, the ancestral home of Mary's father, John's mother, and the current home of the meddling Frane Košanc.

Josip Ban of the Zajčevi household had married a daughter of Košančevi so he was officially related to Mary and John. More importantly, Josip Ban traveled to the U.S. and brought his sons, his niece, and cousins, which led to a chain of perhaps a dozen loosely related people in West Virginia, Pennsylvania, and Ohio who came from the valley and became part of my grandparents' American life in addition to the people they had sponsored.

Marija of Gabrk was the daughter of Ivan Ban of Zajčevi, the older brother of Josip Ban, but she was more than just another Zajčevi cousin. She knew all the travelers to and from America,(her daughter would become one) was well loved and always in the news. Her name was Marija Ivana Ban before she married Anton Jaksetič. His family owned the gostilna at Gabrk, thus she became known as Marija from Gabrk, to distinguish her from all the other Marijas.

Gabrk is a minor elevation at the east end of Povžane, close to the road from Trieste to Rijeka. The gostilna and its inn on Gabrk was a popular spot for weekend visitors from Trieste and people who came to the Brkini forests to hunt. Marija and Anton ran the gostilna while Anton's father, "the old man of Gabrk,"—the actual proprietor—lived with them. He had a reputation for being mean and bad tempered. At a gostilna along the valley road today one can see a whole pig roasting on a spit, eat potatoes deep fried in lard, and drink beer. Perhaps it was the same then.

In 1923, Marija of Gabrk was 36 years old, a large woman with a generous, kind personality. She worked hard, was a good cook, and could make a tasty dish out of almost nothing. She spoke enough Italian and German to communicate with her guests in their own language. People liked to visit with her because she was easy going and helpful. She wore a scarf on her head most of the time, as many mature women in Slovenia did, and always wore two aprons. The bottom one kept her clothes clean and she'd take the dirty one off when visitors came, to display her clean apron. Marija of Gabrk's four children would become integral members of Mary's new inner circle in time. Kristina was born in 1909, and the twins, a boy called Anton or Tonči, and a girl called Mija, were born in 1918. Five-year-old Olga died in November 1918 from the Spanish flu.

The elderly, widowed Trina Mekovka who stayed at Maharinčevi, next door to Biščevi, was also part of Mary's life. She was a friendly, nosey sort, always poking her head in the door to say hello and to send greetings to America. In 1921 she became ill with something that sounds like it could have been multiple sclerosis, a stroke, or even polio, when she improved, she could not walk and arrangements were made for her personal care. She owned property in the middle of the village. Jožef wrote:

> Nearly two years ago, on 16th of May 1921, Mekovka lay down, and never stood up again. She was lying at home for a year and a half, and last fall they took her to Gabrk. She is there, as healthy as ever, except that she cannot stand on her feet, poor woman. She gave the barn and the shed to Maharinčevi, she gave me the slope behind her house, and everything else she gave to Marija from Gabrk. Previously, she had made a Will that left everything to the old man on Gabrk but he has been doing nothing but damage around the house for three years, so she changed her mind, and gave everything to Marija. Since then, everyone on Gabrk hates each other. Whenever possible, they are fighting and complaining.

Life on both sides of the Atlantic remained unsettled. John continued laboring as a semi-vagabond, seeking short-term jobs in the foundries of western Pennsylvania, often living apart from his family. In Brkini and the valley, harvests were poor, taxes were high, would-be emigrants went into debt while preparing to leave, people were selling their land to make ends meet, and the buyers were often Italians. Jožef still struggled in an emotional "push-pull" conflict with his sister. He warned them of the terrible poverty and hard life under Slavnik, advised them to stay in America and then would try to entice them home with news of available property, a nice site for a home, or an investment opportunity. He was still grieving the loss of his father, not only for himself, but also for Mary, who never got to say goodbye.

Pust is the Tuesday before Ash Wednesday, the first day of Lent. Americans call it Mardi Gras. The day is meant to be joyous and mischievous. Colorful characters try to chase winter away with bells, whips, and sticks. But in 1923 things were bad, almost as bad as the hunger they experienced during the Great War, and there was little energy for celebration.

> *13 February 1923*
>
> Today is Pust, but we remain serious. We have a lack of lire but thank God, we are not hungry. We are afraid the hard years from '14 to '18 will repeat themselves. We just received your letter from 7 January; you can see it can take a long time for the mail to arrive. You say you would like to buy a wreath for Ata's grave. A nice one costs 60 to 80 lire. I am not against one, but I think it would be better if we bought a small gravestone. If you want to buy it on your own, we will put whatever inscription you choose on it. If you do not want to spend that much, then I will contribute, and we will add my inscription. I think we could get an appropriate stone for about 150 lire.
>
> Vurh's gostilna has been closed for over a year and he is still in debt. Božidar Kastelic's store has been empty, he hadn't sold much since year '17. I've written to you before about the sale of Ogrnjačevi. Ogrnjač is asking for 7,000, but I think it is not worth more than four. I think the 5,500 you were offering is fair. Suhečeva, who was interested in buying it, will not offer that much.

Uneasiness increased when the new fascist government issued a decree on 23 March that only Italian could be spoken in public offices, post offices, and on public transport. Later, on 1st October,

the Giovanni Gentile Reform dealt a deathblow to Slovene education. The Slovene language was banished in schools, and Italian teachers, most of whom came from southern Italy, immediately
replaced all Slovene teachers. About 500 educators faced relocation
to the interior of Italy or confinement in Sardinia. Most chose to
emigrate to the Kingdom of S.H.S.

The following incident took place in Vrhpolje, in the Vipava
Valley in 1927. It was reported by Louis Adamic, a Slovene émigré to
America who became an acclaimed American author. He received a
Guggenheim Fellowship to write about his travels in the Kingdom
of Yugoslavia in 1932. He wrote:

> Slovene teachers were deprived of their jobs, and in all the
> schools, boys and girls were taught only in Italian by Italians...
> children were forbidden to utter a single Slovenian word...
> They were told that their parents were barbarians and they
> should be ashamed of the tongue their mothers taught them.
> Teachers established spy systems among their pupils and the
> children reported to them to have spoken a word of Slovene
> were punished...The teacher in this village was a young man
> from southern Italy, Sottosanti by name. He was tubercular
> and a passionate fascist. When his little spies reported to him
> a Slovene pupil whom they had heard utter words in his native
> speech, he would fly into a rage, call the offender before him,
> order him to open his mouth wide, then spit on his tongue.
>
> This, of course, enraged the Slovene population of the vicin-
> ity... when Sottosanti had spat into about a dozen children's
> mouths, a group of Slovene peasants—probably the fathers of
> those boys and girls—waited for him one dark night and killed
> him, after which dozens of Slovenes were arrested and tried,
> and several of them are now serving life sentences on Signor
> Mussolini's prison islands north of Sicily, while the Fascist
> organization in the Vipava district erected a monument to
> Sottosanti in Vrhpolje, glorifying him as a Black Shirt martyr,
> a victim of Slovene barbarism.*

*Adamic, Louis, *The Native's Return*, pages 91-92

Planting in the valley took place in late March or April, weather permitting. The ground could not be too wet, and all danger of frost had to be gone before the first shoots were due to emerge. After that, the farmer prayed for rain and turned his attention to other matters. Jožef already had his hands full with John's farm when yet another government decree mandated that all communally held land would revert to state ownership. The villagers of Povžane owned a *Boršt*, or forested area, in common, and they agreed to divide it among themselves rather than allow the government to take it. This task posed a huge challenge because land ownership was the biggest source of friction in rural Slovenia. Jožef, as mayor, bore the brunt of the controversies. He took up this issue with his cousin and brother-in-law, John.

> *14 May 1923*
>
> I sent you a receipt for the grass cut on your farm which brought you 760 lire; the long garden and the big field should bring another 200 lire. When Klemenkova went to Yugoslavia, she leased everything out. The wheat she sowed brought her 580 lire, so you can see your fields have paid well in comparison.
>
> The division of the Boršt is what everyone discusses. According to our plan, you can pay for your part, or we will cut the trees on it and sell them to pay for your part. I need Janez to write back about this decision. It may be true that whatever the wife is, the husband is as well, but it is Janez's name that is listed in the court and it must be in Janez's writing.

Back in America, John received two permanent job offers. The Marshall Foundry closed its operations in Black Lick and offered him a job at their foundry in Sharpsville. The other was at Vulcan Mold, a company that was just starting up in Latrobe. He let Mary make the choice and she chose Latrobe. Mary wrote to her brother about their plan and he responded in the same May letter.

> You write that you'll be moving. Please send me your new address quickly, because Jože Bazle and Skominčič are getting

ready to go to America. If everything goes well, they will leave with the first steamship and it would be right that they know where to find you.

Mary wrote back that they had not yet left Black Lick and that John was still at a temporary job in Sharon. On 24 June, Jožef responded:

> It is unfortunate your letter came eight days too late for Jože Bazle. He had already left. He was worried about how he would find you. If I had known you were still there, I would have sent you a telegram. He may have trouble finding you, but he is smart and young and will figure it out. When he reaches you, please take good care of him, just as if he were one of your own. I told him he should respect and obey you, and he promised that he would. I will send you the bill for everything I spent for him. Jože does not know about all of the expenses. I do not want to send the bill just yet, as the boy first needs to take courage. He might get scared when he learns he owes more than 5,000 lire [$200]. His father might pay for some of it, but I do not have high hopes for that.

In the second half of 1923, the travelers who had been held up by the American consulate were finally able to go abroad. Jože Bazle boarded the *Presidente Wilson* on 16 June and presented his Italian passport with the name Giuseppe Godina. He was 17 years old, deep in debt, and not sure where in America he was going to find his uncle. Boarding the same ship was his friend Jože Fabjančič from Grgurjevi.

Grgurjevi was a house blessed with five sons, but troubled by an extremely controlling mother who hated every young woman whom Jože tried to court. Grgurjova had rejected Marija Bilkoteva, Rezina's well respected daughter, before the relationship had time to blossom. That rejection was a move our Jožef Fabjančič would always hold against her as a personal insult to the extended Biščevi family. When Grgurjova vetoed Marija Rejčeva, Jože Grgur moved out and stayed with the neighbors at Gregarečevi. Persistent aggravation from his mother convinced Jože to emigrate. The two young men stepped onto Ellis Island on 1 July 1923 and went straight to Cleveland where Jože Grgur 's connections helped Jože Bazle find John Fradel working in Sharon, Pennsylvania. Janez Grgur had also had his fill of troubles at home and followed his older brother to Cleveland in November. The new Americans became Joe Godina, Joe Fabjančič and John Fabjančič.

John Ban, a person my Aunt Mary always called "Dad's cousin," was a frequent traveler to America from Mary's village. He was Johan, Janez, or Giovanni depending on who was in charge in Primorska, but to everyone who knew him he was called by his house name, "Skominčič." His first voyage was in 1913. He sat out the war in America and applied for citizenship in 1917, but unwisely traveled home in 1920 before he was granted citizenship. At the church in Brezovica he married Angela Jankovič and they had a son, Stanislas, whom they would call Stanley. Trapped by the 1921 Emergency Quota Act, Skominčič was unable to secure a visa for his wife and son and realized that if he didn't get back to America before the even more restrictive Johnson Reed Law went into effect, he might never get back. John Fradel lent him money for his ticket and he traveled on the *Martha Washington* to the Port of Baltimore on 2 September 1923 without his family.

Immigration successes inspired others to try for America. Mary's niece, Marija Bilkoteva, wanted to go. Her mother, Rezina, pressed her sister for help and her father applied to his brother, Drej Bilko [Andy Siskovič]. Another Ban family pushed Jožef for assistance for their daughter:

> Dear Janez and Sister,
>   I do not want to cause you any troubles in these matters, but Gašper of Grovrečevi and his wife are asking me to write to you, to ask if you could possibly send an invitation and money for their younger girl to get to America. I did not want to do

this and told them they should write to you themselves, but they do not know how to write. Today they both came to me, so I am writing this letter in front of them.

Her name is Rozina Ban; she was born on 7 February 1904. Here is her photograph. Jože Bazle can tell you more about her. They say she is hardworking and smart. Regarding her skills, she knows a few things in the kitchen. She worked in the Vipava valley for a year and now she is working in Trst with fine lords. She has a lot of zest for going to America. So, if you want, and if you can, send the invitation at the same time as you send it for Bilko's girl. If not, please write back to them that you cannot send any more invitations and you are not able to take care of so many people in America. I cannot take any responsibility with this.

Drej Bilko ended up providing the sponsorship and money for Marija Bilkoteva. There must have been some hope for Rozina Ban, but ultimately neither girl was able to obtain a visa for America.

Joe Godina and Joe Fabjančič did not write as often as they had promised and the folks back home complained, with a mixture of anger and sorrow, that they had been forgotten. Frane Košanc wrote to John in regards to Valentin's Will and the cost of the damages done by Rudy at Jurkotevi. Frane wrote: "We have a terrible drought and things are bad, especially for me as I am alone to work and to suffer, since my son Frane turned 21 and was taken into the Italian army." He pointed out that Rudy would also have been drafted had he stayed. Frane Košanc closed with "Give my regards to Rudolf, he also forgot about us. God bless you..."

Pepa Blaževa stopped into Biščevi and Mama persuaded her to write a letter to Mary for her. American life had changed the way Mary viewed her marital role and she had scolded her mother for calling John "her master." Mama always had to have the last word and she was pleased that Pepa was there to deliver it so she did not have to argue with her usual scribe, her own daughter, Tona, about it.

3 December 1923

My Dearest Daughter! I am well now but what I went through in these last ten years would make a cold stone feel sorry for me. You know that there was the War and hard times, and a lot of suffering. Thank you from all my heart for the money you've sent me. I paid for four holy Masses and I bought one apron and a mantle. I bought a liter of slivovic [plum brandy] for the nights when I feel weak.

You were offended when I wrote that I was sending greetings to your master. You now say "my husband," but I am accustomed to saying "master" and that is why I say it now. Pepa Blaževa is writing for me—she let me write about everything that was burdening my heart, therefore do not take this against me.

I remain to you, your Mama.

Pepa Blaževa switched to her own voice:

I am sending regards to Jožek Bazle. Although he has forgotten me and does not write to me, I haven't forgotten him. Give my regards to Jože Grgur when you see him, Marija Rejčeva also waits to hear from him. I wish you all the best. Your friend, Pepca Babuder

The year 1923 ended with an unusually peaceful letter from Jožef with good news of his family:

18 December 1923

Dear Sister and Janez!!! You are glad that we are getting along well with Mama. This is how it should be. Our religion teaches us to respect our parents. We will get old and if we do not treat our parents well, we cannot expect anything good for ourselves. You know how particular our mother is. One needs to be patient and please her, just to have peace. I have to thank God to have such a gentle and patient wife. If she were not the way she is, everything would be different. You ask me to send you the address for our cousin, Karlina from Trst. But

I do not know it. You should have it because her sister, Pavla, wrote to me to get your address, I am sure that she has already written to you.

Dear sister, I have more news to tell you, so that you cannot say that God is not good to us. It is true that the harvest was bad, and that some of our animals died, but God has blessed us by giving us two children on the 15th of this month, a boy and a girl. They are healthy and strong, they came one after the other, as if it were just one. Luckily everything went well and everyone is healthy. They were christened very fast, on the second day. We call the boy Janez and the girl is Milka. I am very pleased that now there are eight of us. I am the only one who can work, but God foresees everything.

CHAPTER EIGHT

1924: Mary's Clothes

On 25 January 1924 John Fradel took the Oath of Allegiance to become a U.S. citizen. I have attended two naturalization ceremonies and even today, when we take our citizenship for granted, it was an inspiring and moving event to watch new citizens become part of the most successful democracy in the world. John was now free to travel. Mary wrote to Tona and Jožef that they would come soon. Tona was so excited she asked for the date of their arrival so she could meet their ship in Trieste. Jožef's hopes were up that John would be there to plant in the spring.—But John and Mary never arrived. Instead, they bought a house.

The family had been renting in Latrobe. On her walk to school in the spring of 1924, eleven-year-old Jane spotted a painted white brick house for sale. The house was a federal style, narrow and tall, with a kitchen and two rooms downstairs and two bedrooms upstairs, not dissimilar in style to homes in Povžane. When it was built in 1840 it was a farmhouse, but the farm itself had been sold off in bits and pieces and the township had grown up around it. A garden patch was all that remained around the house still owned by the original family. On 9 June 1924, John and Mary Fradel signed the deed on 1004 Alexandria Street. The house was a bargain at $3,600, at a time when the average new home price was $7,720.

Tona's letters to her sister between 1920 and 1924 did not survive. In her March 1924 letter, Tona seems to be picking up the
threads of an ongoing conversation. Clearly, their correspondence
had been up to date and many confidences had been shared. Mary
knew all about her disabled nephew, Tona's marital problems, and
gossip about neighbors. From the moment Jože Bazle left Trieste,
his mother worried herself sick about him. She missed him desper-
ately and agonized that he might fail to remember her with letters
and money.

> *1 March 1924*
>
> Dear Sister, I am happy Jože has been saved from the life here,
> although I do miss him. We could always talk and complain
> to each other. If he had one lire, he gave it to me. It is nice that
> he sent money to me, but he sent it to Hrpelje, where they took
> five lire for fees. He should send it to the post office in Materija,
> or to brother Pepe.
>
> Dear sister, I know what you say is true, but you do not have
> a brute for a husband. You have never had to wait for your
> husband to come home from a gostilna. He says that he wears
> the pants and will not be taking orders from anyone. When
> Jože and I confronted him, he told him he could leave the house
> if he did not like it. I am crushed when my husband tells me
> if I dropped dead, he would not care and he would easily get
> someone else. I would tell you every detail but if he found out
> he would become even worse and Jože would be upset.
>
> Jože has not written to me for nine months and my husband
> says I must have done something to irritate him. A month ago,
> I asked him to send us some money. Did he move and not get
> our mail? Does he have a girlfriend? Why does he not write?
> Beloved sister, please tell me about my son. **A**

Letters from Latrobe conveyed their contentment with John's permanent job and the end of nomadic life. The message signaled, without actually saying it, that their return to Povžane was not going

to happen. Jožef wrote at planting time in a tone that could not disguise his frustration with the burden of Jurkotevi.

25 March 1924

You wrote that I should just leave the farm as it is. Well, you are the landowners, and if you have thought about it and decided to leave it this way, then so be it, but if we do not clean the fields, leaves will get into the hay and it will not get the same price if you want to sell it. Or maybe you are planning to use the hay yourself? Molehills and rocks need to be removed to make grass cutting possible. We will soon be making lime for ourselves; it will cost 8.5 lire per kvintal plus something for the men's work. This is how things are, but you do as you wish. The truth is that whatever has lime will grow and what doesn't have lime will stay dead, there is nothing else you can do.

Dear Janez, you have said you would come to put your affairs in order and I wish this would happen. It is hard to get money these days, but if given enough notice I will push people to give me the money they owe you. I've sent you the bill for the money I took from your account for Jože Bazle, but you did not tell me about his reaction. Has Skominčič paid you for that invitation? His wife is ready to follow him, and she has already leased out the farm. Do you know how much she got? Four best pieces of land brought her only 380 lire.

Mary's request for the clothes she left behind struck a nerve in Mama's core. At some level, Mama had already acknowledged to herself that Mary was not coming back, but the actual request made it all too real. Mama had been using Mary's clothes, lending them, and giving some away. On one hand, she felt entitled to do what she pleased with the items she bought for her daughter. On the other hand, she felt ashamed to be caught, and naturally went into attack mode. The complexities of her letter revealed their mother in all the colors Jožef so often complained about: Attack, argue, make excuses, and whine for sympathy because she was so old, so sick, so poor—or whatever.

Tona wrote Mama's next letter. First, came the attack. She accused Mary of not telling her about Sylvia's birth eight months earlier. (Perhaps that letter was lost or Mama forgot). Next, Mama boasted about giving birth eight times, and whined about the loss she had endured, and the insult Mary had inflicted on her, which then permitted her to cry about the poverty that had forced her to appropriate Mary's clothing. Jožef was his sister's staunchest defender. He wanted to keep the faith that John and Mary would return, and that, among other things, she would claim her clothes and they would live at Jurkotevi where they belonged.

25 March 1924

My dearest daughter!! You have waited too long to tell us that you had a new daughter last August! Do not be ashamed to write if you have more children. Healthy and strong children are God's greatest gift to you and a reason for happiness for the father and mother. I had eight of them, even though I was poor. Even if you had three in a year, do not do this to me ever again!

You wrote about the things that belong to you. Just a few days ago I was thinking I would send you a few things, so you would have them to remember me. Now that you wrote about it, I will gather everything that is yours. I should tell you I remade your black skirt for myself when my husband died. During the War, we could not buy any clothes so I gave the one with red dots to Bilkotova to remake, since it had started to fall apart on its own. I tore up one of your shirts, and another one I will keep as a memory of you. Pepe will take care of all these things so everything will be done well and you will get all of them.

The money also arrived, but it came to the post office in Hrpelje. I was a little sick and the weather was bad, so I have not been there yet to pick it up. But it will come in handy, and I thank you from my heart for sending it. I hope God gives you thousands and thousands of times more in return, since I can see you have good heart for me, and you remember that I am your Mama.

Tempers were hot. Jožef wrote a few days later. Mama pampered her granddaughter, Fani, as she grew up at Biščevi and Jožef had long been irritated with his niece. When she was fifteen, Fani had returned to Bazletevi to live with her parents. In the saga about Mary's clothes, Jožef revealed what really happened.

30 March 1924

Dear Sister!!! I can see that the subject of your clothes is hard for you. I understand you feel that what is yours still belongs to you and that Mama has poor judgment in these matters. Once again, I can tell you, my beloved sister, that we were both in one body and therefore my thoughts are in agreement with yours. I've argued with Mama several times, and demanded your things should wait for you. Mama argues she has been taking care of your things for so long, that she has the right to give them to whomever she wants and that I have nothing to say about it. But you know how we have to do things here with Mama, so that all the saints are happy.

When she was ill, Mama said that if she died, I should give all her bedding and all your things to Fani Bazleteva. I told her she could sleep on the floor and give Fani her mattress and the blanket right now, but she should leave your things alone. Fani knows that you told her you would be back and that she should not take your things. It was as if we had a maid who was carrying things out of our house and I could not say anything. Mama was always defending her with things like this: That poor girl, she has to serve! When Fani wore a blouse that I knew was yours to Mass, I could not stand it anymore and I sent her away.

Mother did not give Rezina just the blouse that you mentioned. I was there and I know she gave her the entire dress; I remember you wore it to the *maša hvaležnica* in Brezovica and it matched the dress that Pepa Blaževa wore. Tona is wearing one of your mantles, one I know well. As you requested, I will make a case for your things as soon as possible. But there is no rush, because Mama is now frightened. I wonder on whom she has been eavesdropping. Marija, there is no need to tell Mother you resent her for this, you know her well, she feels remorse for giving your things away. If you write anything to her, then woe is me and my wife!

Dear Sister, if only we could sit down together and talk. You feel as if you are dead to your old home and that saddens me tremendously. There are still memories in my head of things we did in our youth, when we talked a lot and shared everything like we only had each other.

Maša Hvaležnica (Mass of Thanksgiving) takes place on the first Sunday of November. It was an occasion to thank God, family, and friends for everything good that had been received in the past year. In modern times, maša hvaležnica is not used as it was in the past and refers to the Mass in which the deceased are remembered and thanked for their good deeds. Some people translate this as a Commemoration or Remembrance Mass. In the U.S. we call it All Souls Day.

Six weeks later, Mama had calmed down and packed up Mary's clothes to be mailed, or collected when she arrived. Mary knew that money or a package was the best remedy for grievances with her mother or sister.

> *12 May 1924.*
>
> My dearest daughter! I was delighted that you remembered me with a package. I am really pleased with everything. God should return you a thousand times for all your kindness towards me. Pepe was also very pleased and the children were very happy to receive your gifts. Tona is also very happy; it was something she really needed. I also thank you for those lire. Every day I am getting weaker and older, and I have more needs. Coffee now costs 22 lire per kilo so sometimes I buy a quarter [about 8 oz] and some sugar, so I can make a cup for myself. I buy about a quarter of wine [¼ liter] as I need it.

Have no worries at all about your things. Since I always thought that you would be coming home, I made sure things would be ready here for you. Now, we will make a bigger package and I will put in everything that is yours. Also waiting for you is a tumbler, a pad and a night's goblet. I will give you everything, so that you will be happy.

My dear Marija, please tell me if it is true someone in Povžane told you we are getting rich with your fields. It is true we are doing well, but that is not because of Jurko's farm. Pepe is a hardworking and careful master, just like his father was, and he has a hardworking wife. I am old, but I also work all day, from morning till evening. If we have something that is yours, you will get everything back, down to the last *čentižim*.

*

U.S. President Calvin Coolidge settled any questions about immigration as he signed the Johnson Reed Act into law on 26 May 1924. The worldview it laid out redefined foreign policy and became the basis for American immigration to this day. Its intent to restore America's population to the white Protestant majority it had in the early 19th century would also have lasting repercussions in the daily lives of people in Primorska and elsewhere in the Balkans.

Before the 1920s, the United States was party to agreements and treaties that placed American immigration within a larger context of internationally cooperative migration control. The congressional committee that dealt with immigration believed that foreign governments were exploiting this system by issuing passports only to people regarded as physically, mentally, or morally weak. Making plain the contempt for how foreign governments handled emigration, one member wrote, "The kings and potentates should build their own penitentiaries to take care of their own birds on the other side, and not send them to this country." With the Johnson Reed Act, America alone would control its immigration, and it would do so according to a white nationalist vision.

When America shut its doors, a palpable wave of grief spread through the village. People would no longer be able to travel back and forth. Tona was hit hard. Her son Jože had lived with John Fradel in Sharon, but when John and Mary moved to Latrobe, Jože did not go with them. At age 17 he decided to do things his way, which brought the disapproval of his family upon him and unleashed his mother's anxiety. Throughout the fall her grief and regrets poured out in multiple letters.

> Dear Sister, I am saddened my Jože is not with you anymore. With you, I felt reassured he was safe at home. Now we are afraid he'll get lost in America and forget about us. As a mother, I would like to know how much he earns, and has he paid off everything he owes you? Jože wrote to the Gajsčeva, the girl he liked here. He sent her his photo and said he would write again soon, but he has not written. Those who saw the photograph said he was handsome and she did not deserve him. Oh, my sister, if you knew how close he is to my heart, how often I am in tears because I miss him so much! He is often in my dreams, and then I talk to him, but it is unlikely that I will ever really talk to him again.
>
> My dear brother-in-law, please take care of my son so that he does not vagabond around America and waste his good days, please try hard to help him.
>
> Dear sister, please remind brother-in-law that Jože is still young, he should come back to you, so he does not get lost. We regret his leaving. We wonder if it was worth it for him to go. I have worries about everyone. There are rumors things are not as good as they used to be in America.

Jožef wrote:

> I could not have imagined Jože Bazle would cause this trouble. Now I suspect that he is a hypocrite. If you only knew the prom-ises he made to me, how he would never forget me, and never

forget how much I contributed so he could go to America! If it
had been left to his father, he would never have gotten there.
Now he repays me like this! I am not worthy enough so that he
would write to me! The old gratitude of Austria is dead. But in
Jože's case, I should not be surprised as there has not yet been
an apple that would fall from a hazel tree.

The Bilkoteva household was also hurting. Marija, Rezina's eldest
daughter, had long been old enough to marry and her father angled
to match her to a good looking 34-year-old widower with a six-year-
old son. He was a good man, he owned a home and a pub elsewhere,
and came to Brkini to hunt. When he developed an interest in a
daughter from Ogrnjačevi, Bilko reluctantly approved his daughter's choice of a younger son from the Luka household in nearby
Hotična. The couple made plans to emigrate and got support from
her uncle Drej Bilko (Andy Siskovič). Mary and her circle of family
and friends from under Slavnik were ready to welcome them, but
the door to America was firmly shut. Her disappointed father did
not want to throw away money on a wedding and dowry so they
were married without fanfare at the Church of St. Giacomo, on 24
November and stayed in Trieste. With Marija Bilkoteva's departure,
America and Povžane felt the loss of another of their own. Tona
wrote to Mary about it.

> Our mother spent a lot of time with Rezina and her husband,
> but they did not tell her about the wedding. She heard about it
> from someone else. Many are feeling sorry for Marija Bilkoteva,
> she is such a great girl, not spoiled with clothing, and it is a
> pity that she will not stay at home.

*

Settled in Latrobe, John considered his options for Jurkotevi that
fall. He knew it was not a good time to sell, he wanted to keep

options open for a return, and he wanted to provide for Mary and
the children should something happen to him. He knew she would
prefer to return home in that case, and I'm sure my grandmother had
a lot to say in the decisions that were made. Jožef replied to them.

> Dear Sister and Janez, You previously wrote about plans for
> coming home and now tell me it will not go this way. Janez is
> the landowner and he should come home, if only for 24 hours.
> He will learn that land is hard to sell. He might be able to sell
> some of the better pieces, but it would not be right, he should
> sell everything or nothing. This he will understand when he
> comes home.
>
> Dear sister, you say that you do not understand how it is
> that Pepina will become mistress of the house rather than
> you, if Janez and Rudolf were to die, but, unfortunately, this
> is true. Father did not put anything about this in his Last
> Will and it was left to the judge. At the final court hearing,
> the judge decided that in case of the deaths of both brothers,
> Pepina would inherit. I objected, "Where will his wife and
> his children go if Janez dies?" But the judge said this decision
> was in accordance with the Will, and he had to do what the
> law says. When Pepina heard this, she sighed and lifted her
> ears, thinking she is now the mistress of the house. I spoke to
> Jože Jivaninov, and showed him the decision of the probate
> proceedings. He is a lawyer and said that this is valid. Then I
> went to see an old lawyer in Trst, who is from Bazovica, who
> told me the same thing. I will copy the decision so you can
> show it to your best man.

Anger swirling throughout Bač and Povžane about the Jurko farm
was a daily aggravation for Biščevi. Some accused Jožef of misusing
it for his profit. In addition to his disappointments and frustrations,
Jožef suffered health setbacks during the harvest of 1924. A measles
epidemic afflicted his five children all at once. Mary was also sick
but the news was delayed by an interruption in mail service. Jožef
wrote on 28 September 1924.

The mail is very irregular; one letter took 15 days and then older ones came two days later. Dear Sister, I am sorry to hear you are sick. We only learned this when we received these delayed letters. Even when you are in good health, I do not know how you poor women manage a big family. I can see for myself how much work and trouble a mother has with children. Sometimes we need two women to take care of them, particularly now that we have twins.

Speaking of health, I am not doing well either, though I am in my best years and I have not had any accidents. I suffered a lot this year yet I have missed only 14 days of work. I have had a toothache since April, and now I have pain in my back and in my legs. Sometimes it is so bad that I cannot walk or sit or lie. It is probably from all the work on the house. I dug up so many stones, loaded them, unloaded them, I made and carried so much mortar and all this ended on my back. So much wood passed through my hands. All the wetness, all the cold, all my long walks. Now I suffer. If only I had a servant to help me, if only I could rest a little. But you know that here you have to work like an animal and you know that for me work is everything. This is hard on a man. God, I hope things get better.

CHAPTER NINE

1925–1927: We Are in Italy Now

Every March Jožef wrote to John with the same questions. In 1925 his usual urgent tone was replaced with a weary one. Since Christmas Jožef had been waiting for any mail from America. He was weary of winter, weary from yet another death, weary of the messy business of lending and collecting money for John, and weary of asking him what to do with his farm. He used his Italian address for the first time, and announced with sarcastic humor that "We are in Italy now." "Venezia Giulio" is the Italian name for Primorska, which literally translates to Julian Venice, but it is commonly called the Julian March.

> *Povžane 4, Matteria Istro,*
> *Venezia Giulio, Italia, Europa.*
> *8 March 1925*
>
> Dear Sister and Janez!!! I finally received your letter, the one with the postcards and newspaper clippings. It was the first letter since Christmas, but the package from the holidays is still not here. The winter was mild; three times a little snow fell and then quickly disappeared. This was followed by 14 days of a strong burja and cold. Well, why should I write about a mild

winter? We are in Italy now and in Italy there are no winters.
We have oranges growing here!

I was hoping that Janez would come home and do whatever
he pleases with his farm. Tell me what you want me to do now.
Will you rent it out? Please answer me, the time is coming fast
when we need to put some manure on the fields, and take care
of the molehills; there are many this year. Also, please send me
a list of all the sums you have sent me. I think I have all the
receipts except for one that Mama collected at the post office.
I want all the sums done correctly for you, for me, for Janez's
sisters, and the judge.

Tona Bazletova and Pepa Blaževa kept Mary up to date on social
news and served as scribes for Mama. When Tona wrote for Mama,
she would omit messages sure to stir up trouble, but Pepa Blaževa
allowed Mama to unburden herself. Little things such as: Tona
didn't have time to write for Mama, Rezina Bilkotova neglected her,
her son kept secrets from her, she didn't get enough to eat, or she was
unwell, when repeated back by Mary to Tona or Jožef would create
little tempests which they would have to smooth out, and when that
failed, they would attack the messenger, Pepa Blaževa. Jožef would
repeat, "She is not noble," and Tona would say, "She lies."

Jožef's wife, also a Pepa, stayed out of the fray by not writing for
Mama. She remained above reproach. Tona wrote:

> When a bride comes into a house many mothers say, "Why
> should I work, the young ones are here, they should do the
> work." No, Mama is not like that, she works hard and watches
> over everything. She and Pepa get along very well. They do not
> fight like people in other homes, where everybody ends up
> laughing at the bride and stara tašča. Thank God that Mama
> got a good bride.

The women wrote about Marija Grgarečeva, the beloved neighbor
and cousin, who kept a gostilna in Bazovica. In her best years, she

was struck with an illness that put her in the hospital for months. When she recovered, she could not walk and lost some vision and hand dexterity. (Possibly a stroke, polio, or multiple sclerosis). Her husband took her to Kozina where he gently cared for her and their younger son while their older son went to school in Ljubljana. Neighbors, including Jožef, would stop in to see her on their way to Trieste.

Božidar Kastelic, heir to a large and wealthy estate, kept in touch. (photo 10) He attended the village school with John and Mary then went to Ljubljana for secondary school taught in German. His interests were in books, poetry, music and theater, and his letters were written in extraordinarily ornate penmanship. I suspect that he once had a romantic interest in my grandmother, and the letters were composed with her in mind, but he respectfully and eloquently addressed John.

The usual farmer of Brkini was short and broad with a wide, sun-beaten face. Božidar stood out with his slim, tall build, and face framed in sandy curls. He wore a pencil thin mustache aligned with his upper lip that twirled upward at the corners of his mouth, widening his smile unnaturally. His light-colored suits with high lace-edged collars and silk bows gives the impression that he was a bit of a dandy. But despite his education and fine clothes he felt at home among farmers and tradesmen and he was well-loved in the village because of his good nature. Before the war, Kastelic's prosperous store and gostilna in Materija drew people to tables under the shade of its linden tree to eat, drink, share news and do business. In 1908, Božidar founded the Materija volunteer fire department that continues to this day, and is used not only for firefighting, but as the center of social life. Slovenian businesses such as Kastelic were targeted by irredentists but Jožef believed that Božidar's poor management also contributed to his decay. By 1925, Kastelic was falling on very hard times. The topic of *much education*, the local term for gossip, was the birth of a son, Zlato, to Karlina, a maid in his house whom Božidar had not married.

A little further down the road towards Rijeka, but still under Slavnik, is another little village sweetly called Slivje or "Plum", a tribute to this essential ingredient for the local spirit slivovic and home to a man named Josef Ban (no close relation to the Bans of Povžane) who had been separated from his family since he left for Cleveland in 1908. On the *Belvedere* on 10 June 1921 with Rudy Fradel were Josef Ban's three nearly grown daughters and wife. As everyone from under Slavnik, they were to merge into the story. When Joe and John Fabjančič, formerly of Grgurjevi, arrived in Cleveland they boarded with this family.

Grgurjova, the mother of Joe and John Fabjančič, did not change her ways after her sons emigrated to get away from her. The eldest son, Drej, was destined to be the master and the remaining sons, Frane and Miha, still had to find their own fortunes. The eldest daughter, Marija Johana Grgurjeva, had been a romantic interest of Drej Bilko (Andy Siskovič) and some imagined he would return for her. She had been waiting a long time. Tona wrote, "At home her family was treating her poorly, now she can thank God the man from Markovščina she married has rescued her." Joe's girlfriend, Marija Rejčeva, the one Grgurjova hated, expected Joe to return or send for her. Thus when the news arrived he had wed Antonia Ban, the eldest daughter of his landlord, everyone was shocked and disappointed.

Jožef wrote in August 1926, "We heard that Jože Grgur (Joe Fabjančič) got married. Do you know anything about this? If this is true, then he made a mistake. Marija Rejčeva is faithful to him, she is more loyal to him than a wife would be."

Marija Rejčeva was crushed and her hurt would linger for decades. Joe Fabjančič was able to make amends with his mother by sending generous sums of money. How much money a person received from a son or brother in America was an arena for boasting amongst the families left behind. Grgurjova proudly told everyone she had received 100 lire from her son, while Skominčič's wife boasted her husband had already sent her 36,000. Everyone was very impressed.

*

Life was never easy for Tona but the way her husband had changed since the Great War made her life almost unbearable. "Shell shock" was a new term coined to describe exhaustion, tremors, confusion, loss of balance, nightmares, and impaired sight and hearing in battle-fatigued men. A shell-shocked soldier was unable to function but at that time, the less obvious damage of post-traumatic stress disorder (PTSD) went unrecognized. Josef Godina's drinking, difficulty with working, anger about being "told what to do," estrangement from his wife and children, and references to his war experiences were clearly the result of PTSD. Tona's bottled-up hurt, anger, loneliness, and sorrow came out in a long letter she wrote to her sister in America in March of 1925. She sat down with a large piece of graphed paper to keep her lines straight, and with pen in hand, taking unusually great care with her beautiful cursive penmanship, she unburdened herself.

> My dear little Sister, I've wanted to tell you some things about my life for a long time. My husband often tells me if I talk to anyone, then woe is me! He must never know I wrote to you like this, or I will be dead. In the first years of our marriage, he got angry now and then, but I could live with that. During the first year he was in the army, when he was still in Trst, he wrote kindly, and we were never apart for more than eight days. He came to me on vacation, or he asked me to come there. That was the kind of husband he was. After one year, he went to Gradec. His letters were normal at first, then he would write one day that he loved me, and two days later he wrote mean things, and said he did not care about me anymore. He wrote to our son asking him how Mama was doing, asking my son why I did not write to him! Jože was too young; he did not yet know how to read or write; he did this only to torture me. I always wrote back and pleaded with him not to hurt me because I was already sad enough with the poverty and hard

work with the children. He wrote he did not want to see me
when he came home on leave, that I should take the children
and leave. I replied I would not leave because I have not sinned.
When he arrived, he did not speak to me for days. You can
imagine how many tears I shed. He often left to go drinking
and when he returned, he would rage and curse everything in
this world: my blood, my milk, Mother, Father, the earth that
I was standing on. He rants that they are not his children. I
cannot tell you everything, and I do not tell any of this to my
Mama. I do not know why he is angry with Polžane, but he
does not permit me to go there so I visit Mama only when he
does not know about it.

So, this is how my years have been since the war: If the master of the house takes care of things, then some problems can
be anticipated but he goes to drink every Sunday, and often
during the week, he wakes me up in the middle of the night;
many nights I am afraid to go to bed. He always rejects me;
he tells me he is not short of women better looking than me
and that I am too thin. I tell him that he should give me something to eat and then I will look better. If he wanted someone
who was better looking, he should have taken one. I am the
same person that he knew before the war, I have only been at
home. He told me that he had other women when he was in
the army, and what kind of fun he had with them. He says he
should have left us and gone with one of them. I found letters
that he received. I still have one, but what can I do with it? It
is written in German.

For the New Year he told me this: Listen to me carefully,
today is New Year and I will break your head just like I would
do it to a snake. In the evening, he sent others to get me to
join him in drinking, and I did; I had a glass of wine, only
because there were others there, but when he started boasting,
I retreated quickly.

Now, on 8 March, he hit me on my head so hard that I was
sure I would never walk again. He is evil, always thinking of
other women and telling us he will leave. I tell him he could

go to his whores, but he has a responsibility to his children. He says that no, that he would rather kill himself. I am sorry to say this, but I would prefer that he does kill himself because once he is dead, he cannot hurt me anymore. I do not know what kind of death is awaiting me, but I have bad thoughts of shortening my life.

You wrote I should rest more, but he does not give me any rest, I must dig and work and sweat because we cannot survive without my work. I have not had my shoes repaired in three years. Maybe you could send me some of your old shoes. Now, I will conclude this miserable and sad writing. Please, I ask you, please, do not tell anyone. I rely on you as my sister. I only need to complain and I will not do it again, even if I die soon. A

*

On 15 October 1925, a decree was made that only Italian would be spoken in courts, and only Italian place names were to be used. Materija became Matteria; Bazovica became Basovizzi. Povžane and Bač escaped change, perhaps because they were just local place names part of the Materija post office. Jožef wrote to Mary on 1 December 1925:

I received your letter and the photograph of the children on 4 November (photo 8). Dear Sister, you say we should come to America. I would very much like to move away from this bloody government. The Italians always find a cunning way to draw us onto thin ice. They cannot hunt us all down, so they make sure that we will leave on our own. My wife and Mama would like to go, but my children are too small. We should wait until they are old enough to work. Maybe immigration will turn around by then and it will be easier to get visas for America. You will have to describe to me in detail how I could rent or buy a farm. If we are not able to endure it here any longer and if it is possible to get the visa, then we shall go.

On the same day I received your letter about Rudolf's car accident, we were sawing wood up in Slavnik when a beech tree fell on Old Frane Košanc. It squeezed him so hard that he could not talk for two hours and we had to carry him home. He has been in bed for 25 days, only now he is starting to get better. We are still working on dividing the Boršt, so that the municipality cannot claim it. We've been trying to resolve this for three years.

It is December and we have already had enough snow for the entire winter. We wish you Merry Christmas holidays and a Happy New Year, that you may be blessed for years to come, but in better conditions than we have now in this Julian March.

The winter of 1925 to 1926 was bitter cold. Tona sent her Christmas greetings on the fourth of December. The Italian army had come to the house to summon Joe Godina for conscription. When the army came a second time his parents were threatened that they had to produce evidence that he was in America with a visa for at least ten years. They wrote to John, asking for his help.

Jožef wrote on 1 January 1926:

We celebrated the holidays in the usual way. Mama received your letter and I read it on Christmas Eve as we ate that poor *bakalar* [a dried cod soup traditionally served on Christmas Eve]. We wondered what you were doing and imagined all the things that you can get in America. Yesterday, on the last day of the old year, your package arrived intact. I distributed the gifts as you directed. Tona was pleased with everything you sent, including half of the sausage. We thank you from our hearts for remembering us with your gifts. The problem was that you bought and paid a lot for everything, paid for the postage, and then I had to pay 75 lire just to get the package from the post office. Even the postman was surprised that it cost so much. You know that Tona is always poor, and I did not have the money, so I had to borrow it.

Mama thanks you for your previous letter. Unfortunately, my daughter read it to her before I came home; I would have skipped your reply to Mama's story about the parish priests. Mama is sad and disappointed that you do not want to hear about them. There is no need for you to write like this to her; you know that people here, especially women, see priests as the first gods and if someone says that there is no God, well, then he is the biggest good-for-nothing in the world!

On 20 January Jožef wrote again. In quiet defiance of Italian oppression, he never Italianized his name or that of his children.

Dear Sister, Our children also talk about how they would get along with your children if we go to America. Marija will go out with Ivanka, Jožek with Jože, Francka will go out with your Marija, our Janez will take your little Janez around, and that Slavica will take Milka around. Twice you have asked to know the name of the youngest girl. Her name is Emilija and we call her Milka. It is a very Slovenian name, isn't it? This is what I wanted, because more and more they want to make us Italian, and even if they take everything else from us, they will not take our names.

From your description, an American farmer lives like a count compared to us. I've been to Austria, Bulgaria, Romania, Russia, Montenegro, and Serbia. My opinion is that the majority of these people have lives that are worse than ours because they are lazy and lack education. They have fertile land, but they do not know how, or do not want to take care of it. What they grow often goes bad, so that it is not fit for human consumption. You think that I am afraid to come to America, but I am not afraid to travel. Life in America would be good for me. What I fear is that moving to America requires a lot of money. If I had to borrow, I would be a poor man for the rest of my days, forced to choose between feeding my family or paying the loan. I would love to get away from this damn government. I should have done it five years ago, when I could have gotten 80,000 for the farm. But those prices are gone. Nobody is buying land. Therefore, I will remain a slave.

You read about the earthquake here. The first tremor was the strongest. It rattled on the first day of the New Year, in the evening at seven o'clock for five minutes. It felt like we were on the wagon when it hits something and everything jars and shakes. There was no damage, but people, especially the women, were afraid, and many families did not return to bed. To us men, to those who have been in the army, this did not frighten us. We were hit six more times and then for the next four days we felt weak shaking every now and then. [The earthquake that occurred on 1 January 1926 had a magnitude 5.6. The quake's epicenter was near Cerknica, which is 36 miles northeast of Povžane.]

Mary had sent Tona many packages and, in the spring of 1926, Tona wanted to reciprocate with something thoughtful, but she had very little money. She sent seeds: lettuce, radicchio, and beans so that her sister would think about her as she planted and cared for her little garden.

In the spring of 1926, a rumor got around that John wanted to sell Jurkotevi and his sister, Pepina, in Maribor heard it. John received a letter from Pepina. Despite the gracious salutations, she was seething with anger. Her penmanship was poor, and her grammar garbled, but her message was clear.

Na Obrežju 3
Studenci pri Mariboru,
Štajersko, Jugoslavija
8 April 1926

Dear Brother, I am sending you many warm regards from my heart, to you and to your entire family. We are, thank God, healthy, and we wish the same for all of you.

I heard that you were planning to sell everything at Jurkotevi without telling me. I was forced to go down to Polžane and you know that we are poor and cannot afford this travel. I cannot believe that you would order Biščev and Mališko to do this in such a way that I would not know anything about it. And I only find out things by hearsay! Dear Ivan, Are you even aware of this matter?

Because I think that I have not done anything bad to you, I was waiting for you to come home so that we could come to an agreement, and now I see that nothing like this will happen. What a great injustice! I was at Jurkotevi until the very end. I was drudging like an animal through the war, just like Father and our other sisters and brother. And now others are enjoying and building their houses!

I was forced to petition the court so that, if it becomes necessary, Father's Will can be annulled. Unless the two of us can come to an agreement in a peaceful way, Biščev, your caretaker and Mališko, who represents Rudolf and Antonija, can get up to three months in prison for violating the court ruling. It would be better that we come to an agreement, rather than to start suing each other and creating expenses. It would be better to act like brother and sister, because we are all of one mother and of one father and of one blood from Polžane; we are all Jurkotevi!!!

I heard from Mališko that Rudolf was injured when he fell, but I do not know the details. Now let me finish this sad writing. I feel so miserable because of my own brother. Once again, I send you my best regards from my heart and I ask you to please let me know soon what you are thinking, and if it is true that you let them cross the line so far.

Zbogom, Your sister, Josephina Babič

John did not feel compelled to write back to Pepina, not even to set the record straight that Rudolf had been in a car accident, not a fall. That rumor would grow and twist until everyone in Maribor believed that Rudolf had lost an eye. There were other letters from Pepina, usually asking for money, that he also ignored. Instead, John, relied on Jožef to deal with the problem in person. Jožef endured the animosities, accusations, and gossip that arose from it. A year later Pepina wrote again and did not even mention the lawsuit she had persuaded her sister Antonija to join. Pepina offered to drop her claim to Jurkotevi if John would just send her a few *tholars* to help her out of her poverty and misery. *Tholar* were silver coins used in Austria from 1741–1856, and long afterwards they were still considered a valuable coin for trade in many places. The few people who actually had them hoarded them for special occasions. John did not reply.

*

Inflation was wildly out of control in all of Europe. The U.S. dollar, which had been set at 2.27 lire in 1920, had risen to 30 lire. The dollar Mary often slipped in with a letter to her mother or sister bought more lire, but those lire bought less, and the fees attached to changing money, or paying customs on a package, were exorbitant. In an effort to stabilize the cost of goods and services within Italy, Mussolini would deflate the currency in 1927 and the exchange rate for one U.S. dollar would be set at 19 lire. On 15 August 1926, Jožef wrote to his sister about the economy:

> Meanwhile costs are rising. The Italians use every method to rob us. Look at it like this: we sell milk for 85 čentižim per liter, so we need to sell 10 liters of milk to purchase one kilo of sugar. A kilo of white flour was one lire now costs 3½ lire. Salt was 50 čentižim and is now 1.5 lire. Our worst loss is with cattle, the price of beef dropped almost by half and if the meat is not perfect, you almost have to give it away. They pay us only 3 lire for one kilo of meat and the butcher resells it for 10 lire. That gives you something to think about, doesn't it? Everyone complains; we are all worried. Some are saying that war will break out, others are saying these are just speculations by Mussolini's party. What do your newspapers write about Italy?

Skominčič—working in Sharon, Pennsylvania while waiting for his citizenship to be approved so his wife and son could join him—reported to others that work was hard to find and prices were rising. Such rumors caused Tona to fret more about her boy in America. Would he have work? Would he send money? Would he return to marry the Gasčeva girl? Joe had written only one letter to the girl, but it was enough to keep the women guessing about his marital intentions for a decade. Tona had mixed feelings about the girl. She did not think it was a great match, but on the other hand the girl had potential to draw him home. She also worried about the safety of her daughters. Fani had escaped her unhappy home by finding work in Ilirska Bistrica as a house servant. Zora was a servant in Trieste. Premarital and extramarital sex happened routinely and the issue of illegitimacy was generally resolved with a marriage to someone, if not the father of the child, perhaps a widower. A new kind of problem arose when Slovene girls got together with Italian soldiers and policemen. Tona wrote on 9 October 1926:

> Everything has changed since the war. Many girls get together with Italians, and now they have children, but the men do not want to acknowledge them. You know the parents of the Slugar girl from Rožice? She had a child 14 days ago with an Italian policeman. He left, and now she is supposed to hold the baby in her arms. I always fear something like this could happen to my girls. I know it is not possible for Fanika to come to you, but it would please me the most if she could.

Skominčič received his U.S. citizenship and returned home on 16 October 1926. For obscure reasons, Jožef started calling him "Meta," a woman's name that means "mint." Jožef didn't like Meta. He never repaid John for his ticket to Baltimore in 1923. His wife's boast of receiving 36,000 lire was bogus; he had to borrow 5,000 lire from Katarina of Banovi just for this trip. He hoped to expedite his family's immigration by coming to Italy to do the paperwork, but after four months and multiple trips to Pula, Koper, and Trieste in search of the necessary documents they still were not granted the entry permit.

As he made plans to leave on 8 February, Mary and John asked him to bring Mary's clothes but at the last minute it was discovered the travel box the carpenter had made for him was too small. "The carpenter must have been blind," Jožef exclaimed. He would have raced off to Trieste to get another box but it was snowing, so he borrowed some boards and threw one together. Then Skominčič decided he could not leave until March. In the final weeks before his departure, Jožef wrote to John to ask permission for Skominčič to carry cash to John, to avoid the fees associated with the usual international transmission of money. By the time John's letter arrived telling Jožef not to do it, the cash and Skominčič had sailed.

Mary gave directions on how she wanted the rest of her clothes distributed, but Mama did what she thought was best. Tona got the wine-colored dress and the black blouse. Jožef's wife got the striped skirt. The fine blue and yellow dress Tona wanted and the winter shirt with rectangles went to Fani. When enough letters had passed back and forth, Jožef was fresh with anger that Mama had been so generous to Fani, Mama was angry at Jožef for sticking his nose in her business, Tona was feeling sorry for herself, and Rezina, as usual, was angry at everybody.

In his March 1927 planting-time letter to John, Jožef was done with pleading.

> I rented out your fields. This year we will get more than ever: 850 lire. I could not reach an agreement for the Long Field with Pajser. He wanted to give me only 25 lire and I did not want to be told what to do. I have not done anything with the meadows in the last four years, so they are all covered with shrubs. They have to be cleared before we could get something for them which would not be much; it is better left as it is. Dear Janez, around here there is always something new from the

Italians. The government is planning to build a lime storage in our backyard right where your Long Garden is. Two engineers were here for four days. They have already made plans for Ban's property. They will pay us only what they see fit. You must write a request to fight this. I will also write one.

*

Louis Adamic, the Slovenian-American author, observed the laughter, singing, music and public gayety of Slovenian peasants as he traveled in Yugoslavia during these difficult years but underneath this cheerful veneer, he recognized a harshness related to the economic reality of the scarcity of arable land, and the lack of industries that could employ landless younger sons and pay them decent wages. Over half of the land was hilly or mountainous, suitable only for forestry or vineyards. The average farmer owned only seven acres of workable land. A family's wellbeing depended on a very narrow profit margin. Small difficulties and grievances, such as possession of a few feet of ground, or a tool, or an animal, or clothes, or a blanket could cause the eruption of fierce quarrels. The burning of a barn or shed, or even murder, sometimes resulted.

Such crimes were rare, but the vehemence of the disagreements over the deposition of Mary's clothes, or of Jurkotevi with its meager four acres, should not be underestimated. Violence in Primorska became more prevalent during the Italian occupation. When murders took place, as they did in the valley under Slavnik in the next decade, the motivation was unclear. Was it irredentismo or political? Was the climate of rage and violence a smokescreen for a petty grievance?

Jožef revealed his impatience with the tedious details of Mary's clothes, the strain of dealing with John's sisters, and the management of the depreciating four acres of Jurkotevi. But in a lighthearted moment—albeit tinged with pain and sarcasm—Jožef makes a joke about John's large handlebar mustache in a family photo from America. (photo 11)

22 May 1927

Dear Janez, I laughed so hard when I saw your photograph. This is how Italians are shaving themselves—are you also an Italian? You look like an 18-year-old boy. If I were standing next to you, I would look like your father.

Dear sister!!! You write about the things you left behind; you are really good to remember what happened 15 years ago, as if it happened today. About that blanket you asked about; my wife says Mama gave it to Bazletevi and they have worn it out already. Let's forget about this, it is not worth wasting any more words; there is not much we can do about it. As I wrote to you many times, Rezina is not nice. She is angry you do not write to her, and you did not get her daughter to America. She says you are stuck-up and rich. She is too stingy to spend two lire for postage. Even to Drej Bilko, who often sends them money, she writes rarely.

You ask about Janez's sisters. Antonija and Cesar in Art-viže are pretending to be nice to me. They acknowledge they have received what they were supposed to get from Father's Will. They did not want to go to a lawyer, they were not looking for more. Now, their lawyer has sent them the bill, and he also wrote to you. They say Pepina forced them to go to the lawyer and so Pepina should pay the total bill. They talk about all sorts of stupidities that are not worth listening to or writing about: Pepina wants Janez to die, and then Biščev would dance, and that Pepina is angry with me because of you, Marija. They say that Pepina has not been able to stand you since the days when you were still here. I do not know what you have done to her.

As I have written to you so many times, it would be the right thing for Janez to come home, then all of this would be resolved. I know you do not want to spend money, but Janez has been working hard for the last 15 years, just like he was in the army.

Would it not be nice if he would take 40 days off and come to
see his birthplace once more? He could put all his things in
order. To cover the expenses of the trip, he could sell some land
or he could sell the firewood and that house. If there were no
buyers for the farm in the short period he was here, he could
rent it to someone long term. If he can come to an agreement
with Cesar, that would also be good.

*

On 12 June 1927, yet another Italian edict outlawed the use of Slovene language anywhere in public, even in the gostilnas. It required
that surnames be Italianized and children be given Italian names.
Children with Slavic names were randomly assigned Italian names
by their teachers. No Slavic inscriptions were permitted on grave-
stones. Slovenian political, social, economic, sporting, and cultural
associations were dissolved. Libraries and reading rooms were
closed. Three political parties, 31 newspapers and journals, 300
co-operatives and financial institutions were shut down.

*

In the last days of summer Frane Fabjančič of Grgurjevi married
a daughter of Gajsčevi and took up residence at Severlan in Bač,
much to the displeasure of his mother. His brother, John Fabjančič, married Mary Gustinač in Cleveland. Joe Fabjančič sent 800
lire to his mother and reported he was happy with his new wife.
Skominčič wrote from America that Joe Godina had a beautiful
girlfriend, which set loose new worries for Tona. By now, both Fani
and her sister Zora, both working as house servants in Trieste, were
able to give something to their mother.

On 17 September Jožef gave news that would tie Marija of Gabrk
and her children even closer to Mary as soon as the American immigration authorities permitted it.

On Gabrk, they had a wedding this week, and Kristinca [Jak-setič] is now married to Frane Siskovič from Slivje who has come home from Cleveland, but I think it will be a long while before she will see America.

That dry summer of 1927 caused a meager harvest. On 30 October Jožef reported:

> On our end, misfortune is never asleep. As if a poor harvest and high taxes were not enough, on 12 October, my daughter, Mar-ija, was tending a flock, when she fell and broke her right arm between her elbow and her hand. At the hospital in Trst they took x-rays and put her arm in plaster. I had to give them 300 lire on the very first day. They removed the plaster yesterday and she is recovering gradually. So far, I have paid 600 lire. 600 lire is a lot of money these days. You can buy a small cow for this.

At the close of 1927, burdened with poor harvests, high prices, medical costs, taxes, the faltering world economy, Italian efforts to destroy his language, and talk of another war, Jožef allowed himself to muse: "What if I had gone to America?" and wondered whether he should, or could, go now. Mary encouraged this fantasy.

10 December 1927

Dear Sister, You write that you have a lot of expenses with your health problems, but you are fortunate Janez is healthy and capable of earning well. I know you have to work hard and have a lot of worries, but you are lucky to be there. I looked at the prices of farms in the newspapers you sent. You are right that I should have come to America. I should have gone right after the war; our family was small then and there were many opportunities in America. I did not go then because I was afraid to go anywhere. I was devastated by the war. Then things went downhill, our family grew and I got older. I am only four years older than you are, but the war has made me

ten years older. These should be my best years. If I had gone
to America last year and worked two or three days a week like
Meta, would my children and wife and mother be begging or
die of hunger? Even with all this risk, we might be forced to
go. You know even better than we do it will not be long before
another war starts. War is a horrible thing. Those of us who
have experienced it know this best. But just now people don't
care, nobody does anything about it, and they say we'll just have
to wait and see what happens.

Our Francka is now six years old; she was sick in the fall and
she has recovered, but she is still not her old self. Marija is 11,
she can use her arm that was broken for writing and light tasks,
but she will not be able to do heavy work until the spring. Jožek
is seven, the twins are four years old and they are so strong, if
you could only see them, oh, Marija, you would be so surprised!

On 12 November we had snow for three days, but then it
rained and we have not had good weather since. We have not
been able to rake the leaves yet. Mama has been going for
drinks after the evening Mass (**Godmother, one more liter**),
and when she gets home, she says she had only one glass of
wine. If you sent Mama 100 lire, she would praise you in the
gostilna and at home, but since you did not send any money,
she is not happy with you. There you have it; now I know you
will understand how things are. Mother and the old Bazletova
are educating themselves together.

"Godmother, one more liter" is a colloquial phrase used to order
more wine at a gostilna when the crowd is ready to party and drink
to excess and finances aside, there was no way Jožef would have
gotten an entry permit for the United States, but still he imagined
while he worried about his mother's drinking.

*

I remember my grandmother talking with my parents and aunts
about her friends and the people she corresponded with. The names

sounded exotic and musical to me and I had no idea who they were.
There were EYE-vin and Joe Go-deena There was Maria Basioli in
Australia, Fani Colja in Maribor, and Mary Gajst. There were Christina and Frank Siskovič, who seemed to come up in every conversation, and their children, Frank Jr., and Alma Babuder. There were
the names of all the Brkini people in these letters and on passenger
lists for Ellis Island. If they came to America, what happened to
their descendants? Might some of them be knowledgeable about
their family history and help fill out this story? I was to find and
meet some of them.

Alma Babuder was the daughter of Kristina of Gabrk. (Later
called Christina Siskovič in America). Alma told me stories about
her mother, who was the oldest child of Marija of Gabrk and Anton
Jaksetič who operated the popular gostilna on Gabrk. Kristina was
18 when she married 31-year-old Franc Siskovič of Slivje. Six years
earlier, with his name Italianized to Francisco, he had been fortunate to have his visa approved, and arrived at Ellis Island on an
auspicious date, 4 July 1921, just a few weeks after the arrival of
Rudy Fradel and the Ban family from Slivje. He changed his name
to Frank, worked in Cleveland and applied for citizenship. While
this was in process, he returned home to take a bride. Unfortunately,
his wife's application for a U.S. entry permit would not be approved
until he received citizenship, which took another three years. Frank
returned to Cleveland to work and wait for her, and those years
apart caused speculation and rumors.

I learned first-hand that the village women started to conjecture
and plot who their children would marry when they were barely
out of the cradle. When their children emigrated and the village ties
were broken, they lost all control of the matter. The old women were
left unfulfilled, without proof of a marriage, brides or grandchildren to occupy their time, they felt the need to natter on about what
might have been for decades. As the women "educated themselves"
there was lots of room for speculation and misinformation—gossip

that would hang on for decades. Alma told me although her parents seemed to have a good marriage, she always suspected there was something wrong because Kristina had not come to Cleveland for three years after the wedding. I could assure her, a half-century after the fact, the problem had been the Johnson Reed Act, not her parents' lack of devotion to one another.

And the gossip went on. When 17-year-old Joe left Bač, he had some interest in Marija Gasčeva. He wrote to her at least once, and sent her his picture. From this scant evidence, his mother Tona, Mary Fradel, and Gela Skominčič "educated themselves" for years, even beyond his marriage to the very beautiful Jessie Valentinčič in 1929. Gossip swirled around Andy Siskovič and Johana Grgurjeva, Joe Fabjančič and Marija Rejčeva. One could say that such gossip was a major export of rural Slovenia. Even I was to get caught up in it.

In 1956, another Marija Fabjančič from Povžane emigrated to Australia. The mothers and old women "educated themselves" that Marija should marry a certain man from the village who was already there. Marija never had any intention of this, nor did the man. In the end, she met a nice Croatian man, Vladimir Basioli, at the immigrant center in Australia, and they married, had children and a happy life together. But the village women would not let it rest. They circulated a story around the world—to Australia and to America—that went like this: Maria Basioli went to Australia to marry a man from her village, but when she got there she found that he had married someone else, so she was forced to marry a *Bosnian*. As a child, I heard this story more than once, and the emphasis was always on the "B" in Bosnian, as if she was a scorned, desperate woman who had no choice but to marry some undesirable outcast of civilization.

When I was 23, I had a boyfriend in Australia. I decided I would go there to pursue a relationship and satisfy my desire to travel. My application for a work visa based on my nursing credentials was approved. But the story of Marija Basioli was repeated to me by my grandmother and my father as a cautionary tale as to why I shouldn't go to Australia. I went anyhow. My boyfriend had come from post-war Czechoslovakia to Australia as a child and I didn't know what a Bosnian was, but I felt pretty sure I would not marry anyone in desperation. Grandma gave me Maria Basioli's address and I found her and her family in Sydney. They welcomed me in as a long lost cousin. Maria sat me down one evening. "I know what they are saying about me," she said quietly and firmly, and as I enjoyed a bowl of her homemade soup, she set me straight with the real story that had occurred twenty years earlier.

CHAPTER TEN

1928: Resistance in Primorska

When the Roman Empire collapsed in 476 AD, the Lombardi who resided in the Eastern Alps retreated to the Italian peninsula. About 100 years later, in the middle of the Dark Ages, the Slovene people moved into the empty spaces of the Eastern Alps and the western edge of the Pannonian Plain. They maintained their independence there for only a short time. Charlemagne established the Holy Roman Empire in 800 AD and Slovenian lands came under its domain. As the Germanic elements of the Empire came into contact with the tribal society of the Slovenes, the Germans became the lords and the Slovenes became the peasants.

In 863, Cyril and Methodius, Christian missionaries later canonized as saints, arrived from Greece. They created an original alphabet to translate the sacred liturgies into the Slavic language. Pope Nicholas blessed their efforts and Catholicism grew. The Protestant Reformation of 1517 gained many Slovene converts, particularly among the upper classes. In efforts to further evangelization, the Protestants took elements of disparate dialects to create a Slovene literary language and script. At first, nobody knew how to read it and few could understand it. Primož Trubar wrote an eight-page primer to teach the standardized language. In 1550, his primer and the Catechism were the first books to be printed in Slovene and

more books rapidly followed. The unified written language created by the Protestants was the key building block for a Slovenian
national identity. In Slovenia today, Reformation Day on 31 October
is celebrated as a national holiday, with a special recognition for its
role in Slovene nationhood.

Most Slovenes returned to Catholicism during the Counter Reformation. The Slovene Bible written by the Protestants was retained
by the Catholic church. The Jesuits used the new written language
to produce written Scripture and sacred songs and developed an
educational program to help priests deliver sermons in the vernacu-
lar of the peasants. A Jesuit college in Ljubljana, established in 1597,
would prepare men for the priesthood. New Catholic churches were
built and local priests kept written records of marriages, baptisms,
and deaths. The cornerstones of many of the churches in Brkini date
from the 1630s. Catholicism and Slovene language became integral
to Slovenian identity and many patriotic clergy actively defended
against German and Italian influence.

Napoleon founded his Illyrian Provinces along the coast in
1809 to 1813, with Ljubljana as its capital. The language of education became French, and to counter German as the dominant
cultural force, Slovene was also taught. This further awakened the
Slovenian national consciousness. After the revolutions dubbed
the "Springtime of Nations" in 1848, Austria and Hungary joined
empires to quell the growth of nationalism in their minority populations. Austria allowed limited cultural autonomy for Slovenes
and its other Slavic minorities as a means of keeping the empire
economically and politically sound. Under these circumstances,
Slovenian literacy grew, and writers and the arts flourished. Slovenes had not had an independent political or economic life for
over a thousand years, yet their language and culture were completely their own and gave them status as a separate nationality.
Love of language and culture, and their pristinely beautiful homeland, were sources of great pride.

"Slovenia's major products were agriculture and culture," Louis Adamic nicely summarized in *The Native's Return*. In Trieste and Ljubljana, publishers, booksellers, and book clubs flourished—Jožef Fabjančič, Mary and John Fradel were avid readers—and in Ljubljana the streets were named after poets, novelists, and dramatists. The largest monument in town is a statue of Franc Prešeren, a poet and writer from the 19th century. All the towns and most larger villages had public libraries, reading rooms, theater groups, and singing societies. Churches had active choruses and the Austrian-sponsored village schools taught singing in harmony. Bands performed Slovene folk music in the gostilnas and at opasilos. Each area had an individual style of traditional costume and dance. Women engaged in fine sewing and lacemaking.

Thus, Italian irredentism struck at the heart of rural Primorska and Jožef swore that they would not take their names. Tona lamented her son, who was taught in Italian at school, learned neither Italian nor Slovene. Jožef had nothing new to read in Slovene. There would be no evenings with a guitar and accordion, singing ballads over a liter of wine. The *carabinieri* (Italian police), stationed in each village, would be watching, and listening for utterances of the banned language. Worse still were their own neighbors who collaborated with the carabinieri. The girls who consorted with the Italian soldiers were despised, and later pitied. In this milieu, resistance was born.

Initially, acts of violence targeted individuals in the military or police around Postojna and Ilirska Bistrica. Slovene activists joined forces with Croatians in lower Istria and briefly worked with dissidents in Yugoslavia. This collaboration did not last because the Yugoslav dissidents were communists, while Slovenes and Croatians were antifascist nationalists. In September 1927, an informal group met on Nanos Mountain, a sparsely populated plateau looming above the Vipava valley, to unify their efforts. They called themselves the Revolutionary Organization of the Julian March,

"Trieste-Istria-Gorica-Rijeka," or simply TIGR, for effect. The word is the same as it sounds in English, and is symbolic of the mighty and ferocious animal.

TIGR carried out attacks on police, border guards, the military, and members of the National Fascist Party and their Slovene supporters. At night, they burned schools and kindergartens that Italians had built as tools of cultural genocide. TIGR was organized into *troikas* (secret groups of three) to undertake these daring attacks. Each member recruited someone in a neighboring village to start a new troika. Its network was designed to safeguard members from treachery. One can easily imagine the local carabinieri were vigilant for suspects. TIGR received covert support throughout the Julian March. While Louis Adamic stated the Italian teacher Sottosanti was murdered by the fathers of the defiled children in Vrhpolje, he did not know, or perhaps he did not want to reveal, that it was actually an act of TIGR.

In the Goriska region, TIGR was dedicated to producing cultural propaganda and educational materials. In 1926, they produced a primer entitled *Prvi Koraki* (First Steps) to teach children Slovene at home. A reader, *Za Domačim Ognjiščem* (By the Home Hearth), was compiled to help them practice reading. Perhaps Tona used these to teach her son. TIGR published small batches of newspapers for quick distribution on mobile cyclostyles: *Borba* (Struggle), *Svoboda* (Freedom), *Ljudska fronta* (People's Front), or *Straža ob Soči* (Watch on the Soča) were some.

Around Javornik and Snežnik, near the southern border with Yugoslavia, the forested lowlands facilitated the smuggling of newspapers, literature, and propaganda from Ljubljana, an activity financed by Primorskans living there. In Ljubljana, it was called the Union of Emigrants Society, and in Maribor, it was the Nanos Society. One of John Fradel's distant cousins, Marija Fradel, the daughter of a younger son who moved to Maribor before the war, was notably active in this group. Smuggling through the mountain passes of the north was not easy, especially in the winter, but TIGR assisted those threatened by the carabinieri across the border to safety in Yugoslavia.

One of the founding members of TIGR was Jože Dekleva. Born at Bač #4 in 1899, he was distantly related to both the Fabjančič and Fradel families through Ivana Fradel, John's mother. He turned 18 during the last year of the war, and fought with the Austrian army, then graduated from law school at the University of Siena in Italy in 1925.

In November of 1928, Jožef asked his sister if she had heard news about "Ivana's Jože", an apparent reference to Jože Dekleva. He had been arrested that year for his TIGR activities, and was sentenced to five years of confinement on the island of Ponza, not far from Naples. After his release, he emigrated to Yugoslavia and worked with the Union of Emigrant Societies in anti-fascist activities. With the outbreak of World War II, and the Italian occupation of Ljubljana, he fled to Zagreb where he was arrested by the German Gestapo, and handed over to the Italians again. When the war ended in 1945, he returned to Trieste. He was politically active in service of the Slovene minority, and served on the Trieste Municipal council. A tribute to him was placed in the memorial park at Hrpelje-Kozina after Slovenian independence in 1991.

Jože Dekleva was in prison when TIGR pulled off its most dramatic attack. On 10 February 1930 they planted a time bomb in the head-quarters of the fascist newspaper, *Il Populo di Trieste*. It was timed to go off when the place was empty, but some staff were working late. The editor was killed and three journalists were injured. The arrests began in March and April. Altogether 87 men were arrested, though some managed to escape to Yugoslavia. The trial was held in Trieste, rather than Rome, for maximum impact on the Slovenes. Eighteen men stood trial in September for 99 acts of terror. Twelve received prison sentences, and on the 6 September in Basovica four were publicly executed by firing squad. The whole of Primorska mourned. In accordance with tradition for the recently dead, four empty seats were placed at dining tables throughout the Julian March.

TIGR quickly reorganized. They targeted infrastructures, high-ranking military, and police. They built ties with British and Yugoslav intelligence. In 1935 they made common cause with the Italian Communist Party. In 1938 they planned to assassinate Mussolini on his visit to Kobarid, but they were stopped by their British partners, who still thought Mussolini was potentially useful to them in reducing the threat from Germany. After the Anschluss of Austria in 1938, TIGR expanded its activities to Austria. Another Italian trial led to the public execution of more TIGR members near Trieste. By the time Germany invaded Yugoslavia in April 1941, nearly all their prominent members were dead, or in Italian or German concentration camps. Some members joined the Partisans. The goal of TIGR was Slovenian nationalism, which was not fully aligned with Tito's goal of a unified Yugoslavia that included Primorska. Tito wanted to suppress the recognition that Slovene Nationalists might have earned, so when the war was over in 1945, former members were removed from public life, had trouble finding jobs, and were monitored by the Yugoslav Secret Police for the next three decades. TIGR activities were expunged from official historic records and only after Tito's death and the arrival of Slovenian independence did its resistance activity get recognition for its early anti-fascist work. In 1997, the TIGR organization received the *Zlati častni znak svobode*, the Golden Honor Insignia of Freedom of the Republic of Slovenia, the highest state decoration.

*

In the bleak midwinter of 1928 with worries about last year's harvest behind him, and worries about planting his own land, and what to do about Jurkotevi too far in the future, Jožef was able to let go of his impatience with his extended family. He sat at the table in the dimly lit kitchen, keeping warm by the wood burning oven, and simply reflected on his losses and sadness as he wrote to his sister in America. They had been separated now—through a war and poverty, a global pandemic that took the lives of family, and ethnic cleansings—for far too long. His life in the valley below Slavnik was the only home he ever knew and he longed to escape the endless laments of poverty surrounding him by talking to his sister, Mary. She could brighten him with stories of her life in a new world. He wanted to reminisce with her about life before the war, as she remembered home—when the streets were alive with people, and Slovene music and dancing filled the gostilnas. Now, there was much emptiness and misery.

22 January 1928

I had not received a letter from you in a long time, then I got your wishes for Christmas, and then there was nothing, until today. Dear sister, the absence of your letters is hard on me, because when I read them, it is like talking to you. When Tona comes, she has nothing to talk about except her poverty, and you know how useless it is to talk to Rezina. With others, the conversation also goes nowhere; all anyone talks about is poverty. I get tired of it, hope disappears, and everything becomes desperate.

If you came to Trst, Marija, you would not believe how life has changed. Remember how it was before the War? Everything was alive, the streets were full of people, everyone was loud, and full of spirit. And how is it now? Empty avenues, everything sad, people walk absorbed in their thoughts. If you hear two people talking in a gostilna, they speak only about their misery. This is exactly why I wish to talk to you through letters. Even when we have to talk about the poverty, we can exchange ideas without having to see each other's sad faces. You write times are still good at your place, but here we are so squeezed. We have produced almost nothing, we have no income, and nothing to sell. In the past, one could at least sell some firewood, but now we have to pay taxes on firewood. By the time the taxes are paid and you purchase a few items for home, which are always expensive, you end up empty handed! Even this would be a

little something, but recently there is a surplus of firewood, and
then you need to stay in Trst for another day to sell everything.
"The noble ones" do not miss anything when it comes to taxes.

We had cold and snow for 14 days before Christmas, but since
then, the weather has been nice. Marija Bilkoteva in Trst had a
son on Monday 16 January. Mama is sad and angry because you
do not write to her, but mostly she is upset because you do not
send her money, and she is angry with me, because she thinks
I told you there is no need to send her anything! Now she has
started going to Bač to visit Gela Skominčič. Maybe they have
written to you; you can tell me.

In March, Jožef and Pepa had another daughter. "Jozefa" was a glorious example of the repetitive use of first names; her parents were
Jožef and Jozefa (and called Pepe and Pepa) and her brother was Jože.
Baby Jozefa would be called Pepca or Pepka until the time when all
the others in the family called Pepe and Pepa had passed away, then
she would be called Pepa.

The harvests had been poor for years, and by planting time
Biščevi was struggling for seed potatoes and beans. Mary put potatoes and beans in a package along with books, newspapers, and
used clothing. She included candies and little toys for the children.
For a special treat, she sometimes sent coffee. Mary's package was
delayed for months and did not arrive until May which was late in
the planting season.

6 May 1928

I have just received your letter from 14 March, you can see
that it took almost two months to arrive, but both packages
are here. I paid very little for them, only three lire, and ten
lire. The first one had been opened three times because it was
sewn back in three different places, and inside, everything was
mixed up with the potatoes and beans, but I think nothing is
missing. The second one was just as you sewed it, and nothing
has been spoiled. I distributed everything according to your
instructions. Once again, many thanks for everything. I wish

you could see how happy the children were when each of them got something, and they never get tired of the candies, because they so very seldom see them.

Mama is happy with the lire you sent, nowadays she is not home much. She goes to Mass, and has half a liter with the Pajserova and the Blažovka afterwards. At home, they all blame each other for their drinking; Mama says she really does not want to go. She only goes when Pajserova comes by, and insists she will pay for one bottle. Pajserova argues she only calls because our mother wants her to call her to drink. So, every Sunday they go to the sexton or to Rožice or to Sluga's, and then they drink. You need lire to go around like this. Mama is quick to point out it is easy for Pajserova because she always has the money to drink, and Blažovka says it is easy for her because her daughter sends her money. So, you can see why Mama resents you when you do not send her lire. It is good slivovic is hard to get. It used to be she could not live without it, she always had some in the wardrobe, but now she does not have any.

Jože Bazle [Joe Godina] sent 3,000 lire home but his father owes a lot of money to people who are now suing him. Bazle paid Jevanin 1,200 lire, and still owes him another 2,500. Lojze from Oplaz is suing him for 1,000. Someone in Trst is suing him for 4,000 lire. Bazle has no livestock, and as long as his mother stays alive, people cannot take the land because she is the owner. He asked Jože to send more money, but when he gets it, he drinks it up, and the debt remains. The boy is stupid to send it.

Jožef wrote eleven days later. The beans and potatoes Mary sent had just been planted but fortunately, the frost that followed occurred before the shoots appeared.

17 May 1928
On 9 and 10 May it was snowing in the mountains, and they were all covered in white, while we had rain. The days are cold,

and after the snow, the hoarfrost came. Well, if things need to go wrong, this is exactly how it should be done.

Dear Sister, you still remember everything from our youth! You recall when you were in Ostrovica for opasilo without me, you saw my wife, and if I had been there, we would have met earlier and been married sooner. She was there because it is not far from her home in Vareje, but she was far too young; she was only 18 years when we did marry. Marija, do you remember that time we were gathering brin, and having fun, and a man came by with a parrot? Remember he had pictures and pieces of paper in boxes he would sell for 10 coins? The man said to the parrot, "Give me a Slovenian one" and the parrot gave him an envelope. Inside was written what will happen in your future, and in another envelope was a picture of a girl who was waiting for you. I, of course, took one. Do you remember how we showed it to our local girls? We told them this was a photo of my girlfriend I had received by mail. Years later I had forgotten about all of that. I was already married, and in the army, when my wife sent me a photograph of herself. It struck me her photograph was just like the one the parrot had given me eight years before. When I came home for vacation, I found that photograph, and saw they were identical!

So, almost everything in that letter came true. It said I would marry a young girl, we would have a lot of children, and I would work for the good of people in the village and in the municipality. All of this has happened. I wonder if it just happened this way, or was there really something in those predictions?

Marija Grgarečeva is in Kozina with her husband, she still cannot stand on her feet. Her husband lifts her from the bed, and puts her on the chair next to the stove. She can do some small things with her hands. This has been going on for four years now. I would send you her address, but I do not know their house number right now. You ask me what Bilkotevi are doing. They are all hard working, caring, and quick to act. Tona is 15 years old and very diligent; Frane is 13 years old, and the youngest girl is 10 years old. They are a small family, but they all

help. Bilko is now thinking of learning how to be a shoemaker.
If he succeeds, they will be rich.

*

The U.S. was home to 180,000 Slovene immigrants in 1910, and by
1920, there were 228,000. In an era with no safety net for individuals many Slovenes chose to participate in fraternal benefit societies.
These companies sold life insurance and gave some protection to
workers and families in case of accidents or illness. They used their
profits to help immigrants maintain their cultural identity through
social, sporting, and cultural events while they built their new lives
in America. Many immigrants brought the baggage of their political
affiliations with them from the old country, thus fraternal benefit
societies were organized politically, according to Catholic, liberal,
or socialist ideology.

In 1923, Mary and John Fradel joined S.N.P.J. which stands
for *Slovenska Narodna Podporna Jednota* and translates to Slovene
National Benefit Society. Founded in Chicago in 1904 it was composed of individual lodges in areas where Slovenes settled. S.N.P.J.
adhered to liberal ideas and a socialist view of class struggle. The
leading members of the S.N.P.J. were active in the socialist workers
movement in America. It was the largest Slovene fraternal association, with a membership of 40,000 in 1928, outnumbering its
nearest competitor, the American Slovenian Catholic Union, with
membership of 20,000. It published a twice monthly newspaper,
Prosveta (Enlightenment). My grandmother and aunts contributed
articles and letters. Slovenian Homes in some cities contained a theater, ball room, reception hall, reading rooms, library, bowling alley,
and offered space for Slovene owned businesses. Later, lodges built
outdoor recreation areas with camping and cabins, picnic areas,
and dance pavilions. Today S.N.P.J. operates a 500-acre recreation
center in Enon Valley, Pennsylvania that hosts, among other things,
an annual Polkafest.

John and Mary belonged to Lodge 725, called the Torch of Liberty, in Latrobe, where John served as lodge president for 25 years. There were dinners, parties, weddings, drama, singing groups, and the opportunity for John to learn to play the organ. Rudy joined the lodge in Yukon, Pennsylvania, and Joe Godina joined in his city. In May 1928, Mary and John went to Chicago for an S.N.P.J. function where they expected to see more people from Brkini and the valley. They sent Jožef a postcard from Chicago, and his return letter showed with poignancy just how much John and Mary's lives had diverged from the concerns that once were theirs in Povžane.

17 June 1928

I received your postcard from Chicago. I am curious what kind of meeting you had there, that you went so far. You must have had large expenses if you had to pay for it yourself. Things are moving slowly because we have had too much rain. The wheat looks very nice, so does the grass. I hope we will not have a drought like last year. When you have a lot of children, there is always something going on so one can never rest. Our Francka has been sick multiple times, and had whooping cough three times. She often has chest pain so we took her to see doctors and bought medicine, and slowly she is getting better. Jože has been to the doctor twice because he had pain in his eyes for a month.

You asked me about Franca Vršečova. She lived in Markovščina with her husband and two sons. She died three years ago; he died the year before her. They both died from tuberculosis. Now Tona has been sick for 20 days. What is Rudolf doing? I asked about him once before, but you never answered.

Tuberculosis was a major killer worldwide. After the bacteria invades the body, the immune system fights the organism, forcing it to wall itself off in calcified deposits called granulomas. A person is asymptomatic until a granuloma breaks down and releases its contents. Before antibiotics arrived after World War II, treatment consisted of rest, clean air, and excellent nutrition, preferably at a sanatorium. Sometimes surgery was required to remove a granuloma. The disease was not always pulmonary, and might invade other organs or bones. Jožef's Francka was always a sickly, thin child. Whooping cough lasts about six months, then provides immunity, so it is unlikely she had it three times. She was sick with tuberculosis. Tona also had it but I'm not sure she knew it at this time.

In their letters over the summer and harvest of 1928, Mary and Jožef once again indulged their imaginations about his coming to America, even as his health declined. In a letter dated 21 October 1928, 41-year-old Jožef's symptoms and treatment suggest he had stress-induced stomach ulcer and gallbladder stones.

> You propose to me life would be good in Canada, and it would be easier to get there. All this sounds good, but my dear Marija, as I have already written to you, my health is bad. Do you remember when you were still home in the year 1909, when I was sick in my stomach? Since then, my stomach has not been right. When I was in the military it was really bad. It hurts me all the time. There are only a few foods that feel good, and if I eat something I should not, then I feel sick, and I have to go to the toilet all the time. It gets worse when I work a lot, and it exhausts me. I am tired, I do not feel my legs, and I am anxious. I decided I should seek help from the doctors. They sent me to the radiologist for a test, and found my stomach is injured. They suggested I go to the hospital so they could operate on me. Since I know very well how large bills can get, I decided to heal myself at home following doctor's directions. I need to be in bed for four weeks, eat lightly, take milk without cream just like a baby, and take medicine. Therefore, my dear Sister, until I heal myself, I am not fit to travel, or work hard. This is how it is, my dear sister. As if all the poverty is not enough misery, I am anxious because of the illness. When I think about the future, my heart hurts. Everything Italians do to us, all the pressure, I cannot even write about it.

The year has also been hard for Tona at Bazletevi. They have not grown anything, Bazle does not want to work, he even had trouble cutting grass, and the little hay they got, he sold, and he drank all the money. He waits for Jože to return home in the spring, and bring him thousands.

Bedrest, his special diet, and medication must have helped because he sounded like he was feeling a little better when he wrote a few weeks later, on 10 November.

What do you think, now that you will have a new president in America, will it be easier to enter? If this were the case, I would be ready to go. Nothing will change here; they will destroy us. Marija, when you write, tell me if you read anything about **Ivana's Jože**. If there was anything in the newspapers about him, send it to me so I will know what happened. *Edinost* is not published anymore, and others are not writing about him. You know, he got five years of prison time because of his political views, and he will be sent to Sardinia. Also, would you kindly send me *Čas* if it is still published?

Herbert Hoover was elected on 6 November 1928, and Jožef dreamed, "Now that you have a new president will it be easier to enter?" In fact, Hoover was the third Republican president in a row who promoted draconian anti-immigration policies. President Warren Harding, the architect of the immigration quota system, died in office on 3 August 1923, and his vice president, Calvin Coolidge, took over. In 1924, Coolidge was elected on anti-immigration campaign promises, and happily signed the Johnson Reed Act. In late summer of 1928, he announced he would not stand for re-election and Hoover stepped in.

In this short letter, it is probable "Ivana's Jože" was Jože Dekleva, the founding member of TIGR from Bač #4. Jožef did not say his name for a couple of reasons. Some of the envelopes Mary received bore the marks of censors, so Jožef was careful not to draw attention to his association with a known TIGR member. Jožef had confidence his obscure reference was sufficient to remind John and Mary that Jože Dekleva was related to them through Ivana Fradel. Jožef heard he had recently been arrested and sentenced to five years imprisonment. Jožef thought he might be able to read about it in *Čas*, (Times) a Slovenian newspaper published in Cleveland, since *Edinost* (Unity) was no longer published.

Edinost was the last Slovene daily newspaper of Trieste. The newspaper and a political society with the same name had been housed in the Narodni Dom before it was torched, but they stayed afloat for another eight years despite the repression. Jožef was a regular reader, and *Edinost* had kept him up to date with local and world events. The newspaper was shut down by the fascists on 4 September 1928. Access to knowledge of the outside world had effectively ceased, and Jožef relied on newspaper clippings and magazines his sister sent and perhaps newspapers smuggled from Yugoslavia, or the leaflets printed and distributed secretly by TIGR. The Secretary of the Fascist Party in Trieste had written in 1927:

> We have to do away with the last remaining classes in schools, disperse all Slovenian organizations, both sporting and cultural, destroy all Slovenian newspapers and books, introduce compulsory enrollment of all Slovenian children in Fascist youth organizations, prohibit Slovenian language in church, and confiscate the property of all Slovenian businesses, unions, and banks...

On 19 November Edinost, the political society, was shut down. The Slovene-owned Trieste Savings Bank, where Jožef did his banking, was liquidated, and merged to an Italian bank.

Jožef had only a brief reprieve from his maladies. Two weeks later he was suffering from sciatica. His mood was dark and impatient, so when John wrote he wanted to collect all that was owed to him, and sell the farm, Jožef could not hide his feelings.

23 November 1928

Thank God, I only have problems with rheumatism! All summer I had pain in my teeth, and in my head, and now I have horrible pain in my leg and stabbing pain in my back, and I cannot go anywhere. If I do not move, then I can almost endure the suffering. I hope God turns this for better. Dear Sister, as you are writing to me, you are also having health problems.

You now say you would like to sell the farm. Both you and I would like to sell, but it cannot be done. Janez needs to come home. I hope this will be soon, because I am tired of it. I was forced into taking this upon my head. If I had known it would be for such a long time, I can tell you honestly, I would not have accepted it. Those stupid sisters of Janez are still complaining they were thrown out of their home, and that Biščevi is getting rich using their land. They are blaming me, as if they actually owned it, that I took it from them, and forced them to go away. Because of words like this, and other stupid people who hold their hands, I suffer. I am saying it once again I wish, and beg, for Janez to come home, and end this once and for all, so they can see how things are at Jurkotevi.

In regards to your questions about the money, I took it to Hrpelje on 2 November, but they would not accept it. They advised me to take it to Trst, so I went there on 17 November, and deposited 10,300 lire, (say it, ten thousand three hundred lire). Now, I need to recover debt from others. Once this is done, I will add what is missing from my side and deposit all of it. Could you please wait a little while, or until Janez comes home, so we can make the balance sheet, and I will pay everything at that time? Right now, I do not have it, I do not have any goods to sell, and I have nowhere else to take it from. If only I were healthy. But I do not earn enough to buy salt. I had to borrow 600 lire; we have to live, pay taxes, and I will have to make this money back by selling goods next year. With a little bit of luck, things will be better. If you request everything be paid immediately, we will have to do whatever is possible. The money is deposited in Trieste Loan and Savings Bank, Via Torre Bianca No. 19. You can withdraw it whenever you wish, the bank will notify you.

Two days later he wrote again:

> I can see each of us has troubles. You wrote you were locked in
> quarantine for one month. This is hard even for healthy people
> to be inside a house all the time. I am curious if Slavica recov-
> ered from her illness, and if they removed the card from your
> door. Dear Sister, If I take care of myself, and eat light meals, I
> start to feel better. But I have to work, and if I work then I need
> to eat. If I eat heavy meals then I feel sick, my feet are numb
> and I feel like I want to vomit. Milk and mush please me most.
> Now in the winter when there will be no hard work, I will slow
> down, and maybe things will turn for the better. Everyone else
> is healthy, except for our Francka, who is always thin. It is hard
> to be healthy if you do not gain any weight.
>
> You asked me once before for the address of Marija Grgarečeva.
> I went to Trst yesterday, and I was in Kozina around 7 o'clock in
> the evening. Their place was completely dark, and I felt for her
> in my heart, I thought about what the poor woman was doing,
> either sitting next to the stove or lying in the bed, suffering in
> either case. Her address is: Marija Dobrila, Kozina No. 4. Pepa
> Blaževa, your friend, works in Materija at Cerabin, she is the
> same as ever, which is not very noble. Bazletevi are no worse
> than they ever are, except that one month ago the carabinieri
> took Bazle's gun away because he did not have any documents
> for it, and he got six days of jail and 600 lire fine.
>
> I already knew what you told me about the presidential elec-
> tion because I read it v Malmu. Some who were campaigning
> for the presidential candidate threatened if the workers did not
> vote for him, then the capitalists will close the factories, and
> starve people to death. It is always the same, those who have
> money give the orders, and they direct water to their watermill.
> When will the equality come? I think never. Woe is the poor
> man. It's been like this from the beginning of the world, and it
> will be as long as the sun will shine.

"*V Malmu*" is the exact presentation in the letter which translates to
something like "in the small one," perhaps something smuggled from

Yugoslavia. It has the ring of propaganda to it, and we can see how
socialist ideas were disseminated to even isolated, rural populations.

*

Catholic priests in previous centuries had actively defended Slovenian national rights, culture, and language against the pressures
from Germanization. Many priests in occupied Slovenia resisted
Italianization, and participated in the anti-fascist movement, in
disobedience of Achille Ratti, known as Pope Pius XI (eleventh).

Until 1860, the Papal States had stretched across the middle of
the Italian peninsula. While other states peacefully joined the Kingdom of Italy, Pope Pius IX (ninth) refused, even when his subjects
overwhelming supported unification with Italy. The Papal States
were seized by military force, and Rome was made Italy's capital.
Pope Pius IX and his successors retreated behind the Vatican walls,
and fought the Italian state with every means possible for the next
60 years. They excommunicated the King, government officials, and
Members of Parliament. The popes directed Catholic citizens not
to run for office or even to vote. The popes declared themselves
"prisoners of the Vatican" and never set foot outside it. The popes
did not really want the burden of civil rule over their formerly large
kingdom, but they did want a foothold on the earth that was not
subject to any rule other than their own, along with the restoration
of the church's prestige.

Benito Mussolini was a rabble-rousing journalist with inordi-
nate confidence in his own ability to make Italy great again. He
was an atheist, anti-clerical, and especially hateful of the power and
prestige held by bishops and priests. In 1904, in his publication
entitled "God Does Not Exist," he attacked the church and claimed
priests were "parasites and black microbes." He changed his tune
in 1921, when he needed Catholic support to solidify his power. In
his first speech to Parliament, he suddenly embraced the idea of a
Catholic nation, shocking everyone with his change in attitude. His

logic was this: A source of Italy's greatness was the fact that millions of people across the world recognized it as the spiritual home of the Roman Catholic Church, and Italy needed to treasure that identity. He saw that coming to terms with the Pope was a means of making Italy great again.

Achille Ratti, Archbishop of Milan, was elected by the cardinals in 1922, and took the name Pius XI. Like his predecessors, he refused to support the Italian state until the separation of church and state ended, and the privileged position of the church in society was restored. While serving as an emissary to Poland after the war, Archbishop Ratti developed a visceral opposition to communism. He also mistrusted democracy, which he believed was a gateway to communism. However, Pius XI, led by his authoritarian nature, was ready to negotiate with Mussolini, whom he viewed as the kind of authoritarian he could respect. In Mussolini, he saw the person sent by God, "a man of Providence," who would end the separation of church and state, restore many of the prerogatives of the church, and defend against a communist takeover of Italy. As a precondition for negotiations, Mussolini demanded closure of the Catholic Popular Party and the Pope complied, he could not control the party anyhow, and believed Catholic political activity brought democracy into the Church through its backdoor. The closure of that political party along with some socialist parties, allowed membership in Parliament to shift in Mussolini's favor, for him to become a dictator, and ultimately to stop any pretense of elections. He required everyone call him Il Duce, the leader, and that it be printed in all capital letters.

Mussolini agreed to the Pope's petition to allow a lay organization, Catholic Action, to continue under his direction, as long as it did not include any political activity. Thus, Catholic Action conducted "a battle for morality" that served the interests of both the fascists and the church. Members scoured their towns and villages to identify anything the church found offensive, and report back to authorities. Public display of female flesh was at the top of the list:

bare legs, bared backs, revealed bosoms, dancing in swim suits, bur-
lesque performances, and female participation in sports offended
both church and state. Books critical of Catholicism, or containing
anything erotic, including ones just offering marital advice, or films
with sexual appeal, especially American ones, were banned. Theaters and plays were subject to moral review, and proselytizing by
Protestants was forbidden. Meanwhile, schools were required to
have crucifixes and teach the Catholic religion, and children were
required to join fascist youth organizations. Holy days of the church
were made national holidays, and Mussolini made a belated show
of faith with his own church wedding of his long-time wife, and
the baptism of his children.

In February 1929, Mussolini and Pope Pius XI signed an agreement called the Lateran Accords. The Vatican was made an independent nation and Catholicism became the state religion. The church
was financially compensated for the loss of the Papal States with
generous annual payments. All bishops were required to be Italian
citizens, speak Italian, and take an oath of fidelity to Il Duce himself.
With this, two Slovenian bishops were removed from their offices.
All parish priests were required to speak Italian and every Mass
mandated a prayer for the Prosperity of the King and the Italian
State. Until the signing of the Lateran Accords, Catholics who were
unhappy with the dictatorship could argue that the Pope was not
enthusiastic about the fascist regime. With the signing of the Lateran Accords, the Holy See put its stamp of approval on it.

CHAPTER ELEVEN

1929: A Very Cold Winter

Something strange going on at Oplaz that winter of 1928 was the subject of many letters between Jožef and Mary. Oplaz was a cluster of four houses a few hundred yards west of Povžane, alongside the valley road. Lena and Janez of Oplaz had a daughter and three sons. Their firstborn son was in Yugoslavia because of the Italians. They were devastated when their daughter who had married someone in Beka near Trieste, and the youngest son who lived at home, both died from tuberculosis in the preceding year. The only son remaining at home in Oplaz, the middle one, had recently married. He had the same problem that Rudolf Fradel had at Jurkotevi; the absent firstborn son might return at any time to claim his inheritance. Why should the middle son till the soil for the eldest? He needed to be established in a home of his own.

The odd Janez Durc owned Durčevi, an ancient duplex that shared a wall with Bilkotevi, and a few acres. He lived alone, wandering the village in ragged clothes, perhaps he was depressed, mentally ill, or had dementia. He had been unable to look after himself, his house, and his farm for many years, and the poor economy and high taxes threatened his ownership. Rather than lose it to the Italians, Janez and Lena of Oplaz made a deal with Janez Durc. They would care for him in their Oplaz home, and in return their middle son and his

young wife could make a fresh start at Durčevi. Unexpectedly, Durc
died soon after moving to their home. He was buried on a Wednesday in late October 1928, and on the following Saturday the police
dug his body up again. Someone had raised the suspicion Lena
and Janez had starved him to death. Janez of Oplaz and his middle
son were put in jail and forty people were interrogated during the
month-long investigation. In December, without any conclusions
made, the two men were released, whereupon the son went back to
Durčevi. Within days there was a fire. Jožef described these events
on Oplaz to Mary and finished the story with this twist:

> Let me tell you on Gabrk everything burned down on 14
> December. Everything burned, only a few things that could be
> moved were saved, everything else went to ashes, only the bare
> walls remain. The burja helped the fire spread and everything
> at Durčevi burned down, and, surprisingly, only Jurkotevi,
> which is falling into disrepair, and has only hay stored in it,
> did not burn. One more thing to tell you, on another evening
> Matežin's barn burned down. Every fire happened on a Sunday
> evening; I wonder what this means.

What started the fire at the prosperous Gabrk? Questions remained
over how the flames spread to Durčevi—at least a quarter mile from
Gabrk—with lots of houses in between. Could the burja have picked
up sparks that skipped over Jurkotevi, the prosperous Pajserevi and
Klemenčevi, and ignited Durčevi? In fact, there had been a pattern
of structure fires on Sunday evenings that winter. I'm not saying
any locals talked of a connection between the fire and the fascists,
it is my own musing. Irredentismo was seeking to displace Slovenes.
One could also imagine malice or jealousy of neighbors toward
Janez and Lena as a motivation. Their older son had already been
forced out. Could a fascist collaborator have created the suspicion
of murder to prove the middle son's ownership of Durčevi was
fraudulent and when that failed, set fire to the place? Jožef may have

feared to speak his suspicions in a letter destined for inspection by censors. In time, Durčevi was repaired, life went on, and the middle son from Oplaz lived there for decades, sharing a wall with Rezina and her family at Bilkotevi.

Alma Babuder, the granddaughter of Marija of Gabrk, recalls what her mother, Kristina, who was present when Gabrk burned, told her about the fire. The gostilna's heavy wooden floors were scrubbed until they shone, and the inn was a popular spot with weekend tourists from Trieste. Marija's husband, Anton Jaksetič, was a bit strange, loathsome at times, and he drank too much. Kristina said because he hated the place, he prevented people from putting out the fire—he just stood by and laughed as Gabrk burned. After the fire, the Jaksetič family moved to Kastelic, since Božidar Kastelic was pretty much destitute himself, and willing to rent part of his spacious house to them.

Thus 1929 began. Jožef's only sources of information were the fascist and TIGR newspapers—all were tainted with propaganda of one sort or another, and in this darkness, conspiracy theories abounded. In the next letter Jožef checked with his sister, and she confirmed there had been a major flu epidemic in 1928-29. Like all conspiracy theories, the possibility that new immigrants in America might be driven out had a grain of truth in it. President Hoover had ordered mass deportations of Mexicans under the guise of saving jobs for Americans. Would the despised Italians be next? Jožef wrote in the new year.

3 January 1929

Until the new year, the winter was fine, then snow fell heavily for a week. The mailman from Materija had to stay here for three days, and we had to clear the snow before he could move on. Now the weather is nice again, but because of the deep snow we cannot go anywhere.

We have not received a letter from you since 4 December, the one with the newspaper clippings. Mama has been crying, she says you have forgotten us, but I am afraid you are sick. I read in the newspapers more than 10,000 people in America have influenza, and I am afraid you are among them. Tell me if this is true so I will know if I can trust the newspapers. Now, people are saying, and we have read in the newspapers, you will have to leave America, just like they chased Jews out of Germany and sent them to Italy. If it comes to this, perhaps it would be best not to sell your farm so you can return to Povžane and help us suffer. Jews are millionaires many times over, and the Noble Ones rob them. They leave them with just 25,000 lire, the rest they need to forfeit to the state. It would be wise to protect yourselves before the new law comes into place. You can transfer your biggest assets into money. One of you could bring it to Europe, and buy an apartment here, an investment to earn some money. That would be my plan. But you know better than I do how things are, because you are able to read the newspapers. Z Bogom.

Dear sister, after I finished writing this letter, the *Novi Čas* and the books you sent on 6 December arrived. First, let me thank you for everything. Mother is angry you sent magazines and books rather than old clothes for the children. She is even more bothered by the fact Grgurjova received 400 lire from her sons, and Drej Bilko sent 350 lire to Bilkotevi.

25 February 1929

I just received your letter from 13 January. We never received four of the letters you described. I mailed a letter to you 14 days ago but it has been such a bad winter the mail could not leave Materija for eight days, so I am sorry you will have waited a long time to hear from us. It is so cold here; on Shrovetide Sunday it was 25 degrees [Celsius] below zero and it continued for eight days. There is more snow here than anyone remembers! Across the street at Grgurjevi and Grgarečevi, and at Blažečevi, the snow is as high as the houses. They made a tunnel to enter their homes and had to remove the snow in front of the windows. At our place we did not have quite that much, although it was as high as I am along the entire street. I am sick of it; we have been wrestling with it for 56 days. Fortunately, just yesterday, the wind started to blow from the south and some snow started to melt.

There was so much snow at Jurkotevi the roof caved in. The ridge between the pillar next to the barn and the side ridge broke. You should know which one that is, Janez, you helped to chisel it. Now it looks like a bowl. It is not safe to enter as it can collapse. It cannot be fixed; new wood is not worth the expense. It would please me most if Janez would come home and sell it. Dear Sister, you wrote you would like to sell the firewood from the meadow but everyone is cutting firewood this year and the price is not good, maybe next year it will be better. But even then, I would like Janez to come and do it because I do not want his sisters to say Biščev is selling it.

Tona wrote on 15 March:

Dear Sister, There is great poverty here for everyone. The cold and snowy winter this year was hard to endure. The Old People say they do not remember anything like it. My dear sister, for two months I had to break ice in the pail with the axe, there was ice on the shelves and I was so cold it still hurts me all over my body. I was crying and cursing the master for not fixing the kitchen since before the War. **A**

The fortune of Božidar Kastelic was gone. He no longer had any sheep, had only three cows, and could only work on half of his land. He needed to borrow to get salt and sugar, just like everyone else. He and Karlina, his former maid, were now married and had two children: Zlatko was seven and Dana was four. Marija of Gabrk and her family lived with them during the winter after their home burned down. Božidar was so desperate for money he wrote to Mary about selling some of his antique books in America. His letters were written in an ostentatious penmanship with phrasing reminiscent of the formalities of the Austrian Empire. His letters are best read aloud; then one can hear the poetry in his efforts.

> *On the advice of your brother "Pepe" I have the pleasant occasion to be able to write a couple of lines to you. It is dear to me to hear that things are going well with you and that you are situated in these times in America in a place with income and blessedness.*
>
> *Lively memories still awaken to me of you from those rosy blossoming days when we strolled to our singing lessons, to dance at our home opasilo, etc. But everything passes. Times are changing and we with them.*
>
> *We have had a terrible winter here, and it is said that there has not been one like it for 100 years. Now the field work is starting. But the poor people do not have seeds. But patience, we have faith in a better future.*
>
> *I would like to place before you a certain proposal and I hope that you will have the knowledge to achieve a satisfactory outcome. I have for sale two old books. They are English-German dictionaries, the first from the year 1805 and the second from 1809. The books are of great value, namely up to 2,000 dollars and even more each individually, due to their antiquity, and inside is the signature of some historical aristocrat; the books were previously his property.*

Božidar wrote several times with the details of these books. Interestingly, the dictionary he wished to sell is of value today, at least in a scholarly sense it is considered an important historical document of the German language. But Jožef thought differently.

I went to see Kastelic to talk about his proposal to sell his books in America and give you part of the profit, but to me it seems like he is dreaming. He is really stupid to think he would get thousands for those books. It seems to me its value is no more than the value of our old books, the ones from Mohorjeva [an educational publisher]. Do you remember them? We still have all of them.

Tona wrote:

> My dearest sister, Thank you so much for your letter and for the
> money. The 87 lire helped me more than you can ever know.
> You wrote that last December you sent me a letter with a dollar
> inside but I did not receive it. Pepe told me there were many lost
> letters. I sent you a picture of Zora. Did you get it? I am always
> sad and broken hearted. I wish I was closer to you and my son
> so we could talk every now and again; that would make all the
> difference. Receiving a letter from you or one of our friends
> is my biggest pleasure. I would like to hear everything and if
> necessary, I will throw the letter into the fire. I need to hear
> about my son. When is he getting married?
>
> My husband imagines that Jože will send him some 3,000
> lire. I do not know why he thinks this because he doesn't even
> write to Jože. My stara tašča is also becoming a bigger and
> bigger devil. My girls are earning, they are hardworking, but I
> am always afraid that something bad will happen to them in
> these troubled times.
>
> Marija Rejčeva is doing well, and her husband loves her, but
> she cannot forget about Jože Grgur and she is always cursing
> him. She had a son 20 days ago, but he died on the eighth day.
> Her husband has one boy from his first wife, but Marija does
> not care about him and they treat him poorly. We do not hear
> anything about Skominčič. His wife is still waiting to go to
> America. Kristina from Gabrk is waiting to go and if anyone
> needs help, it is her. Her husband left for America after our Jože
> did, but he is not a citizen yet. He tells Kristina he will send
> for her shortly, but people are saying he has a wife and chil-
> dren there and will not send for Kristina. Pepa Blaževa worries
> about you, she sends regards and asks you for forgiveness, as
> you were angry with her. **A**

Jožef wrote every three or four weeks, usually on a Sunday afternoon, with his children milling around him. The older ones helped
their mother prepare meals or did homework for school while the

younger ones squabbled and played noisily under the supervision of their grandmother. Marija was thirteen and the brightest in her class. Her Italian was good and at home she was taught to read and write Slovene, practicing by writing letters for her grandmother. Jože, age ten, did not like school but he was hardworking and showed promise as a farmer. Together the children helped with the plowing by leading the oxen while their father held the plow. Francka remained a thin and sickly eight year old, the twins were robust at age six, and Pepca was one year old.

8 April 1929

After this terrible winter we had about 20 nice days; now on Saturday, 6 April, we had snow falling the entire day, it was cold and the burja was blowing as if it were Christmas. We went to Mass yesterday and it was so cold the stream in Brezovica was solid ice. Some of us have already planted potatoes! The wheat is looking bad, most of it died from the cold. The meadows look dry, we have not had rain in four months, and soon we will have no water. We may soon wish for a Flood to come again, just like it once happened in the Bible. Mama is sour-faced, and you know why.

As it just so happens, every man has some luck every now and then, even Bazle. Jože sent them money, and Fani and Zora are earning. Bazle catches some lire here and there from people who come to hunt. Tona does some work for Marija of Gabrk, who is staying at Kastelic right now. Thus, they endured the winter; but I do not know what they will do now, since they have nothing to plant.

You want the details for selling your farm. This is how I see it working. The house and the firewood will sell. The adjoining neighbors, Suhečevi and Zvrtevi, would each buy one half of the house. People from Povžane and other villages would buy the firewood, and some might use it to make lime. I might even buy some to take to Trst. People have no interest in buying land. If Janez came home he would become the sole owner, then he would be able sell the land any time in the future. He could even authorize someone to sell it for him by writing from America.

The intent to sell seemed real. Mary wrote of plans to visit Povžane and Jožef's letters were full of details about their arrival, selling firewood, and renting the land. Then a thunderclap of news reached Povžane and Bač.

Joe Godina had married without telling his parents. He wed Josephine Valentinčič on 4 June 1929. In Slovenia every Joe, Joseph, Josephine, or Josefa was called Pepa, but this Josephine broke with tradition and called herself Jessie. She was born in Colorado to Slovene immigrant parents, before the family moved to Pennsylvania. The wedding picture shows a beautiful, dark-haired woman in a modern wedding dress and an appropriately solemn groom. Mary recalled in a letter to Christina Siskovič many years later she and John had just bought their first car and had driven to the wedding in Sharon, Pennsylvania. Tona's heart broke upon hearing the news of the wedding, knowing fully for the first time her son was never coming back. Her letters to Mary during 1929 were incoherent with despair.

> I cried so hard I could not read your letter, I had to put it away for two days, I was so sad and I was also sick. I wish I had five lire at that time so that I could buy a liter for myself. God give them happiness, more than I got. But still, he has not written to me. If he only knew how many tears I have shed, how much I cry when I remember him. He forgot about me, I have only these few days of suffering left; it won't be long anyways, and he forgot me.

Joe Godina's father was also grief-stricken. He was irrational in his expectation of receiving great sums of money from his son, and his drinking and abuse accelerated. His daughters stayed away as much as possible. Tona, nine-year-old Ivan, and the mute 14-year-old Karel, were left to suffer from his tirades.

Two months after his marriage, Joe sent his mother 170 lire and a photograph of the wedding. (photo 12) The entire neighborhood was awed by the beauty and wealth revealed in it. But true to nature, people gossiped with disappointment that "their" Jože Bazle would not be coming back for Marija Gasčeva. The biggest gossip of all, Gela Skominčič, prepared to leave for America to join her husband and Tona put together a small wedding present for her to carry to Joe and Jessie and wrote to her sister.

> You will receive a package Gela will bring to you. It includes a small bottle of honey, so you can put it in your tea when you have a cold. The identical two cups are for you, and the handkerchief I sewed is for Ivanka. For Jože and Pepca, there is the set for black coffee, with six cups and plates, a sugar bowl, a coffee pot, and napkins to put on the table; this is how the noble people do it here. I am sending them a small cheese so the two of them will remember me sometimes. Give them my gift any way you can and let me know what they said; tell me if they were pleased or not.

Skominčič had returned to America two years earlier carrying 2,000 lire Jožef expected him to give to John, but he had not delivered the money. Jožef went to see Gela and threatened to report the theft to the courts. Gela feared this might interfere with her final visa so she swore to take care of it. While Jožef expressed skepticism and complained again, "The old gratefulness of Austria is dead," Gela left for America on 6 August, promising to pay up when she got there.

In September Mary broke the news John was not coming to Povžane as planned. Jožef was seriously trapped in the problem of Jurkotevi and its not quite four acres. At the same time he was physically suffering. He had begged John to return and take Jurkotevi off his hands but he could not just quit the caretaker job and he had no power to hand it over to Antonija or put it up for auction. He had an innate drive to make things right, to do the right thing by the land itself, even if John and Mary were not doing the right thing by him.

19 October 1929

You tell me that Janez will not come as planned. And what will happen to your house? I always thought Janez would come home, but as I can see, he does not want to come here. But the winter will come soon and the snow and the burja will destroy everything. It would not be right to let the straw roof and wood be destroyed—they are still worth something. Therefore, we have it insured; it costs 35 lire per year. It is hard to pay this, but until it collapses, it is hard to stop this. Write to me what you think.

I was feeling well while we were cutting the grass, but now I am starting to hurt again. There was not much hay. The drought has turned everything brown and there was no second cutting, and the livestock have nowhere to graze. We have half of the beans and some corn. The potatoes are really nice. From the seed potatoes you sent us, last year we had 22 kilograms and this year we have three kvintals.

If you could only see how Povžane looks, you would not believe it. It should be called *razolrta*, [the ruins]. Mekovka's house is leveled, and Tancetevi, Nankevi, Durčevi, Brčinevi, yours, Klemenčevi, Zajčevi, half of Blažečevi and half of Zlogartevi will soon be. Fourteen homes do not have livestock anymore. In the village only 50 cows and 50 sheep remain. Can you imagine the difference from 90 cows and 150 to 200 sheep we used to have? Mama always has a sour face because you do not send her anything. If you do not mind, send her a few cents so she will be in a better mood.

Drej Grgur planned to marry in the spring but it had to be delayed because he was sick with tuberculosis he got when he was in the Italian army. He recovered a little bit and got married on opasilo [August 11] to the daughter of Berhan, who will come to live at Grgurjevi. My wife's sister is the Bride at Berhan and we know Drej will have a good Bride. But Drej's health is still weakened from the tuberculosis. He has not been cutting grass at all, he does not do anything, he is protecting himself, but there is not much hope.

Jaksetič have started to build a new house on Gabrk, even bigger than before. The roof is done, but when it will be finished, and who will have it, who knows?

*

The Wall Street stock market crashed on 29 October 1929. As cataclysmic as it was for the wealthy of the world, it did not earn a remark amongst the poor in Povžane and Bač.

*

24 November 1929

I received the letter you wrote on 6 October. I did not reply immediately because I was sick. I had stinging pain in my back, and I was in bed for eight days, then I had a wooden neck, and then pain in my teeth and in my head. All together it lasted 50 days.

I feel better now, but I am not healthy because my blood is spoiled from all the suffering. Everyone else is healthy. The children are going to school, but only going, not learning; they teach them in such a way so they will not know anything. We produced a little more than we did last year. If the snow buries us again, we will at least have potatoes and mush to eat. They are predicting a bad winter; it has already showed itself. We had some snow followed by rain every day. Why can't we have it during the summer when we really need it for our crops?

I heard those who are not citizens must leave America, is this right? If this is true then Kristina from Gabrk will get her husband home because, as one can hear, he cannot get citizenship. Well, he can come now; Jaksetič have rebuilt the house on Gabrk, and they will move in tomorrow. Franciska, the older daughter of Franc Košanc, went to Argentina. Many from around here have left to go there, but not all of them are happy. Pajser went to Yugoslavia; he will rent out one of his farms; he left one girl and his mother at home. Mama is shouting from the house you should write to her, and if you do not have five lire to send to her, you should just get it, and send it.

As Italian oppression grew, Jožef watched the political and economic movements of neighbors with wealth and status comparable to his own, such as Pajserevi and Klemenčevi at the east end of the village. One false move could bring scrutiny from the Italians. He said nothing and kept his head down. Biščevi was modestly well off and, of course, he had enemies because of his caretaker role at Jurkotevi. He felt at risk. He knew his dreams of America or Canada were unrealistic and he had no desire to start over in Argentina. Pajserevi, Klemenčevi, and others were sending family members out of harms way, or renting their fields and taking refuge in Yugoslavia, usually in Maribor. His family was young and he wished not to be displaced. What did he have to do to protect them?

1. Marija Fabjančič around 1910.

2. Mary and John Fradel with baby Ivanka in Cass, West Virginia, 1914.

AUSTRIAN HUNGARIAN ARMY
FOR 'CESAR' KAISER FRANZ JOSEF

John Fradel - served with 14th Field Company - 97th Infantry Regiment (5 months) 1912-13 - KARLOVEC AUSTRIA

3. Janez Fradel, 97th Regiment, 14th Field Co., Austro-Hungarian Army, 1912–1913.

4. Jožef Fabjančič, 97th Regiment, Austro-Hungarian Army, 1915.

5. Marija Fradel aged 19, while waiting to leave for America. 1915.

6. Marija Cergolj and Josef Fabjančič with Pepa Rošanc, Jožef's new bride, and Fani Godina, their grand daughter in 1915.

7. Rudolf Fradel in America in 1920. (Emilja Kljun photo)

8. Sylvia, Mary, Joe, John, and Jane Fradel in Latrobe, Pennsylvania, 1925.

9. Jožef Fabjančič and his family in 1925. From left: Nona, Marija, Francka, Jožef, son Jože, wife Pepa, and twins, Janez and Milka.

10. Božidar Kastelic (Slavko Gerželj photo)

11. John Fradel with an Italian style moustache.

12. The wedding of Joe Godina and Jessie Valentinčič in June 1929.

13. Jane Fradel, graduation from Latrobe High School 1932.

15. Franjo Fradel, Yugoslav soldier in 1938.

14. Mary E. Fradel and Jane Fradel strolling in Maribor in 1937.

17. Lada Babič, son of Pepina Fradel, in better times before the Second World War.

16. Jože Fabjančič age 20 in 1939 photo. (Marinka Fabjančič photo)

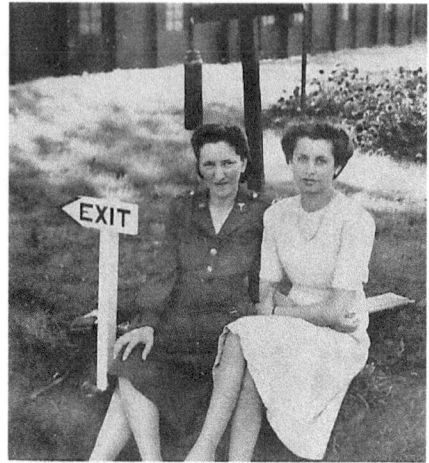

19. Lt. Jane Fradel and Dr. Franja Bidovec in England in 1944.

18. Joe Fradel, 526th Ordnance Co. of U.S. Army in 1943.

20. John Fradel, Army Air Force instructor in 1943.

22. Francka Fabjančič (1921–1945) in a pre-war photo. (Marinka Fabjančič photo)

21. Tony Laurich in Trieste with Pepa Fabjančič on right side of photo in 1953.

24. Milka Fabjančič (1923–2000). (Darko Mezgec photo)

23. Janez Fabjančič (1923–1996). (Marinka Fabjančič photo)

25. Ivan and Danila Godina and their children in 1950.

26. John Fradel, poster boy for Vulcan Mold.

27. John Fradel retirement from Vulcan Mold in 1958.

28. Mary and John Fradel with family in 1936. From left: Mary, John, Jane, Joe, and Sylvia.

29. Rezina (seated) and Tona Fabjančič around 1900.

30. Rezina and her son, Frane, in 1955.

32. Antonija Fradel of Jurkotevi as a young woman around 1920. (Nevenka Karba photo)

31. Tona around 1930.

33. Mary Fradel with her grandsons in 1950.

34. Antonija Fradel with some of her children: Amelja, Frane, and Slavica in 1950s. (Nevenka Karba photo)

Potpis vlasnika

35. Pepina Fradel Babič. (Pina Babič photo)

CHAPTER TWELVE

1930–1932: *Bad Weather and High Taxes*

The American economy took a nosedive immediately after the stock market crash of 1929 and spiraled downward for years. Farm prices plummeted and the demand for manufactured goods fell. The steel industry, where John Fradel was employed, was considered recession proof. In the expectation that the economic downturn would be brief, President Hoover encouraged factories to keep workers employed and maintain wages. He attempted to protect American industry by placing tariffs on foreign goods, but this only led to retaliation, decreased global trade, and a worsening recession. Matters were not helped when the worst drought and heat wave in 300 years destroyed agriculture in half of the country and turned farmland into "dustbowls." Banks failed and ordinary people lost their life savings. Many became homeless and hungry and lived in shanty towns built from crates, old autos, and other scraps called "Hoovervilles" in honor of the President. "Bread lines" were a common site as people waited in long lines for handouts. Farmers and miners were the hardest hit by unemployment. Nationally, 25 percent of Americans were out of work, but in Pennsylvania unemployment was 37 percent.

John's work at Vulcan Mold continued as the factory stayed open filling back orders until mid-1931, then the shutdowns began, and for years he was laid off for days or weeks at a time. His teen-aged children got after-school jobs. All talk of going to Slovenia stopped. Whatever happened at Jurkotevi was trivial compared to the immediacy of paying the mortgage, keeping food on the table, and covering health emergencies. Despite the austerity the family in Latrobe experienced, Mary slipped an extra dollar into letters to her mother and sister.

All five of the Fradel children attended public school. Sylvia, the youngest, was eight in 1930, and Jane, an excellent student, and the apple of her parents' eyes, was 16. Slovene was spoken at home. Although the children had American friends at school, the family focus was on Slovenian friends and S.N.P.J. activities. Mary and John clung to people from Brkini and the valley, and had very few acquaintances from other parts of Slovenia. Slowly but surely, they acquired American tastes and outlook, and the gap in understanding and sympathy between their new world and their old world widened. John and Mary were immeasurably grateful that they had come to America, but Mary's heart ached for the life left behind.

The beginning of the new decade was bleak in Primorska. Weather extremes caused decreased crop production and taxes were destroying farm ownership. Italian fascism was in full swing, and education and social life suffered. Harassment by the carabinieri caused some Slovenes to quietly move to Maribor. Young adults faced a dim future, and some headed to Argentina.

Families in America had their own economic problems, and expectations of their loved ones back home for regular gifts of money were burdensome, and perhaps annoying. A letter from home, formerly greeted with delight in America, was now met with dread of more bad news and yet another request for aid. Many Slovenes just stopped writing home. Mary never paused. Tona's daughters, Fani and Zora, were now young adults and began writing to their Teta Marija. Tona's letters, which had been a source of welcome girly gossip, turned bitter and sad. Her marital situation was tragic; she suffered under her stara tašča's bad temper, and she painfully missed her eldest son. She was insanely jealous of Gela Skominčič who enjoyed living close to Mary in Pennsylvania. "If only it were me," she cried to herself. Her health had been poor for years, but it was only now that she suspected tuberculosis. She wrote in the new year:

10 January 1930

Dear Sister, I wanted to write to you and my son for the holidays, but I could not afford the postage. If Jože had not sent me a few lire just in time for Christmas, I would not have had anything. He would like to bring Ivan to be with him in the spring but I do not know how he can do this since nobody can get the permit to go to America.

Gela promised she would tell me honestly how things are in America, but in some ways, I do not want to hear from her because she is so childish! She wrote all about her fine clothes. She already had a nice coat, but her husband quickly bought her a new one. People remark if her boy is as bratty in America as he was here, he will be left with nothing but a basket full of manure sitting in front of his nose. But there is no need to tell Gela any of this, tell her only that I am sending my regards.

Fani has been home for a month with a painful arm. She could not eat and did not sleep for 12 days; it is now improving. During the same time, I had bloody dysentery. I suffered like a dog, all my bones were hurting, it was like giving birth. Now the pain has moved to the side, and I am afraid that it might be tuberculosis. I cannot see the doctor because we have not had a single čentižim in the house. My beloved sister, I know you have your family and expenses, and that times in America are hard too, but nonetheless I am asking you kindly to send me some money, even if it is only a dollar. **A**

As for John, there was no nagging spring planting letter from Jožef, who had resigned himself to the fact his brother-in-law was not coming home. Jožef gave the sorrowful news of a little girl's death at Jakovinevi after a long and expensive illness. Children were actually dying all the time. By examining the status animarum, I estimate almost half of the children did not live past their third birthday. Mary's mother lost four of her eight children, Ivana Fradel lost six of her twelve, and her mother, Marija Dekleva, lost five out her eleven children. Measles and diphtheria showed up routinely. Cholera and other diarrheal diseases were major killers of children then, just as they are today in developing countries. The deaths went unmentioned because the sorrow was too vast for words. I have heard of a folk belief that until a child reached a certain age people kept a little coffin waiting under the bed.

On Gabrk, the new house was complete and the Jaksetič family reopened the gostilna, but there was little peace on Gabrk. The *stari tast* [Marija of Gabrk's father-in-law] was angry and wanted to recover what he had put into the new venture. Young Kristina was still waiting for her much older husband in Cleveland to send for her. Rumors that Frank Siskovič was not an honorable man abounded, and some said Kristina was no longer satisfied with her husband. Stories spread she and Marija Vrh, a fellow waitress at Gabrk, spent their time looking for boys and partying in Trieste, Koper, and Rijeka for up to eight days at a time. Oh, how the women *educated themselves* on Kristina's young life!

Then Frank Siskovič became a U.S. citizen on 22 November 1929, and three months later, Kristina was on a ship bound for America, destined to become a good friend of my grandmother. Biščevi asked her to carry little wicker baskets for Mary's girls in Latrobe, *klobase* (sausage) for everyone, and two *koserice* (pocket knives)—a big one for John and a little one for Joe Fradel. Jožef did not have time, or perhaps the cash, to purchase new ones in Trieste, so he persuaded Jože and Janez to part with them as gifts to their cousins, and consoled them with the promise of new ones.

Even with Kristina gone, the gostilna on Gabrk was a hotspot for the flirtations of young people. Jožef ended his spring letter in 1930 with the comment, "Fani Bazleteva is home this winter. A man from Kras who works at the gostilna on Gabrk is making a fool of her." Despite all the bad things that Jožef thought about Fani Godina, Mary had a special place in her heart for Fani, the "little sister" she had abandoned when she went to America. When Tona used Fani's ailments as an excuse to ask her sister for money, she was usually successful. Fani was now a young woman and Mary was delighted to get a letter from her. Fani addressed her Teta (aunt) with the formal plural "You" rather than the familiar "you." She used Italian words such as "Trieste" rather than the Slovenian "Trst." My translator commented that Fani's letters lacked the archaic language of the other letters and could easily have been written in more modern times.

Trieste, 4 April 1930

Dear Teta! I am sure You will be surprised to receive a letter from me. I was working in Trieste, but I have been home for three months because of my arm. It is better now and I can work just fine, but my dear aunt, I would be much happier if I were a trained seamstress, as I was once eager to be. My family expected Biščevi would send me for training, but they have their own children to consider and my family did not care, so I was left with nothing. Now my only thought is to get away; there is not much life in Italy. I wish I could be with You in America, but I know this is not possible. If all goes well, I will get married and go to Yugoslavia, but Nona Biščeva is not happy I talk to that boy who works at Gabrk, but You know well, my aunt, what love is. I have been talking to him for eight months. He is good and attentive; he is not a drunk or spendthrift. He loves me and I like him. He is from Gorica, from the village of Lipa. My uncle Pepe [Jožef] and Nona say such a boy, who rides a bicycle on Sundays with his head uncovered, is not a good boy. My brother Jože rode with his head uncovered, and he is now hard-working and doing well in America. My own family is happy with my boyfriend. Dear aunt, when You write to the Biščevi in Povžane, You do not have to mention I have written to You about my boyfriend, or even that I wrote to You at all. Z Bogom *Fani Godina*

More letters from Fani followed. She worked hard for her lady in Trieste, sometimes from six in the morning till eleven at night. On summer weekends, she and Viktor Colja took the train from Trieste to Kozina and walked or caught a ride on a wagon to an opasilo in one of the Brkini villages. On her birthday on 4 October, Viktor gave her a gold necklace, her friends filled her room with flowers, and her employer gave her 50 lire and the day off. She and Viktor spent the beautiful fall day outdoors and they went to a movie theater in the evening.

Joe Godina wrote to his mother every few months with a few hundred lire. His father complained and cursed his wife because his son did not send thousands. Tona worried her husband would read the letters, so the sisters adopted the practice of writing messages on scraps of paper they could hide from their husbands.

> [on a scrap of paper] My dear sister, it is good you have not mentioned my husband in your letter, because he thinks I am writing about him. He read your letter and was pleased. Then he said he is also sending his regards. When you write the next time, please add a few words I can show him.

Tona wrote the harvest looked promising, yet there was only polenta to eat on Easter, instead of the usual festive foods. To make matters worse, during the summer when the hay needed to be cut, Bazle was arrested for hunting without a permit. He went to *pržane* (prison) for 50 days because it was his second offense and had to pay 600 lire in fines. Tona wrote more:

> My dear little sister,
>   Tears flooded my eyes when I read the letter you wrote to Mama. You asked if there are flowers growing on our Ata's grave. I plant many different kinds of flowers on his grave, and on the graves of Ivana and Valentin Fradel, that bloom from Easter until the Day of all Holy Ones. [1 November] As long as

I am alive, I will do this regardless of all my sorrow. But once I
die, I don't know who will care for the graves. Our family from
Povžane say they want to do it, but do not have time. I recall
my beloved Ata's words, "Remember well, you will be crying so
hard that a cold stone should feel sorry for you, but there will
be no mercy." And this is exactly how it is.

In the new year of 1931 Jožef Biščev was full of hope and determi-
nation, but excerpts from the letters he wrote throughout this desperate year reveal that by harvest's end the proud man was reduced
to writing secret messages on scraps of paper to his sister, begging
for firewood he could sell, as well as used clothes for his children.

18 January 1931

You tell me about great poverty in America and I can tell you
here there are no earnings and no money. The Italian government takes our money to pay off its debts and to prepare for
war. Those of us farmers who still have pigs have to pay a 15
lire tax per year for each pig and 47 lire for each one that we
kill. The last newspaper stopped publishing in November and
while they only printed what was allowed, it is still hard for
us. We are like people from 500 years ago because we do not
know what is going on around the world.

Last week I demolished your house; one of these days I will
put that wood up for auction. It is all rotten and crumbled, and
firewood is cheap so it won't fetch much. While I was working on it, I cursed myself for not setting it on fire. If it burned,
perhaps the insurance might pay some money. It was not easy
work; inhaling the dust burned my chest, everything was dirty,
and there was constant danger something would fall on me.

Zupančič left 40 days ago to go to Yugoslavia. He is afraid;
he is a thorn in the heel of the Italians and they are watching
him. Pajser wanted to come home from Yugoslavia because he
is not healthy, but he is afraid they will stop him at the border
in Postojna and lock him up.

22 February 1931

The winter was mild until the start of February, and now it has snowed all month. All the children had an illness where their necks were swollen on the outside, but they had no problems swallowing. [mumps] Except for my stomach I have been the healthiest. I took care of everything outside of the kitchen while everyone was sick.

Marija has finished school. She will soon be 15. She is smart and very helpful inside and outside the home. Jože is now in charge of the wagon when we get firewood. He and Janez are both hardworking, brave, and very strong. When I was sick and could not carry the hay after we cut grass in Dula, I told Marija, Jože and Janez to rake the hay and carry what they could to the pen and leave the rest. When they came home in the evening, they had raked and carried everything! If they continue to be healthy and hardworking, I will be saved. Only Francka has poor health. She is 10 years old, skinny, eats almost nothing, and cannot do anything. We will have some expenses because four of our children will be administered the sacrament of Confirmation this year; I am sure you avoid things like this.

8 April 1931

March was cold, and a cold burja came on the last days of March and the first days of April. We had to plow with our gloves on. Just now it is getting warmer.

Dear Janez, you have not written to your sister at Cesarevi in two years. She and her husband have not spoken to me but I have heard from others they plan to sue me because they believe I ordered the house to be destroyed. Now, Frane Košanc is stirring up trouble by saying I cut down your trees for firewood. The year before last, there was a big drought and four small trees dried up in your meadow and this winter a few more rotted away so I cut them down. If I had known Frane and others would be sharpening their tongues over dead trees, I would have left them to rot.

Župančič rented out his entire farm for just 1,600 lire when he left for Yugoslavia. I offered your farm for rent for a very low price, but nobody wanted it. There are many farms to choose from. I would so terribly like you to come here, Janez, to see how things are with your own eyes and finally take this load off my mind. You can give it to Cesar. He is angry because he believes that I am against it but there is nothing true in this!

Fani Bazleteva is earning in Trst, she will soon follow her boyfriend to Yugoslavia. He went there because of the politics. If he had not left, he would now be in prison.

31 May 1931

March and April were cold and rainy and since mid-May we have had ten good warm days. The grass is looking good. It should be a good harvest. You write I should just leave things on your farm as they are. This sounds odd to me, because we still have to pay taxes. Do you know how much they demand? There are six installments per year and if you are late, the penalty is eight percent. If you miss three installments, they start to sell your property. They charge 20 lire per hour for the office work and soon you owe ten times more than the original payment. This is how the Italian government becomes the landowner. Therefore, dear Sister and Janez, it is necessary and smart for Janez to come home. After so many years of work he could take 50 days off to see his hometown once more. He would fulfill the terms of his father's Will, become the sole owner, and then he could sell whenever he wanted. The land currently has no value, but it will in the future. The sale of firewood and that hovel of a house could cover his travel expenses. If Janez does not come home and dies in America, Rudolf will inherit Jurkotevi, and your children will have nothing.

Stefan Cesar from Artviže is going to court to try to get more money from Jurkotevi to cover the dowry and wedding expense. His lawyer insists Frane Košanc appear at the courthouse on 10 June. If Košanc decides to stir things up, then they will also call me and every party will need to have his own

lawyer. I cannot represent you. I will send you the address of
a lawyer. You can send him an authorization to permit me to
present to him your side of the case.

[on a scrap of paper] Dear Sister, when Mama received those
two dollars, she was as pleased as if she had never seen money
before; she has prayed entire litanies for your health and happiness. I also thank you greatly. Dear Marija, as I've written in
the letter, please try to convince Janez to come here. I would
very much like to have this resolved and I hope he will listen
to you.

1 August 1931
     Prospects in May were good for the harvest, but after May
there were only two light showers, followed by a burja that
dried everything up. We cut grass on 20 June, ten days earlier
than normal. The amount of hay was good, but there will be
no more pasture, and no second cutting of grass. The beans
are good only for seeds, and the best potatoes are the size of
walnuts. We reaped the wheat 14 days earlier than usual; the
grains are tiny and only half the amount we usually get. There
is half the usual amount of corn. It is truly sad, everyone is
crying and sighing about our future.

[on a scrap of paper] Dear Sister, as you can see, we have poverty
and there is nothing we can do to help ourselves. Will you ask
Janez to give us some of his firewood so I can take it to Trst to
sell? The price is only seven lire per kvintal, but when there is
not much, a man must be satisfied with little. You do not need
to tell him what I wrote. Just make the suggestion sometime.

In America, S.N.P.J. had a youth section with its own magazine
called *Mladinski List-Juvenile* published in both English and Slovene to engage the children of immigrants in Slovene language and
culture and to promote its socialist views. The magazine presented

translations of Slovene literature, poetry, and biographies. Louis Adamic, the renowned Slovene-born author, was a regular contributor. Social news about picnics and dances for Halloween, Valentine's Day and *Pust,* the Slovene version of Mardi Gras, were covered. My aunt, Jane Fradel, was a politically active member and contributed her first letter to the magazine in 1928. She campaigned for socialist candidates for local offices, and for Norman Thomas, the socialist candidate for U.S. president. Mary and John were immensely proud of Jane. She was well-spoken, beautiful, hardworking, she helped with her younger siblings, and was a positive role-model for them. Thoroughly American, she helped her parents bridge the gap between cultures. Mary proudly wrote to her brother about Jane's letters to *Mladinski List* and in this return letter, her Uncle Jožef commended her. Jane was a bright student in the college preparatory program and was entering her senior year at Latrobe High School. (photo 13) After graduation she started a three-year program at the Latrobe Hospital School of Nursing.

20 September 1931

You wrote that Ivanka is very intelligent. I admire her interest in her nation and her knowledge of what life is about. While everyone else complains how bad things are in America, how is it Skominčič are always writing everything is great? Gela wrote to Rožice they have a nice house and a garden and they earn a lot. Is this nothing but a lie? Are they still just people from Bač who always boast? Vašte from Skandanščina came back after 24 years with his wife and two children for one week to see how things are. He lives near Chicago; he has a farm and 38 cows and two horses.

[on a scrap of paper] Dear Sister, I thank you for the offer of firewood in Štrpet; I think there will be enough for one wagon to Trst. Dear Marija, if you have coats and winter clothes your children have outgrown, would you send them to us?

In Ljubljana, Fani had settled at Galjevica Number 210 with Viktor's parents when she wrote to her aunt again on 23 Nov 1931.

> Dear Aunt!!! After I returned home to Bač from Trieste, I had to wait 40 days for my passport. I earned everything I have by myself, and even from my small earnings, I gave some to my family. I had to spend as little as possible, I did not write to you because I could not afford a stamp. Those days were so long; I was sick and tired of everything, but when the time came to go, it was hard to leave my parents, my youth, and my beautiful hometown.
>
> Since 14 October I have been in Ljubljana. It is rather cold here, but there is no snow yet. The law requires I be in Yugoslavia for six months before we get married so I need to find a temporary job. We are living with Viktor's parents who have moved here from Gorica. I am beginning to like this foreign place. It will not be bad here; we are young and love each other. We will have to worry and work all the time, but we are used to that. If God gives us health, all will go well. *Fani Godina*

In America, Andy Siskovič, remembered as Drej Bilko in Povžane, was never far away from my grandparents. They lived together in Cass and he worked alongside my grandfather in Black Lick, Sharon, and Pittsburgh—in between jobs he returned to the sawmills in West Virginia. He was godfather at my father's baptism at St. Michael's Byzantine Catholic Church in Farrell, Pennsylvania. He came for every special family occasion but Andy remained the unmarried vagabond.

In 1931 Andy was 46 years old and likely considered to be a very old bachelor. At the S.N.P.J. Lodge in Latrobe my grandparents introduced him to a new widow with four children, who lived just a few blocks away from them. She and her first husband owned a hardware store in Latrobe that was in the process of failing in the midst of the Great Depression. Andy married Louise Znidarsič on 3 March 1931, and the following year he took his new family to West Virginia.

*

After the Great War was over in 1918, hundreds of thousands of veterans in Italy were unemployed. The government was broken and paralyzed with bickering. Socialists had taken over municipal governments while right-wing thugs attacked the socialists and Catholic clergy. The possibility of a communist revolution—similar to the 1917 revolution in Russia—was on everyone's mind. Benito Mussolini, a demagogic politician full of magnetism and confidence in himself, with widespread popularity and armed mob support, stepped into the chaos and took control of the Italian government, with the blessing of the King.

Under his leadership, by 1925 the economy had grown by 20 percent and unemployment fell 77 percent. In addition to certain economic and trade reforms, he made extravagant investments in the public sector and infrastructure that provided employment for hundreds of thousands. Canals, roads, and railway stations were built. Forests were planted and swamps were drained to decrease health risks, as well as to reclaim farmland that would increase grain production. Hospitals and orphanages were built and health services were improved. He aimed to make Italy great, and self-sufficient, and families were encouraged with financial incentives to have at least five children. Those with more than five children paid no tax at all. Evidently, this incentive was not extended to the Slovene minority—Jožef had six children and got no tax break.

Italy did not begin to feel the effects of the American stock market crash until 1931. Historians have credited the economic measures taken by Mussolini with delaying and reducing the effect of the world-wide depression in Italy, but largely because of the trade war instigated by U.S. protective tariffs, its industries and banks began to fail. The crisis peaked in 1932, and in response, the government took an even larger role in directing the economy. By 1939, Italy had the second highest rate of state ownership among all nations—only the Soviet Union had a higher rate.

Primorska had no industry. The rural economy had been sup-
plemented with the foreign earnings of returning workers or overseas family members, but émigrés were struggling themselves and
unable to send much home. Similar to the American agricultural
experience, unfavorable weather throughout the decade added to
the decline, along with the unrelenting Italian taxation. During
this time 100,000 people fled Italian-occupied Primorska and Istria.

Mussolini's infrastructure projects in the valley under Slavnik
were built with the advancement of Italian occupation all the way
to Ljubljana in mind. The twelve-mile stretch of road from Kozina
to Podgrad was made wider, flatter, and straighter. Water resources
were developed. With few exceptions the projects employed only
Italians. Jožef described how these projects progressed in his letters
throughout 1932:

> The Italians finished the barracks and the hospital, and they
> are also widening the road. They have not reached Materija
> yet, but they have measured it. They will throw out our cherry
> trees in Oplaz and take one meter from our garden, but they
> will not pay us anything...
>
> The government is building the road just like a railroad,
> with embankments, even where it is flat. They destroyed some
> houses, dug up the properties of others, and built embank-
> ments in front of some of the houses. The bank in front of
> Prucet's house is three quarters of a meter high. At Župančevi,
> they demolished the barn so that the road could go straight. In
> front of the house, they dug so deep that six stairs are needed
> to get in the door, and the road is only two meters from the
> house. It is so damaged, and so close to the road that it is not
> worth half of what it was. In Oplaz, the bank in front of that
> house is 75 cm high.
>
> We also had many fires here in the month of August. On the
> 18th, Jevanin's barn burned down. The next morning a barn
> and shed burned down in Slope, and in the evening, everything
> belonging to Lojze Rejčo, who now lives on Oplaz, burned

down. Five days later, it burned at Sever's in Tublje. To the person coming down the road it looks like a war is raging. Everything is dug up, houses are burned down along the road, Župančič's home ravaged; it is truly a sad view.

In the spring of 1932 Jožef fretted as rain fell for two weeks straight when he should have been plowing. Then two weeks of fine weather improved his mood, only to be crushed with 20 days of continuous rain. Through the summer, intermittent rains encouraged hope for a good harvest, but it was not enough to make up for the bad start. Hay was always his economic bottom line. There needed to be enough to feed the livestock and enough to sell to pay the taxes. Jožef did the simple math. Hay sold for 10 lire per kvintal and taxes were 212 lire so he needed to sell 21 kvintals of hay to keep his land. Every one of his letters was a repetitious litany of prices, taxes, and poverty. "I will not even write to you about the penury here. If things continue like this even the poverty won't be able to survive."

Immigrants in the Americas continued to struggle through 1932 as well. Toni of Gašper from Brezovica did not find luck in Brazil, he had to borrow money for the return ship, and arrived home empty-handed. Joe Godina wrote he worked three days a week and Skominčič worked three days a month. Skominčič still owed money back home and his wife continued to irritate everyone with boastful stories of throwing leftover meat away and buying new clothes. Rudy was still single and flexible in where he lived. He labored in foundries and coal mines, boarded with families, and lived frugally. He had no one in Povžane he wanted to send money to, in fact he did not write at all. My grandparents were doing well enough they could drive to visit their friends in Cleveland, including Kristina of Gabrk and her husband, who had just had their first child.

Pepa Blaževa and her family rented or did housekeeping in exchange for a roof over their heads. She collected 300 lire per month as a pension and earned something on the side doing farm labor or laundry. Her daughter earned something as a seamstress. In this manner, they could do well enough until her husband, Ogrnjač, got sick that winter of 1932, and those 300 lire could not cover everything. Jožef paid them to give Franca Biščeva, his frail tubercular daughter, sewing lessons at their house after school. It was less than a true apprenticeship, but Franca enjoyed it and gave hope that she would one day earn money because she certainly was not going to make it doing farm labor. Pepa's sister, Tona Blaževa, the one who ran off with the Poklukar boy in 1913, died that winter in Zagreb after suffering from colon cancer.

Fani married her boyfriend, Viktor Colja, in the summer of 1932. Nobody seemed to be embarrassed about her pregnancy before marriage. In fact, it was a common event. For some reason, whenever Fani's husband was mentioned in my family, it began with the same phrase. I can still hear my Aunt Mary's voice saying, "Viktor Colja," and in an undertone, "(*you know*), the Partisan..." My mother echoed the words as if it had to be whispered. He was from Gorica, a hotbed of antifascist activity, and God only knows what he actually did and why he was working in the gostilna at Gabrk. Perhaps he was a communist operative on a mission, delivering propaganda or messages. He was a young man "who rode a bicycle on Sundays without a hat!" Communist and/or antifascist activity must have forced him to go to Yugoslavia. Tona wrote to Mary about Fani's marriage, and then, more bad news.

8 Nov 1932
   My dear and beloved sister, I have not written to you in a long time, because I am in a state of a deep sadness. I am either sad or angry all the time, and there is always something that postpones my writing from one day to another. You ask me about the children. Zora works in Trst and Fani is in Ljubljana; she got married on 10th August. Shortly before she was supposed to get married, she went into labor at seven months. She was in the hospital in Ljubljana for 14 days; she is healthy

now, but the child died. Ivan is at home, he is in 5th grade at the Italian school, and studies Slovene at home.

My dear sister, Karlo is 18 years old, and I cannot even write about him without shedding tears. He was four years old before he started to walk and he remains mute. Now in the month of May he lost his mind; he made a mistake, and he was dangerous. On 25 June they put him into a hospital in Rijeka. Before he went to the hospital, he was a beautiful strong boy, red, and well fed, when I went to visit him on 15 September, he was so thin; he looked like he had tuberculosis for two years. Now I would like to go and visit him again, but I cannot afford to go. And so, my beloved sister, I cried my eyes out for him. I wrote to Jože two months ago about his brother and have not received a single word. Is it possible his wife gets the letters and does not tell him? Tell them only that I am sad I have not received any of their letters. My stara tašča is meaner than ever. I never thought I would have to suffer this long with her. She still tells me I am living in her house and I am eating her food. As master of Bazletevi, my husband has managed things so we do not have a single cow. Fortunately, the harvest was a little better than the one last year

I hear you sent a photograph of Ivanka to Biščevi. I would tell you more about our family, but I do not want to be reproached. When you have not written to brother for a while, Biščevi say I must have told you some lie, and this is why you did not write to them. **A**

CHAPTER THIRTEEN

1933–1934: *Under the Heel of Fascism*

Franklin Delano Roosevelt defeated Herbert Hoover in a landslide victory in November 1932 and took office in January 1933. Voters were hopeful that FDR and his New Deal would bring positive change. Within days of his inauguration, he closed all banks for four days and reorganized them to restore confidence in the system. He took steps to stabilize prices of agricultural products and consumer goods, then proceeded to lower unemployment with infrastructure projects such as the building of dams, rural electrification, conservation, construction of public buildings, and arts projects.

6 January 1933

Dear Sister and Janez!!! Judging from the things you write about, times are not good in America, either. But you have had elections, your new president might be a better one—one who will look after workers and poor people. I think you have a good life, despite all the poverty. You have freedom and connection to everything that happens in the world. To be able to sit at home and listen to what is going on around the world is really nice. We live in darkness, just like people a couple of centuries ago. When we learn about something that has happened, it is from other people, and days and months may have passed and even then, it is only half the truth. This kind of life is not suitable for the 20th century.

I can see you are doing well; you have electricity, a gramophone, and a telephone. Only a few rich people here have any of these things. There is a radio in the township building in Materija, and there is one at the top of Gabrk, but they are weak and do not get a signal from outside of the country. Despite the shortages you experience, you still have a good life in America, with the freedom to speak and celebrate in your native language. Here in Materija it is a little easier to talk in our own language or sing folk songs in a gostilna than it is in other places, but I think you know how things are here overall.

You say Ivanka is studying in the hospital. Is she studying to be a nurse or a doctor? The nurses here do not go to school but they can still earn a living. During the war, the Sisters of Mercy did the work of both doctor and nurse, but nowadays they only assist. What kind of vocation will Janez choose? Will you send him for advanced education? Our children only learn how to suffer even more than their parents do. They teach in Italian, without any translations to Slovene. This means children learn how to write and read, but they have no idea what it means and, in the end, they know neither Italian nor Slovene. We teach them how to read Slovene from old newspapers since there are no books published in Slovene. They study from our old books from Mohorjeva. When I start thinking about their future, it breaks my heart. There is no money to put them in schools and there is no future in being a worker. Here, when sometimes work is available and they need 10 workers, 100 Italians show up and our people are the last in line.

Mama received the money you sent; she was very pleased. If you were to send it more often and if there were heaven, you would be the first one to go there. I am impressed you remember so much; you described how we walked to attend Mass. All that remains the same, but very few children go to tepežnica anymore. They do not do it in Bač, only a few in

Povžane do. It brings back memories. Do you remember what
kind of Tepežnica we got from Janez's mother?

Tepežnica, or "beating day," was an old Slovenian custom observed
on 28 December. Children got up early to go around to wish their
adult relatives good health and beat them with a hazel rod until
they were given presents that included dried fruits, walnuts, dried
sausages, and money.

Jožef and Tona followed the progress of the Fradel children. The
children started school not knowing English, though it is unlikely
that they were alone. Latrobe was full of young immigrant families
speaking different languages. This did not hold any of them back,
except Joe, my father. He said he had to repeat first grade because of
his poor English but I think because of his late November birthday
he was too young to be in school. His slow start left him feeling
inferior but ultimately, he found his niche in the industrial program in high school, learning carpentry, plumbing, electrical work,
and auto mechanics. John studied general education and Sylvia and
Mary's course work through the commercial program earned them
skills in typing, shorthand, and book-keeping, as so many girls did
in those times. John and Joe worked for the Lencoski dairy during
the school year and they brought home free milk. Mary got an after-
school job at a law office and Sylvia worked in a shoe store. Joe
also worked in a gas station and in the summer, he was a lifeguard
at Idlewild Park on the weekends. For two summers, John worked
at the saw mill in Slaty Fork, West Virginia with his uncle, Andy
Siskovič. He returned healthy, tanned, strong, and made the varsity
football team his senior year.

At home, my grandparents were avid readers and loved music.
My grandfather played the organ and loved birdwatching. He kept
a birdbath in their tiny yard. I never saw that they had a vegetable
garden, unlike most Slovenian immigrants.

When my grandparents played matchmaker between Andy Siskovič and Louise Znidarsič, they thought they were doing a good

deed. The aging Andy could settle down, a widow with four children would gain a clean, sober husband, and my grandparents could secure the happiness of their friends. When the store failed and Andy took the family home to West Virginia, the marriage went sour. The situation provided an opportunity for everyone to *educate themselves* at Andy's expense.

Jožef was quick to point out Louise was, after all, a *Kranjinca* (a woman from Krain, another part of Slovenia, not Brkini) and that's what happens when you do not marry your own kind. He believed Drej Bilko was rightfully angry he had been tricked into marriage out of a sense of social propriety, rather than love. A widow of one of Louise's grandsons told me Louise and the children hated West Virginia, and even 75 years after the fact, suggested Andy was deficient as a husband. Andy wanted to stay in West Virginia and Louise wanted to return to Latrobe. My grandparents sided with Louise, arguing that everybody was out of work from time to time, and Latrobe was a better place to live and find work in the long run. This put Andy at odds with my grandparents, and Mary announced to her brother Jožef they and Andy were no longer friends.

Jožef was a man of the old school. He sided with the Drej Bilko he knew. He wrote, "I never thought the law in America would allow a wife to lock her husband up on a short leash and, as you write, do it so easily. I find this ridiculous." When Louise left Andy, he wrote, "What you wrote about Drej Bilko surprises me, he seemed so reasonable. He married a widow and put himself under her control and now regrets it. I agree he looks like an *abandoned uncle* wandering around America. I never thought it would turn out like this for him."

Andy finally gave up on West Virginia, returned to his wife in Latrobe, and repaired his friendships. During the Second World War, both Andy Siskovič and John Ban came to work at Vulcan Mold, alongside John Fradel. After the war, Andy was working at Latrobe Hospital when he died suddenly on 9 March 1953, at the age of 68.

*

The farmers in Brkini and the valley were so hard-pressed some could not survive. Any stroke of good luck—like the favorable potato harvest of 1934—was negated by an increase in taxes on that product. The price of owning and slaughtering a pig was already prohibitive and now cows were targeted. The best cow could be purchased for 700 lire, but the ownership tax was 100 lire every year. The taxes on Biščevi were 212 lire in 1932 and they increased to 600 lire in 1933. This was *irrendentismo*, ethnic cleansing, the plan to rid the Julian March of its Slavic people.

Urhevi, the home of the now deceased Josip Ban, the man who had led his family and friends to West Virginia, was sold by the tax office for 1,700 lire to an Italian who already owned the co-operative in Materija and had his eye on the financially troubled Gabrk. Ban Bubnič still had debt after he sold everything but a small parcel of his land he wanted to hang on to. Tone Ban had nothing after the government took his home. He stayed with Lojze in Oplaz in the autumn and on Gabrk in the winter. Marija Urheva picked flowers to sell in Trieste, Jakovina made clothes, some picked brin despite the low prices, and others stole firewood to peddle. The problem with trade within the village was no one could pay cash, so they bought on credit or bartered, which did not pay the taxes. Others sent family members to Yugoslavia in hopes of getting some cash flow.

Pajserevi already had a daughter, Marija Nedoj, in Maribor. Now, they sent their son Janez Nedoj, in hopes he would send money. At Zajčevi, the widowed master was destitute. He had only one cow left, his 20-year-old son had tuberculosis in his bones and walked with crutches, and he needed his 14-year-old daughter for work in the house, so he sent his older daughter, Pepa Ban, to Maribor to look for work. Pepina, John Fradel's sister, helped her get settled. As Jožef watched these villagers leave, he saw the social structure of the village slowly breaking apart, and worried for his own family.

Košančevi held together. When Antonija became the nevesta of the younger Frane Košanc, there were two Franes, two Francas, two

Tonas, two sheep, and two oxen. The nevesta and the mother turned the house into a battle zone over the small annoyances of life, but when they needed to work, they pulled together. The house was repaired, three children were born, and 18 sheep, and five cattle were added.

Bilkotevi also managed to hang on. Notably, they kept to themselves and were seldom willing to help anyone else, but they had healthy, strong children who worked hard. They were also regular recipients of the generosity of Drej Bilko, the American Andy Siskovič, who remembered them even as he struggled with his new wife.

At Bazletevi, Tona's dreaded stara tašča had a stroke and lingered unconscious for eight days before her death in March of 1934. Tona would no longer be able to curse her for her troubles but her death brought harder times for Josef Bazle. His mother was the actual owner of the house and as long as she lived people could not do anything about the money Bazle owed them. Now they came after him through the courts. Bazletevi was losing their children: Joe was gone to America, Fani to Yugoslavia, and Zora made her own way in Trieste with domestic services. Karol was committed to an asylum. Only Ivan remained at home. Old Aunt Terezija in the formerly Slovene suburb of Rocol in Trieste lived under the heel of Italian fascism. She had one married daughter nearby in Rožice but Paula was gone to Argentina, and soon Marija would leave for Maribor.

Italians made life unbearable for dissidents. Jože Ivanin of Materija was locked up during a local election in the spring of 1934 and he was watched after his release. He could not go to Gabrk or Poljane (supposed meeting places for dissidents) and he had to be home by 8 p.m. They checked on him every hour during the night to see that he was home.

On Easter Sunday of 1934, at 9:30 at night, a fire in Bač destroyed the houses of Skominčič and Tenel. Each had family in America, people Jožef Fabjančič and John Fradel had assisted to get there. Everything burned; their clothes, their furniture, their pigs. Only one cow and one wardrobe were pulled to safety at Skominčič.

The harvest in 1933 was again poor. The price of hay dropped from 10 lire to 5 lire per kvintal. Given the increase in taxes to 600 lire, Jožef needed to increase the hay he sold from 21 kvintal to 120 kvintal. To rub salt into his wounds, his eldest daughter Marija broke her arm again, the same one she broke five years earlier. In the early fall she came home from Mass one evening, and after scrubbing the floor, she joined her girlfriends for a walk down the slope to the pond just as the cows with their tinkling bells were coming home. She climbed on the stone wall to get out of the way but slipped. Jožef wept. He was sorry for her pain and bad luck, sorry for the loss of her labor, and sorry that it would cost him more than 700 lire—more than a year's worth of land taxes. Hoping to recover his losses by selling brin, he and his sons collected ten kvintal of the berries used to flavor gin. In 1933 brin had sold for 85 lire per kvintal, a bonus of 850 lire to pay the taxes, but in 1934, when he needed it more than ever, it fetched a mere 24 lire per kvintal.

Mary sent used clothes and shoes. He replied, "We received the package, thank you so very much for it. The boys are very pleased, only Mama was not in a good mood because there was nothing for her. You know, Mama still does not want to accept poverty is present here and all around the world."

Italian soldiers added to their suffering that summer when they took over the fields around Povžane for artillery practice almost every day, which meant the farmers could not work in their fields until shooting drills were over. It felt like a war zone, with the earth trembling beneath their feet. The soldiers left their cannons at the bottom of the slope and failed to repair the trenches they dug. There was no compensation.

The road was widened by 1934 but they were still working on the water distribution system intended only for the military. The water came from Pazin, in the highlands of Istria which is now Croatia. It flowed down from the Čičarija plateau, through the villages of Vodice and Golac, to join the valley road around Hrusiča, where the military barracks and depot were located. The water system then ran through the valley east to Podgrad, where there were more barracks, and west to Kozina. In 1934 they were just beginning the stretch from Lubek to Gradišče, which included Materija.

In the port city of Rijeka goods were cheaper than in Trieste and many people went there to shop, even though it was much further. They risked losing everything at the customs station on the return trip, and if they were fortunate to keep their purchases, they walked in fear all the way home along paths through the valleys and the forests of Čičarija, carrying 40 to 50-pound packs. Jožef remarked: "They would not go if they did not have to. Still, you may read in the newspapers how good life is in Italy. Yes, it is good to die of."

*

Jožef wrote to tell the sad story of Frane Grgur—an account that pulls on all the threads in the social fabric holding Mary and John Fradel and their fellow expatriates to their homes in the valley under Slavnik. The story widely told blamed the highly educated but under-achieving Božidar Kastelic, who lived in a decaying house once the center of village social life, for instigating the event. His wife was about to give birth to their third child but the creaking of a broken shutter made him fearful someone was breaking in. Without fully considering the alternatives or the consequences of his actions, Božidar called the carabinieri, who came accompanied by a local man named Sarč, one of their fascist collaborators who felt important marching around with his gun.

Frane Grgur, one of five brothers who lived under the thumb of their demanding mother, was hunting that night. Drej, the eldest, was debilitated from TB but fortunate to have a good wife from Berhan who also enjoyed his mother's stamp of approval. Two middle sons, Joe and John Fabjančič, had recently been home from Cleveland to visit, bearing gifts. The youngest Grgur son, Miha, had just returned from military service in the Italian Army. Frane, also a middle son, married a girl from Gajsčevi, and with the support of her family, they lived in the house called Severlan in Bač.

As desperate as any farmer in Brkini in 1934, with a pregnant wife and five others depending on him, Frane was hunting rabbit that night to add meat to their next meal with a gun that was unregistered. Knowing that the penalty for an unregistered gun could be 600 lire and 50 days in pržane, when confronted by the carabinieri who were investigating Kastelic's broken shutter, Frane ran. Jožef wrote about this story on Christmas Day, 1934:

> This is how it happened. On 13 December, at Kastelic, one of the shutters was a little cracked open, it was rotten from old age. But when Božidar Kastelic saw this, and being the coward that he is, he reported it to the carabinieri. While the police were walking around and guarding the house, Frane, who was out hunting rabbits, came down from Bač and crossed the road. When he saw the police, he was afraid because he had his gun, so he started to run. They ran after him, and shot him in the back right next to that mulberry tree where we go to *kolina* [a place where pigs are butchered in November]. He died immediately. They dragged him into the store and announced he was dead.

There was irony that his body was laid out in Kastelic's home, the formerly prosperous gostilna and store, and the former social center for all of Materija, Bač and Povžane in those peacefully nostalgic days before the war when they were citizens of the Austrian Empire. The symbolism was too poignant, even for the hardened Jožef.

> The son of Šarč from Materija shot him; he is a municipal servant and a municipal policeman. He was carrying his arms and often walks around with the carabinieri. Šarč no longer is permitted to carry arms and the commission of inquiry has already assembled four times; it is a big investigation; it is not

known what will happen. People are very sad and upset, but cannot do more. If someone were to say anything, the police would quickly take him to the barracks and lock him up, but so far, they have not locked up anyone.

Left in Severlan in Bač is the poor wife of Frane, who is about to give birth, and their two small boys; one is six years and the other is seven years. One of her sisters is 15 years and she has been sick for 13 years; she does not walk on one leg at all. Another sister is 18 years, she has been struck by something [unspecified mental disability]. Her father, Piro, is still alive, he has 80 years. So, you can see, without a father there are now three orphans; seven people depended on Frane. Grgurjevi are suffering a lot because of this, they will be sick from their grief.

Grgurjova, the mother who had done so much to contribute to the unhappiness of her sons, was distraught and, at least in Jošef's mind, she was partly to blame because the family had quarreled with Frane and driven him away. Grgurjevi had a different understanding of what happened. Frane was not the only local man to be hunting illegally that night. Šarč particularly disliked Frane and was waiting for him to separate from the others so he could shoot him. He saw Frane cross the road in front of Kastelic and took aim. When the carabinieri arrived, they decided Frane's murder by their leading collaborator would not look good, so the story that Božidar had summoned them about a broken shutter and an intruder was fabricated. They dragged his body inside Kastelic and said that Frane had been caught in the act of robbing the store, but everyone could see the marks where he had been dragged in from the street. There was never any chance for justice. Before long Šarč disappeared, some say he went to Italy.

CHAPTER FOURTEEN

Why Go to Yugoslavia?

The lure of fast money in America in the decade before the war caused a significant change in migration plans for the men of Povžane for the first time in centuries. Most went alone with every intention of returning to purchase and claim their own farms, marry, and carry on as their forebearers had, but after the Great War, the economy in Primorska never returned to its 1914 baseline. In addition to inflation and a worldwide depression, irredentismo actively worked against the return to prosperity. The middle class, the educated, and the politically active were early targets for harassment, imprisonment, or exile. Unrelenting taxation assisted by poor weather created impoverishment unlike any previously known. Denied a meaningful education and the use of their own language, young people struggled to see a future. Implementation of a military draft in 1935 for foot soldiers in Abyssinia was an immediate reason to leave one's homeland. They fled to Ljubljana and Maribor, the two major cities in the eastern two-thirds of Slovenia within the Kingdom of Yugoslavia.

Before the First World War, in the days of the Empire, Maribor was a city with an ethnic German majority. Only 14 percent of its inhabitants identified as Slovene, just 13 of its 205 businesses were Slovene owned, and there were no Slovene schools. However, the

German speaking majority was limited to the city with the surrounding rural areas being 100 percent Slovene. The Primorskans who came before the Great War were painted by the press as intruders competing for jobs meant for ethnic Germans. Only less prestigious jobs in civil services and police work were open to them.

At war's end, the city council proclaimed that Maribor and its environs would be part of Austria. The very next day, 23 November 1918, a day destined to be a national holiday, Rudolf Maister, a major in the Austro-Hungarian Army, a poet, a painter, and a Slovene, assembled a volunteer force of 4,000 soldiers to take control of the city. Maister was proclaimed a general by the Slovene Council and a week later, when the Kingdom of S.H.S. was established, King Alexander confirmed his command. In January 1919, while awaiting the arrival of an American military delegation that would broker the peace and decide on partitions, Maister's forces fired upon the waiting crowds, resulting in the death of nine civilians and the wounding of 60 more. The ethnic German population, numbering about 10,000, fled in fear to Austria.

By 1931, the Slovene makeup of Maribor was 80 percent. The shift occurred not just because of emigration, but because many of those who were German speakers were actually Slovene born, and resumed speaking in their native tongue. The population void left by the German exodus was filled by refugees fleeing irrendentismo in Trieste and Primorska. Intellectuals, artists, writers, journalists, musicians, teachers, choir masters, business owners, and dissidents of all sorts, as well as the simply impoverished, found haven in Maribor. Favorable housing and employment in police work, the civil service, the burgeoning electric industry, hydroelectric plants, railways, textiles, and manufacture of vehicles were to be found. Maribor was the fastest-developing city in all of Yugoslavia.

In "Primorskan Slovenes in Maribor, 1918-1941," Dragan Potočnik described the arrival of Primorskans. Initially wary of newcomers, the residents were won over by the openness, cheerfulness, and goodwill of Primorskans. Slovene schools were opened.

Primorskans established an organization called Jadran (Adriatic), reflecting their origins along the coast. Best known for its choral societies, their goal was to entertain and to promote their culture. Performances raised money to help the poor and they traveled to venues all over Yugoslavia delivering their cultural message. Jadran planned events for everything worth celebrating or commemorating in Primorska or Maribor: Grape Harvest Parties, St. Nicholas Evening, the founding day of the Kingdom of S.H.S., as well as Easter, Christmas, and the usual saints' feast days were occasions for music, theater, and dancing. The remembrance of the signing of the Treaty of Rapallo, which awarded Primorska and Istria to Italy, the torching of Narodni Dom in Trieste, and the Victory of Rudolf Maister were opportunities for music, poetry, and educational lectures. Primorskans changed the culinary scene of Maribor with Teran, the traditional karst wine, true karst *pršut* (prosciutto), sea fish, polenta and other Primorskan dishes. Tomatoes and chicory became part of everyone's garden. Primorskans awakened in Maribor a new identity as a Slovene city and renewed cultural pride among its original residents.

Under the rule of King Alexander, Jadran promoted the ideal of a new Yugoslavian nationhood. Some might have favored a Yugoslavian republic, or a federated republic, but (especially in the 1920s, as noted) loyalty to King Alexander was challenged by only a few.

In 1932 a new organization called the Nanos Society was formed. Its goal was specifically anti-fascist and political. Its name reflected its support of TIGR, the anti-fascist terrorist organization of Primorska, which had its founding meeting on the Nanos Plateau in 1927. Jadran and Nanos had an overlap in membership and goals, but young people with activist goals joined Nanos. Every year, they held an event mourning the four TIGR members who were executed in Basovica for their participation in the 1930 bombing of the fascist newspaper. They sponsored lectures such as "The Struggle of our Minority in Italy" and "Fascism and Schools." They held dinners and entertainment events to raise money for Primorskans who arrived with nothing during the worst of the financial crisis. In 1935, they assisted a new wave of refugees fleeing Italian military service.

*

Mary and John Fradel's connections to Maribor ran deep. John Fradel's second cousins, the younger sons of Fradelevi, were among the early Primorskans in Maribor before the Great War. The three Fradel brothers had tried their luck in Trieste around the turn of the century. Josip found work as a mechanic and stayed. Anton Fradel was truly a wild child, acting out just as Rudolf had done when he was desperate. About 16 years prior to his move to Maribor, Anton worked in Odolina, the tiny settlement two miles below Bač where charcoal was made, and just like Rudy, he liked to party in Trieste. *Edinost*, one of the Slovene daily newspapers of Trieste, in 1898 reported:

> Nineteen-year-old charcoal burner A. Fradel from the district of Materija wanted to join a joyful, loud party of gypsies who had just camped near Montella. They had just let him join in, when the police approached, arrested him for vagrancy, and put him in the slammer.

Anton later spent four months in prison for stealing from a pasta factory, then headed to Maribor, where at age 35, he married Alojza Hlade in 1914. A bad construction deal found him in court again in 1929, and in the 1930s, he was working at the hydroelectric plant at Fala on the Drava River, at the north end of Maribor. On 17 November 1937, as he was examining some equipment, a wooden block fell and crushed his head, killing him instantly. He was just 58.

His brother, Frane Fradel, married Josefa Černak in Trieste, where their first child, Marija, was born in 1913. Following his brother to Maribor, Frane found work as a railway policeman. Their second child was a son, Franjo. I discovered glimpses of their lives in scattered newspaper stories. Franjo played soccer for the rail-road workers' team. Marija was an excellent student and graduated from secondary school. She skied with her friends on the local slope called Pahorje and became a committee member of the Nanos Society. She accompanied groups of school children to the King Alexander I Youth Hostel on the Croatian coast, where the children learned to swim and sail and were taught what being a Primorskan was all about.

When my Aunt Jane visited Maribor in 1937, she met Marija. At the time, both women were 24 years old and a photo snapped as they strolled along a city street in Maribor shows a type of image that was in vogue in the 1930s. (photo 14) Franjo joined the Yugo-slav army and died suddenly in 1938 of an unknown cause during peacetime. Marija sent his picture (photo 15), and another one of his grave stone, to Jane. Frane Fradel was promoted to a municipal policeman in 1938 but everything he had was destroyed in the war. He was imprisoned, and his wife and daughter, the beautiful blonde Marija, were deported. I found Marija Fradel in the Kozina phone directory in 2012 and wrote to her; I did not realize that she would be nearly 100 years old. The letter came back marked "*umrl*"—dead.

Josef Babič, husband of Pepina Fradel, worked in the port of Koper, but following his participation in an unsuccessful strike, he was not safe from fascist thugs and the carabinieri. The family took refuge in Maribor in 1920, settling in Studenci, a part of town near the factories and the railroad where Primorskans congregated. Their first son, Jože, born in 1917 before they left Povžane, was destined to become part of the lively theater scene in Maribor. Their second son, Stanislas, or "Lada", was born in 1922.

Another family member in Maribor was Milan Godina who was the younger brother of Josef Godina (Bazle, Tona's war-scarred hus-band). Milan found work in Trieste but kept company with Marija Nedoj from Pasjerevi, one of the more prosperous households in Povžane. A daughter was born before the marriage. After Milan survived his time in the Austro-Hungarian Army, he returned to

Trieste but watching the defeated Italians lord over him was intol-
erable. In Maribor he found police work, and his wife, Marija Nedoj,
found her old friend, Pepina Fradel. Their children Jože Babič and
Milena Godina would blossom in Studenci, then a working-class
neighborhood filled with talented people who had fled Trieste and
Primorska. Jože studied set design with Ernst Franc and Milena
studied opera, and was performing onstage in 1934 and '35. Both
attended the drama school of Vladimir Skrbinše, and both were
involved in communist activities, which got them into trouble. Jože
was expelled from school and briefly considered going to Spain to
fight, but found work in 1938 in the avant-garde theater in Ptuj,
where he became the artistic director. Milena was banned from
work in the theaters of Maribor, but was able to get theater work
in Skopje, Macedonia, until the Yugoslav police caught up with her
and stopped her from working in her craft.

Jože Babič was destined for fame in Slovenian theater. After the
war he brought a new and unconventional approach to theater
in Maribor. He expanded his creativity in the Slovene Theater he
established in Trieste while it was an international territory under
Allied governance. When the Italians took over the city, the theater
moved to Nova Gorica where he directed hundreds of plays, acted in
some, and later turned to film and television. He received accolades
from all sides and is immortalized with a bust displayed in front
of the theater in Nova Gorica and a plaque in the village where
he was born. True to the actor's stereotype, he was married three
times, fathered three children, and had at least one affair—all with
leading actresses of Slovenia. His daughter, Barbara, describes him
as very charming.

Milena Godina returned to Maribor in 1945. Her mother Marija
Nedoj had died during the war. She performed in operettas, puppet shows, on radio and stage. She also taught drama and worked
with children. Her son, Karpo Godina, became a well-respected film
director. Karpo told Babara Babič that Milena was there to care for
Pepina in the last months before her death in 1971.

*

The parts of Slovenia and Croatia not occupied by Italy had little
choice but to join with Serbia at the end of the war. An independent nation of southern Slavs was not a new concept and was not
totally unwelcome in Croatia and Slovenia, though the union was
not based on any notion of a federation of equals. For Serbians,
the Kingdom of S.H.S. was the realization of their ancient goal of
a "Greater Serbia," and the triumphant liberation of their Slavic
brethren from foreign domination. From a self-serving point of view,
the addition of Slovenia and Croatia, former Austro-Hungarian
provinces that had participated in the brutal 1915 invasion of Serbia,
could be viewed as compensation for Serbia's tremendous losses.
After all, one in five Serbian men had perished during the war
and Belgrade was in ruins after the departing armies vindictively
destroyed it.

The Kingdom of S.H.S. was a constitutional monarchy with a
representative national assembly, but Serbian King Alexander I
was an authoritarian. The economy was a plutocracy of less than
a hundred mostly Serbian families headed by the King whose
racketeering methods were compared to a glorified Al Capone by
a contemporary of Louis Adamic.* War reparations and foreign
aid, particularly from France, poured in to rebuild Belgrade. King
Alexander awarded building contracts to his friends who enriched
themselves at the expense of the country. Croatia and Slovenia were
taxed heavily in a punitive spirit. The foreign aid and tax revenues
were used to build military force and secret police that worked to
eliminate any opposition to the monarchy. To maximize fear and
control amidst common folk, soldiers from one region were sent to
police another, and the army was brutally maintained by officers
recruited from warlike tribes in the borderlands of Albania. The
regime was oppressive toward dissidents, mainly separatists and

*Adamic, Louis. *The Native's Return*, p. 256

socialists, who were imprisoned and subjected to barbaric torture
in King Alexander's prisons.

The National Assembly with its two dozen parties, was a mad-
house and a circus—the butt of international disdain and humor.
Rather than strive towards unity, King Alexander played factions
against each other. Ministers were changed every few months, fos-
tering a climate of inefficiency and instability. Many party leaders
were demagogues and, egged on by the King and his agents, they
called each other vile names and engaged in fistfights, which esca-
lated to more irrational and scandalous behavior.

Stefan Radič, a charismatic leader of the Croatian Peasant Party,
sought independence for Croatia, and many Croatians revered him
as their uncrowned king. Radič stirred emotions so much that in
June 1928—during a shoot-out in Parliament—he was hit in the
stomach and died soon after. In response to the ensuing crisis, King
Alexander abolished the National Assembly and the constitution
in January of 1929, and established a dictatorship. The name of
the country was changed to the Kingdom of Yugoslavia, a subtle
yet symbolic move to indicate that federation or autonomy of the
provinces was not open to negotiation.

Yet, in spite of all this, King Alexander enjoyed widespread
popularity among the people during the 1920s for his wartime
record and his charm, although as a dictator, he fueled widespread
hatred. With French insistence, he presented a new constitution
but he maintained all executive power and essentially hand-picked
the members of the assembly. On top of this, continuing Croatian
demands for independence threatened the survival of Yugoslavia,
and the growing economic and military might of Italy and Germany
after 1930 added new pressures. Many believed the death of King
Alexander was all that was necessary for Yugoslavia to fracture
and achieve its separatist goals. In October 1934, while on a state
visit to Marseilles, France, King Alexander was assassinated while
riding in an open car, by a Macedonian separatist believed to be in
league with Croatian separatists. The assassination was captured

on film and is remembered as a landmark in film history. Prince Paul Karađorđević, the King's cousin, was appointed as regent for Alexander's son, the eleven-year-old Prince Peter.

Prince Paul accepted the regency reluctantly. He was more inclined towards democracy than the King had been, and sought neutrality in foreign affairs but in the next few years, exports of minerals and agricultural products to Germany would pull the Kingdom of Yugoslavia out of its economic depression and straight into the German economic sphere.

CHAPTER FIFTEEN

1935: Caring for the Sick

After a decade of reading and studying Jožef's letters, I feel like he is someone I know. I know how he thought and some of his innermost feelings. I know how he experienced farming and the weather. I imagine what he might think as I toil in my little garden with lettuce, tomatoes, beans, and a few other vegetables. When the lettuce is germinating and the soil is dusty and cracked, an afternoon shower is a godsend. When the lettuce is bushy and fresh, the same rain will flatten and ruin half of it. One year, my kale faltered through a long, dry, aphid-ridden summer and a wet autumn was its salvation. I looked forward to a winter of glorious fresh kale salads, then the deer finished it off overnight. I think of the devastation Jožef would have felt. I am thankful for my grocery store, for California kale, and that I do not depend on my garden to stay alive.

His letters over the decades are filled with lamentations and obsessions about the weather: too rainy, too dry, an unexpected frost, too cool, too hot, too windy, crushing hail. But these events were his world, his life, his family's survival. He was not exaggerating. Climate conditions in the 1930s were objectively worse than ever before for the rural economy of Eastern Europe. Summer temperatures were extraordinarily high and periods of drought decreased agricultural output. The same thing was occurring in the United States, where farms were turned into dust bowls and people were forced off the land to seek employment elsewhere.

Jožef's writing style included triple exclamation points at the end of each salutation (!!!) and I could sense his feeling of hope and enthusiasm as his words reached across the ocean to his dear sister. But in early 1935 the pointed punctuation was infrequent, and I felt his depression, his despair. Without books, and little news, he lacked a global perspective, and relied on Mary to keep him informed. He knew little about the leader of the right-wing party in Germany, an admirer of Benito Mussolini, who aspired to become the absolute ruler of Germany. He was unaware that when Adolph Hitler gained power as chancellor in January 1933 and president in August 1934, he would forever change the world by eliminating his enemies through extermination, confining them to concentration camps, and suspending political rights. Jožef was however, aware that for centuries the Jewish people had faced hatred, blame, and persecution at every turn, and that their persecution was on the upswing.

He also knew about poor crops, taxes, inflation, widespread poverty, Italian surveillance, poor health, and death. The stress from all of these things took its toll on his health.

3 February 1935

Dear Sister and Janez, I have not yet received the almanac you promised. You worry sending Slovene literature might create problems for us, but they do not suspect me of anything. If they find the books, I have the good excuse my sister knows I like to read and I do not know Italian, and thus she sent me books in the language I learned. If you could prepare a small package and put the book inside some old clothes, this would work.

Božidar Kastelic is now a widower; his wife died on New Year's Day. He goes to confession and communion every day, and cries over her grave. He was confused before, but whatever sense he possessed has been destroyed by the clergy. You know the government promotes big families and the priests say to be childless is the biggest sin. A few years ago, the doctor told them if he wanted his wife to live, they should not have more children. He and his wife always went to confession and they preferred to listen to the priest. When she was eight months pregnant her blood went bad and she was in bed for 20 days. When the time came to give birth, she went to sleep forever.

Božidar's wife, Karlina, had high blood pressure in her previous pregnancies, and the doctor correctly advised her the problem would get worse with each pregnancy. She had eclampsia, the most severe form of hypertensive disorder of pregnancy. Swelling began in her feet, then spread to her hands, face, and her whole body as her kidneys failed. Her blood pressure skyrocketed. Seizures, and possibly a stroke may have occurred before her death. Disruption and early separation of the placenta often result in fetal death, but this child did survive. He was named Božidar. Jožef continued:

> Marija from Gabrk is also a widow. We buried Anton Jaksetič on 30 January at the church in Brezovica. He was always such a healthy person. He was in bed with pneumonia for only three days and died. With her Kristina in America, she has just her boy and girl with her, they are 17-year-old twins, Tonči and Mija. Their stari ata [Ivan Ban, Marija's father] is often sick, he will soon leave this world. This winter took many people, and many others are nearing the end. Sluga from Rožice died today; he was 99 years and two days. Edo and his wife in Brezovica, died this month within five days of each other, each was 86 years. Jakoper from Brezovica died last week, he was 87 years. Šimina from Brezovica, died eight days ago with pneumonia. This is how people move on, and make space for others.
>
> Košančevi are hardworking and doing well; they have lots of livestock. Their life should be good but they fight every day. Franca, the stara tašča, wants to have total control of the house-hold, and Markovka, the bride, wants to do the same. They say

to each other "It is your fault... no, it is your fault..." and so they fight all the time.

At the far end of the village, Zajčevi still live in poverty. The older boy is sick with TB; he has been walking with crutches for four years. They depend on the 16-year-old girl who is still at home.

Mama is the same. As much as she is healthy and old, she is equally grumpy, more and more every day. She is stubborn, she wants to give the orders, and if someone does not obey her, then everything goes to hell. We suffer through this, even when it is unfair, because we know it will not last forever.

17 March 1935

Tona is doing better this winter. Zora is home, her 15-year-old son, Ivan, is cooking for the policemen, and she is washing clothes for them. This is how they earn money for polenta. Bazle does not step out of the house and he does not earn one čentižim, but he demands everything and when he does not get it, he curses.

Bilkotevi are special people, they keep to themselves, and nobody knows why. A few days ago, Bilko told me you have been angry with them ever since that time, so long ago, before you left, when we were all cutting grass together in Skadanščina. We were all going to get an equal share of the money but Bilko complained Janez did not do his share of the work. Bilko insists you continue to resent him for that. He complains you never write to sister Rezina, but I know you wrote to her and she never replied. You cannot say anything to such people, it is best to leave them alone.

At Gašper's, they spent a lot of lire making arrangements to go to America, but when that became impossible Gašper and his son went to South America. While they were gone Marija managed the household, and like a woman, she created a large debt. Gašper and his son did not have luck in South America and when they returned home it was hard for them to help themselves, so they live in poverty; they have only one cow.

Despite all this trouble, Marija Gašpereva is still young and good-looking.

Many people are scared war will come, but people want change, even if it means war; we cannot live like this anymore. What do your newspapers say about this? We do not know anything and if we see it in the newspaper, we cannot believe it, because the newspaper prints only what they are told to write.

I am in bad shape, as I have told you, my stomach is getting worse and worse. Now for a few months, the pain is coming during the night and many nights I cannot sleep. I am taking medicine and if I do not improve, I will have to go to the hospital. This will be a hardship because the children are not yet strong enough to work on the farm, but if I do not get better, there will be no choice.

Jožef had stomach ulcers and gallstones, nonetheless he struggled through the spring planting before going to the hospital. The removal of his gall bladder in April instantly made him feel better, and a soft, low-fat diet was necessary. In those days, ulcers were treated with a "sippy diet" that consisted of milk, cereals such as cream of wheat, oatmeal porridge, or polenta, eggs, and pureed vegetables. A person was advised to eat a little every few hours to keep the stomach lining coated. The medication that Jožef used would have been liquid calcium carbonate, magnesium hydroxide, or aluminum hydroxide (we know them by brand names such as Tums, Maalox, or Mylanta). Such things were the mainstay of ulcer and gastritis treatment up until 1976 when Tagamet, the first medication to actually prevent the stomach from producing acids that burned holes in the stomach lining, was introduced. Nowadays a gall bladder surgery is a one-day procedure done with robotic tools that leave two or three tiny holes in the abdomen. In those days there would be an eight-inch full-thickness incision on the right side of the abdomen. Jožef was in the hospital in Trieste for 18 days, and needed several more months for the abdominal wall to completely heal.

17 June 1935

I do not feel that sickness anymore, and now that I have gained weight, I look 10 years younger. I do as the doctor ordered. I drink milk, tea, and water. Wine and all alcohol are forbidden. I cannot eat any lard or pork so we need to buy special meat for me. Nothing can be prepared with butter or oil; therefore, they always cook separately for me. This is prescribed for six months. It is expensive so I will keep it up only as long as I can afford it. I have not worked at all and the grass needs to be cut, so I will try to see if I can be of help. We are lacking rain, everything is so dry, and we are afraid the harvest will be poor.

17 July 1935

For two months after the operation, I protected myself. I did not do any work until 20 June. The easiest thing for me is to cut grass, so I have been cutting every day, and I do not have the slightest pain in my stomach. The scar is still hard and I feel a little clumsy with strenuous work. Raking does not feel right and I just cannot load hay. Since St. Peter's Day [29 June] we have been cutting dry grass. We have not had any rain. Soon everything will be brown, just like during the winter. We continue to work, but everyone is desperate and full of worry about what they will eat. Some are afraid that this is the end. For sure, the end comes soon enough for all of us.

Tona received health care at the tuberculosis clinic in Materija twice a week, but she was getting worse, and in July she was moved to the hospital in Rijeka. Although the hospital in Trieste was much closer, and transportation was cheaper and easier, Materija was now part of the Rijeka administrative district, so she had to go there for free care. Zora came home from Trieste and Fani came with her one-year-old son. Jožef did not give Tona a good prognosis. "We do not know if they will cut her open or not. I suspect she will be cured only when she is in the casket, behind the mayor." (Traditionally, the priest and the mayor led funeral processions.)

11 August 1935

Your letter and package traveled for 40 days but everything arrived intact. We all thank you kindly for everything. I feel like I have been born again since I got rid of that pain. We ran out of water 20 days ago and now we need to haul it in. The harvest is so bad everything from the fields will be good only for pigs. We fear this year will be as bad as the years between 1915 and 18 when the people at home were asking the Lord for the plague or the war, just to be relieved of their hunger. It seems we will soon have all of this, but no Lord to save us.

The doctors at the hospital in Rijeka say Tona is a little better, but I believe she will be cured only when she dies. Fani and Zora were fighting at home, so Fani has been staying with us for four days now; maybe she will return to Yugoslavia next week. One can see she is happy to be married. Zora has some work in Bač, but she is unhappy there. She prefers to look around for boys.

*

A year had passed since the murder of Frane Grgur by Šarč when another homicide took place. Anton Škerjanc from Artviže was among those who had been to America twice and returned. His first trip was in 1906. In 1913 he traveled with John Fradel on the *Polonia*. He was someone John and Mary knew well.

On a hot day in early August, Škerjanc walked from Artviže to Skadanščina, but never returned. Artviže is at the crest of the Brkini ridge and Skadanščina is on the opposite side of the valley, on the lower slope of Slavnik, a distance of six or seven miles. Most of the way is an easy walk by road straight downhill from Artviže through Materija. At the back of the village a shortcut on a path eastward through the fields behind Povžane would take a traveler up the slope of Slavnik to Skadanščina. (see map) Soldiers said that they saw Škerjanc on Grgur's Hill, and they searched the meadows for the missing man for three days. On the ninth day, Pajserova found him dead just outside of Povžane near Bilkotevi's hazel trees. His body was hidden in a bush not more than 30 yards from the path. The log used to kill him came from a fence along the path that belonged to Biščevi. Jožef was called to the barracks four times for questioning. The commission of inquiry interviewed almost everyone from Povžane more than once. Frane Rejčo and Bubec from Materija were suspected, but witnesses confirmed they were loading hay up in the hills behind Bač, way on the other side of the valley. The two men were held in jail for 72 days, but no charges were issued. Jožef told the story over the course of several letters as tensions and suspicions grew amongst the villagers, the carabinieri, the collaborators and the Italian authorities. The climate of political violence perpetuated by the authorities could easily cloud what may have been a grievance over money or land. Jožef wrote, "Here we are not allowed to talk, but we cannot be quiet."

Decades passed before the murderer was known. A man from Golac, a village three miles or so beyond Skadanščina near the Croatian border, hoping for forgiveness before he met his Maker, made a deathbed confession. He was a friend of Škerjanc and during a quarrel he hit him on the head with the fencepost and hid his body in the thicket.

Tona was in the hospital in Rijeka for six months. It was too far to walk and transportation alone was 30 lire and expenses to stay in Rijeka were 50 lire. Bazle went once and Zora saw her mother three times. They reported she was weak and had no appetite. Johana from Oplaz and Marija Rejčeva visited her because they were in Rijeka for other reasons. Jožef recalled when he was in the hospital, he always wanted people to visit but when they left, it was doubly hard and he cried every time. He did not go. The silver lining was Tona could see her son Karel who was housed in the same building. Her presence was everything to him because he recognized only a few people, did not talk, and did not appear to hear. In mid-November 1935, Tona was sent home. Her Mama went to see her, but Zora saw her coming and barred the door, saying they did not want Mama or anyone from Biščevi in the house.

The holidays passed and the year 1936 began. A package and a
few dollars for Mama came, and letters of greetings and thanks were
exchanged. Jožef wrote:

19 January 1936
   Dear Sister!!! The last time I wrote to you, I said you could
soon expect a letter that would say that sister Tona died. Today
is that day. She died on the 16th in the morning. We buried her
on the 17th, on St. Anton Day. She has done her work, now she
is saved. The evening before she died, we were all with her, but
she could not talk anymore. From six o'clock until midnight she
did not talk, then she woke up a little bit and called for Mama.
Mama came to see her and she recognized her, and at four in
the morning she let her last breath out.

                                  *

My grandmother grew old in her own home in Latrobe. She was age
71 when she was widowed and lived another 21 years. At first, she
spent a lot of time with friends, continued with S.N.P.J. and even
had a gentleman companion. But over time she slowed down and
had some small strokes, which set her back. Her daughters, Mary
and Sylvia, insisted she live with them at one of their homes, but
she could be ornery and difficult, and preferred to be in her own
place. A neighbor stopped in every day and others called regularly
to check on her. She was extremely slow of movement, though her
mind was sharp. I visited a few times during this period and we
sat in the kitchen at her heavy wooden table painted in a colorful
peasant floral design, with solid matching chairs. I loved that table.
There was a print of some parakeets with a pink border in a faux
bamboo frame on the wall. She insisted on making the tea, so I sat
and watched. Light filtered through the curtain sheers of the tall
windows. It was always a little dim.
   "What do you do all day, Grandma?" I asked one time.

"I get out of bed, I make the bed, I dress, I make a little breakfast, I eat it, then I clean up." She smiled as she slowly recalled her morning routine in a tone indicating that she was a little insulted that I should ask such a silly question. By then, she had answered the phone at least once and it was lunch time. Meals on Wheels, a home service program, delivered enough food for lunch and supper. It took me years to figure out for a 90-year-old woman who had suffered several strokes, her independence and activity level were remarkable.

She had a bigger stroke, and her recovery was not good. She refused to live with her daughters, so went to a nursing home. Additional small strokes caused her memory to fade and she did not always recognize her children and grandchildren. She stopped speaking English, and held conversations in Slovene with people she mistook for her Mama and her sister, Tona, who had died from tuberculosis in 1936 at the age of 50.

CHAPTER SIXTEEN

1936: Family Divisions

Mussolini invaded Abyssinia, what is now Ethiopia, in 1935 and instituted a draft of all men over twenty-one. Frane Bilko was deployed in March of 1936, the month of his 21st birthday. He was admired as one of the tallest, strongest boys in Povžane. All the Bilkotevi children were tall, they worked hard and cooperated with one another, so the family prospered. Jožef often cited cows as a measure of family wealth, for example, Bilkotevi had six compared to Zajčevi, with one, and Bazletevi with none. Despite the relatively good fortune of her children and her home, Rezina Bilkotevi had driven a wedge between herself and her parents and brother Jožef at Biščevi, the family of her sister Tona at Bazletevi, and her sister Mary Fradel in America. Rezina had no patience and ruthlessly said whatever was on her mind. Mama was easy and pleasant to talk to on her good days, but she was often cranky, and those around her needed to be forever conciliatory to keep peace. Rezina was unwilling to do that but Jožef and his wife, Pepa, worked hard at it. Mama was unreasonable when Mary sent a letter without a dollar, so Mary tried hard to send the expected money. Tona and her mother had spats but managed to get over their differences. Rezina held onto her grudges and resented that Mama favored the Bazle children, especially Fani, over her own.

Jožef used an old expression, "The Bilkotevi are like *Podgorci*." Podgorci are people of Podgorje, a little Slovenian village on the other side of Slavnik in Čičarija. Men went up Slavnik only to cut wood and collect brin, for there was no other reason to go near Podgorje. What Jožef meant was that although the Bilkotevi household was footsteps away, they visited as often as someone from Podgorje might visit them, or they "might as well be living on the other side of the mountain."

Misfortune never seemed to be far away from Biščevi. Every year nests of caterpillars appeared on the pine trees and a few days each winter were spent removing them. One day, thirteen-year-old Janez climbed a pine tree to cut off a branch filled with nests and accidentally struck his hand with an axe. It was so bad it could not be treated at home. The severe injury required a hospital stay, where they sewed him up, put a cast on, and kept him for a few days. Every day cost 25 lire (about one U.S. dollar).

At harvest in 1935, the grass was burnt and only cabbage, a little rye, and barley remained to eat through the winter. They purchased beans and potatoes to plant in 1936, but that growing season was too dry, and then it got too wet, so new potatoes sprouted out of the ones already growing. The old ones were glassy and the new ones were too young. "It was double the number of potatoes, but none to eat in the end," Jožef lamented. In the fall of 1936, there was no grass to cut and the harvest yielded only a little corn, turnips, and cabbage. In early autumn, four pigs, including two pregnant sows and a big one ready for kolina (butchering) died. They had never been without a pig to slaughter in the fall, but now there was none and no way to get one. There would be no meat at home and no cash from the sale of other pigs to buy clothes and shoes and pay taxes.

The military was still conducting training exercises around Povžane. Almost daily soldiers fired their cannons and the farmers could not get to their fields to cut grass till eleven in the morning. The gostilna on Gabrk went bankrupt. Marija of Gabrk took charge of another gostilna in Materija for Župančič. Božidar sold Kastelic to someone from Hrušica, took to drinking, and was soon out of money.

Meanwhile, life in America was improving. John had intermittent work at Vulcan Mold and the children were thriving. In fact, there was much to celebrate in 1936. One can imagine the pride of John and Mary, immigrant parents whose two children had graduations in June—Jane graduated from Latrobe Hospital School of Nursing and John graduated from Latrobe High School. Mary hosted a graduation party and wrote to her brother about it. In Slovenia, a *veselica* is a public festivity that includes live music, dancing, eating, and drinking. The word means "to be happy." Jožef responded:

> *2 August 1936*
> Dear Sister, You wrote you had a veselica. We don't know what this word means anymore. Boys sometimes try to organize a dance, but the carabinieri must always be present and they each have to be paid ten lire. The municipal officers are slaves to the fascists and will lock into the barracks anyone who has had too much to drink, even if they haven't done anything wrong. They are locked up just for being drunk, and then they have to pay 60 lire or more to be released. If one were to complain, well, you know what happens. So, what we have here is not a dance, it is a trap. You can see, dear sister, life here is such that your heart hurts, and there is no help to be found anywhere.

Every letter contained news of people in their international network. *Bučansko* was a word Jožef made up. *Bačansko* is a resident of Bač. *Buča* is a pumpkin. The saying *"ima trdo bučo"* means that she has a hard head like a pumpkin, is obstinate or even stupid. By combining *buča* and *Bačansko* into *bučansko,* Jožef made a play on words to express his opinion of the two women.

I agree Ferbova and Gela Skominčič have always been as obstinate as any Bučansko. It is amazing after so many years of being away from home, they have not changed. It is not right what they said about Marija from Gabrk. Marija may be fat; she has about 100 kilos [220 pounds], but she works hard and her life is not easy. This spring was especially hard for her since the gostilna she is managing was closed for a few months. Now that they have reopened, they are living a good life. She had a letter from her Kristina about a month ago; she says she and her husband bought a house and they are doing well.

You ask about Aunt Terezija in Rocol. I last talked to her when I was in the hospital. Her daughter Marija is now at home; she has a hardworking and a sensible husband and a daughter who is seven years old. Karla is in Yugoslavia. The youngest daughter, Paula, is in Argentina. Fani Colja is in Ljubljana and her husband is a mason, or a painter when needed. Pepa Blaževa lives at Prucova, she is doing well, and continues to receive her pension. Her daughter is a seamstress and her boy trained to be a blacksmith.

Dear Sister, you've always said you will come to visit us sometime, but now you say it is unlikely we'll ever see each other again. I would really like to see you, all of you. It would also be the right thing for Janez to come, because of the farm. Mama sends you special greetings and thanks you for the dollars. These tiny leaves are from Tona's grave, there are no flowers at this time of year.

Sometime after the summer of 1936, Jožef"s daughter, Marija, got a boyfriend, who was none other than Miha Grgur, the youngest of the five sons at Grgurjevi. He was 26 years old, had served his time in Mussolini's army, and was ready to marry.

In traditional village life marriage was more than just an agreement between a man and woman. A good match promoted harmony within the family and improved the tone of the village, so as a matter of course the elders in the family were consulted. All relatives and friends were at liberty to offer their opinions, suggestions, and gossip, and they always did. For weeks (and in a few cases, years) the betrothed couple were the focus of scrutiny and speculation, but in the end it was the father who decided who the child would marry, unless the process was derailed with an unexpected pregnancy.

Everything we have heard about Grgurjevi took on new importance as the union with this house was considered. Grgurjova was still loud and controlling. Jožef remembered his virtuous niece, Marija Bilkotova, had not been a good enough match for her son. Marija Rejčeva had not been good enough for her either and despite the hurt Rejčeva had endured because of her fidelity to Joe, Grgurjova could not find it in her heart to say a kind word to her. Could she be equally cruel to his daughter? Grgurjova had driven her sons, Joe and John, to Cleveland although she could now praise them for the money they sent. She had been opposed to Frane's marriage, disinherited him, and forced him to move to Bač. Now he was dead, shot in the back by an Italian collaborator, his sons orphaned and embittered. Jožef still felt Grgurjova was partly to blame for Frane's death. On the plus side, Drej, the new young master of Grgurjevi, was married to a daughter from the house of Berhan, with the blessing of his mean-mouthed mother. This had merit in Jozef's eyes because his wife's sister was married to the master at Berhan. The mutual respect they felt for their Berhan connections had potential for creating a bit of harmony in the village.

A big sticking point in any Slovene marriage was the dowry the bride's family gave to the man's family. Jožef would have to negotiate this with Drej, the young tubercular master who Jožef still viewed as a boy. It was not just whether Miha would be a hardworking sober man ready to support a family, but the thought of giving money, livestock, or property to Miha's family to jumpstart his life was hard to swallow. This is what Jožef had to say:

22 November 1936

You ask me about my daughter Marija and Miha. She is 20 years old and Miha is 26. He is small and wide; his height is unlike the other Grgurs and his behavior is also very different. Overall, he is knowledgeable, people like him, and he does not let anyone resent him, so you are surprised we were against it. I am satisfied with the boy, but I know what opinion the rest of the family has about Grgurjevi, so we held back until we could see if the old ones were satisfied with the marriage. Marija and Miha were sad we were against it and now we will let it be. You wrote in your opinion his brother, little Drej, was a nice boy. He was, but when he came back from the military, he was sick, thin, green, and without muscles. I liked Frane, and I like Miha. The old ones like Miha.

They would like to get married in the spring. The last thing we need is a wedding and for Drej Grgur to come and negotiate the dowry. The first time I talked to that boy, I told him he should not expect to get any money from us. There are nine of us, and for many years we have had to pay the hospital and bury the livestock in the pit. The dowry will be difficult for us. The bigger the kids are, the bigger the problems and expenses. Franca trained to be a seamstress so we bought her a machine. We have to buy clothes and shoes and we pay high taxes, and if I have to give large dowries, then the old ones should go and start begging.

Miha and Marija did marry, and they were given, or bought Maharinčevi, the house next door to Biščevi and directly across the street from Grgurjevi. They had two children, Marija and Josef (what else?). I met Miha and Marija in 1977. Miha was a small pleasant man who was always hitching up his pants to keep them from falling down as he went about the business of his farm, and caring for the animals. He was notably humble, and hardworking.

Jožef usually wrote to Mary just as soon as he received a letter, but the Christmas of 1936 passed without a package containing treats, magazines, used clothing, or a dollar for Mama. Jožef wrote on 10 January 1937 and diplomatically mentioned the absence of holiday letters.

> It seems odd we have not received any letters from you for the holidays. The last letter I received was the one from November, when you sent a couple of dollars to Mama. I replied to that letter, and Mama also wrote back, and we wished you happy holidays and New Year. I would think that you would have written to us for the holidays, but maybe Postmistress Gastjova took it, and read it.
>
> Winter weather is mostly rainy and generally unhealthy. Many people have been sick, and five of us were in bed for a few days. This sickness makes your head hurt, all your limbs numb, and you have no appetite. Pneumonia develops from this sickness and a number of people in Trst died from it. But here, so far, nobody has died. So, you can see we had bad holidays and we are struggling through this winter. I will finish for today, as I am not in the mood for writing. I am still sick; my head hurts and I am waiting for your letter.

The following week the mail arrived, delayed by a world-wide influenza epidemic that struck over the winter of 1936–1937. Jožef described its symptoms perfectly. It was during this outbreak the first influenza virus was isolated and work began on a vaccine.

> *17 January 1937*
> I received your letter from 27 December. Now I know the reason I did not receive your letter! I was blaming the post mistress but she was innocent. As one can see from the letters, the cause of the delay is the illness here is the same one as you have in America. The winter has been very mild and the illness is everywhere. Now for a few days we have a little snow, but the cold is not harsh.

You wrote Ivanka is thinking about coming when my daughter gets married. We would like this immensely. Mama cried from happiness! You and Janez should also come. I think Janez would like to see these places again and he should come because of the farm. The wedding is planned for the month of May. The exact date does not matter; we could set the date for 20 days after she arrives. That time would be nice for Ivanka because the month of May is the most beautiful. All nature is alive and the sea voyage should be nice.

Everything else is as usual, health is progressing slowly, and we are all fine. We are sending you our best regards. We wish you lots of fun for *Pust*—the young ones should enjoy it. Once they are my age, they will have no will for such things.

CHAPTER SEVENTEEN

1937: Jane's Visit

J ane Fradel's first job after becoming a registered nurse in June 1936 was at the Montefiore Hospital in Pittsburgh. Her mother wrote to her often, "Just so that you know that we are alive." In addition to her relatives in Europe, my grandmother stayed in touch with her friends and children with regular letters, a habit she continued even after telephones became a standard feature in American homes. In my childhood home my father received a letter from his mother every week, even in the 1970s. The first words "Draga Joe," were all I could understand and I bet the last ones were "Just so you know that I am alive..."

The influenza epidemic of 1936-37 swept through Montefiore Hospital six months after Jane started her job. She contracted the illness which exacerbated her asthma. She took time to recover at home under the care of her local doctor, and her mother. In Pittsburgh, Jane lived in the nurses' residence, her employment was steady, and she earned enough to buy blouses for her sisters, help pay some bills, and still saved for a trip to Europe to attend Marija Biščeva's wedding. Her mother, on the other hand, worried about paying the two-dollar doctor's fee, though she frequently managed to send two dollars to her mother in Italy. Her brother's laments about poor crops, dying livestock, taxes, and hospital bills would certainly make anyone want to help him, but he never asked her for money. He was grateful for used clothes, books, and magazines. No mention is made of financial agreements between Jožef and John for his role at Jurkotevi but I imagine Jožef got some compensation from the Jurkotevi account. Jane had only recently returned to work when her mother wrote her this letter in Slovene containing the quiet chatter of daily routines and minor events.

> *Tuesday, 12 January 1937*
> Draga Ivanka,
> It is now 18 minutes past nine. I just sent the little birds off to school. Father is not working and he is getting up just now. I told him a healthy person should not be allowed to sleep so late. Last week he worked two days; there has been nothing yet this week, and he doesn't know when there will be. Johnny has not worked this week either, so there will be no money for us this payday, which makes me angry. Mary worked for Mahady in his law office for seven hours on Friday, but he has not paid her yet. Mr. Funk said he has to pay at least 30 cents an hour and he will see that she gets that.
> Yesterday a parcel came from Gimbels. Sylvia and Mary were so happy with the blouses, they immediately tried them on. I think they are beautiful. Thank you so much! Now the girls and Joe are at school, Father is sitting by the radio and Johnny is in the kitchen reading. On Friday, I got a letter from Mary Ban in Pittsburg. She told me you visited them; they can hardly wait until you come again. How are things otherwise, have you recovered from your asthma? Just now we got a bill from Dr. Eiseman; it was almost two dollars, but you are sure to help? I would like to start to pay it off, but what cannot be, will not be; nothing is left for the family to live on other than the hope perhaps things will be better again soon.
> Today I have nothing more to report, but I wanted to write, just so that you know we are alive. *Mother*

On 1 February, Marija Biščeva, the bride-to-be, sent a wedding invitation.

> My beloved Aunt,
>   I'm very excited Ivanka would like to come to my wedding. I cannot express how much happiness this would bring me! But even more, I would love to have You and Janez in our company for my wedding day. Among all our relatives, we have very few who will come. On my mother's side, there is just the bride and small children, and You know about my father's side. Bilkotevi keep to themselves and ever since Aunt Tona died, Bazletevi do not know us apart from Fanika who does write to me from Jugoslavia; the poor girl often writes she is homesick. Now I hope and expect at least my first cousin, Ivanka, will come, and we will spend a couple of happy hours together.
>   *Marija Fabjančič*

Aside from the cost of the passage, the Fradels had other things to consider. John was barely working and if he went to Europe, he might not have a job when he returned. Mary did not feel up to going on a voyage with Jane, and leaving her husband and three high school children to fend for themselves. Circumstances arose that required Marija and Miha to be married before May, so Jane was unable to attend, and her travel dates became flexible.

Jane and Anna Mae Sweeney, another nurse from Latrobe, were in high spirits when they went to New York to board the steamship *Champlain* on 3 June with all the other elegant travelers bound for Le Havre, France. They each spent $159 to travel in tourist class. Jane was 24 years old, curvaceous and beautiful, her Slavic facial features framed by wavy dark hair cut in an ear length bob with a side part, and she had chosen her wardrobe carefully for the trip. Her personality was strong, not the least bit shy, and although her parents thought of her trip strictly as the triumphant return of their daughter to their homeland, Jane and Anna Mae planned to have fun. They arrived in France on 10 June and headed straight to Paris for a few days, then by train to Trieste. They arrived in Povžane on 22 June, where everyone knew Jane as Ivanka. After a few weeks under Slavnik, the two friends traveled to Ljubljana, Maribor, and Vienna, then back to Povžane to depart from Trieste for the voyage home. Altogether, they were away for 12 weeks.

Jane's letters to her mother were in Slovene, but she had learned to speak the language, not to write it. Her spelling and grammar were often incorrect and some phrases were so inconsistent with written Slovene they could not be translated. Other words were made up, apparently jargon used within the family. For example *Naneta* refers to her father. *Nane* is a common nickname for John and I would guess it translates as "Little Johnny." She also affectionately calls him "Blue-eyes" and calls her mother "Little Golden Mother."

Povžane Number 4, 25 June 1937

Dear Little Golden Mom,

We are in Povžane now. Nona, Milka, and I, are in front of house number four. We are drinking coffee, and now I think it is time to write. This is how it was...

In Trieste, we stayed the night in the Hotel Metropol. On Tuesday morning we went to the station in a *karet* [cart], and by electric train to Hrpelje Kozina. The station was full of Italians. Tell father we saw Johanna Mekleva in Hrpelje; she is a nice, beautiful woman, only too fat. She has already outlived three husbands. In Hrpelje, we met a Slovenian man driving a car. He asked me if I knew a blacksmith from Hrpelje in America who had not written home in twenty years and he wanted to know why. I did not know what to tell him. He took us through Tublje and then to Povžane.

When we came to your house, Nona was standing at the big tree. As soon as she caught sight of me, she had tears. I did not cry then, but my eyes would not be dry at the end of the day. Little by little, we met the whole family. Nona told me what a pure, sweet, kind, hardworking, good girl you were (and I cried) she talked of Tona (and I cried). She said my father was a good man, a hard worker from when he was very young. She told me you and Father planned to come back after three years in America and she showed me where you intended to build a house (and we cried). In the evening when we sat down to eat supper, Nona prayed. She asked me if I knew what she was praying for, and I said yes.

The first night we heard singing in Materija. The voices from Kastelic were so loud it was possible for people in Povžane to hear. And then I went to sleep in your bed in your room which you left 24 years ago. Whoopee!

The next day, Rezina's daughters, Franca, and Tona, came to welcome me and gave me a big bag of strawberries, four eggs, and flowers. I am told the daughters sometimes visit Biščevi, but Rezina has not been there for three years. Frane Košanc brought a nice big bag of cottage cheese. Tell Father the Košančevi asked very much after him. At Liparjevi in Bač, father's Aunt Margeritha was so happy to see a photo of Naneta. Tell Rudy Fradel the Košančevi and Liparjevi and many others asked after him.

When I saw Rezina on the street, she gave me a kiss. I presented her with one gray cloth and gave her daughters three beautiful handkerchiefs. Nona was very happy with the money. I presented the other gray cloth to Uncle Pepe's wife, and gave the other cloth to the Biščevi girls because I know they are more in touch with you than Rezina and her daughters. I think the gifts are adequate for everyone, but if you think not, tell me.

Let John and Gela Ban know I gave a skirt to the Jakatova and I will give a skirt to Karolina on Sunday when we come home from church. Nona does not go to church every Sunday. Many people asked after Gela Ban and were surprised about how fat she has become. Maria of Gabrk asked after Kristina, her daughter. I had to tell her you wrote to Kristina two and a half months before I left, but she did not write back. Yesterday at Bazletevi, Bazle offered us wine, bread, and pršut. I was not hungry but I took a piece of bread so he would not be offended.

His son Ivan works in Lujzit but he came home for the night to
visit with me. His father is truly a very <u>mean</u> person. Ivan has
not lived at home for two years because of him. We talked a lot
and I have much more to tell you when I see you.

I met old Theresa Pajserova. She told me she just had a
dream that Jurkotevi and Grgurjevi had come from America.
Marija Rejčeva walked with us to Materija. She laughed as she
told me when she was a little girl, she carried letters from my
little blue-eyed father to you and she said Nona threw a stone
at her once.

I saw Pepa Blaževa and she lives on the street below Materija.
She said to me, "You look just like your mother." Almost all your
friends say that! When they look at your photo, they say you
have not changed at all. You can be pleased because all your
friends look at least 20 years older than you do.

On the eve of St. Ivan's day [June 24] they burned crosses of
juniper wood. Every village at least had one cross. We could see
the one from Hrpelje Kozina. The son of Maria of Gabrk [Tonči
Jaksetič] and the son of Drauftevi [August Babuder] have come
on their bicycles to visit us on two evenings. Last night they
serenaded us under the window to say good night. It was very
<u>cute</u>. Now it is already eight o'clock and I think I will finish this
letter. With love and kisses to the whole family, and of course
to you and Daddy.

Your daughter, *Jane*

Jane's 16-year-old sister Mary wrote back for the family in English.
(I'll call her Mary Elizabeth to differentiate her from all the other
Marys and Marijas.) Her first letter was there to greet Jane on her
arrival in Povžane.

Latrobe, 15 June 1937
Dear Jane,
Everything's OK in Latrobe and I hope you are, too. I went
to Canton in Ohio with Rudy, his parents, his aunt and the
Morellas. We traveled in two cars. We left for Canton at eight

o'clock Sunday morning and got home at eight o'clock Monday morning. On the way, we had a flat tire, and coming home we had a blowout.

It was swell, and I'm very sure you would have had a nice time. Many asked for you. Ludwig Zupančič was dressed "spiffily." He told me he has two jobs, one of them is working from four to ten on the Democratic payroll. Frank Uranker was with a girlfriend. John Alick, looks very nice since he gained some weight and seemed very much interested in me.

Mr. and Mrs. Ban [John and Gela Skominčič] were there. She said you're going to get it from her when you come back because you told her you'd see her before you left and you didn't, and you have not written to her. Mr. Vider asked about your trip. Mike Kumer thought your trip is swell and it's something he, too, would like to do. Rudy Zornik and his mother asked for you. John Grabenja was sorry he missed seeing you before you left.

We liked your card from New York. Mother is on a ride with the Bells, Sylvia is washing her ribbon, Joe is with Frankie, and John is at Geary's because this is his day off. Pop is working. I wanted to write to you about Canton before it got stale. But maybe it's stale to you already, considering all the exciting things you're seeing!

Your sister,
Mary Elizabeth

Interestingly, her mother instructed Mary Elizabeth to write her letters to Jane in English, so the folks in Slovenia would not be able to read them. She said she didn't want her family in Slovenia to know "how wild" they were, but what was the real reason? Did she fear the cultural gap between them had grown too wide and they no longer understood each other? Perhaps she thought people might think they were less generous than they should be. The Fradels in America had unimaginable luxuries: electricity, a radio, a car and leisure to drive two hours just to attend a picnic or dance. John spent

his earnings on flying lessons at Latrobe airport. They purchased
a porch glider and an electric fan while Jane was away. Consider
the price of their purchases: an oscillating electric fan cost $8.00
(160 lire) and a padded-back porch glider sold for $17.50 (350 lire).
By comparison, Mary sent a monetary gift to Mama $2.00 (40 lire),
while Joe and John Fabjančič sent their mother, and Andy Siskovič
sent his brother and sister, regular gifts of 100 lire or more.

Latrobe, 29 June 1937
    Dear Jane,
    Mom told me to write to you last week but we were too busy
cleaning the house: wallpaper, washing and polishing the floor,
and cleaning windows. On Saturday evening we sat on the
porch to watch people as they came and went to the Firemen's
Parade right on Spring Street. We have a new two-seat glider
on the porch that makes it very comfortable. We all like to sit
on the glider, so unless Mom and Pop want to sit down, we
scramble to get there first.
    We talked with Cecil Kobes at the parade while he was eat-
ing popcorn. He looked nice. On June 20 we went to a picnic at
Rillton, on Shuster's Farm. Martin Serro and his Trio [a polka
orchestra] were glad to see us. We also saw Louis Drop and he's
a lot of fun. On June 27 there was a picnic at Republic but it
rained so hard we sat in our car all afternoon. The hall was an
open-air pavilion, so the Trio decided to dance at someone's
house. That did not work out well, so we sat in the car with
Martin Serro and Rudy and had lots of fun while they thought
of somewhere else to go. When they finally found a place to
dance it was too late for us. It was two hours from home, so we
left. So, we didn't have any picnic or dance, but it was a good
crowd with plenty of boys and lots of fun.
    John quit at Vulcan Mold on June 15 and got a job at Geary's
the next day. Now he's almost as black as a negro! John is still at
his flying and on the night of the Firemen's Parade, he flew over
town and did a trick with his plane. Everybody just stopped

and looked at him. We felt great because we knew it was him, and you can imagine how proud Mom and Pop felt to see their own son flying!

Mom asks if there are many cherries there? You know, the big, juicy ones Mom and Pop always talk about. Mom wants news about our grandmother. Every day she thinks about what you are seeing and doing in Povžane, Bač, and Materija. On Sunday 27 June you were probably at church in Brezovica. We got your postcard from Paris today and like it very much.

Mom's ironing shirts now, Joe is painting the screen door and last week he cleaned the yard and cellar. Sylvia is working on an article for the *Mladinski List* and John and Pop are earning money. We're all so busy. July fourth will soon be here and I wonder what you will be doing. *Jaz mislim da je pa cel svet ahcet na tisti dan, pa ne.* [I feel that the whole world is waiting for this day, but it's not]. We hope that you are enjoying yourself <u>much too mucha!</u>

Your sisters,
Mary Elizabeth and Sylvia Rose Fradel

The scenes of everyday life Jane described in letters home gave her homesick mother a measure of relief but raised her father's anxiety about his neglected house and farm. Visiting their loved ones, enjoying traditional foods, music, dancing, and walking to church, brought back memories John and Mary could savor through their daughter's eyes.

Povžane No. 4, 30 June 1937
Dear Little Mother and the whole family,

Yesterday I went to see Daddy's sister, Antonija, at Artviže. She is a really great woman. She was happy to see a Jurkotova again, the daughter of Naneta and Marica. She gave me a big piece of butter. She has four beautiful children, especially two-year-old Slavica, a boyish blue-eyed blonde. It is very nice here, but we are going to have to leave on the 12th of August if we

want to go on that steamer. If not, we will have to wait until
the 2nd of September. I want to be sure to save enough money
so father or you can come to the old place another summer.

On Sunday, we walked to church in Brezovica. I saw the
Biščevi and Jurkotevi graves. The church is surrounded perfectly by the linden trees and its interior is beautiful. The singing is truly moving, and the bells sound wonderful. On Monday,
we took the bus to Trieste and stayed with the Bilkotevi's Marija. She had a big banquet for us and showed us all of Trieste
including the American Consulate. She wanted us to stay longer but we could not, so we will go next Saturday and Sunday
to visit her again.

We danced at opasilo in Gradišica. Zora Bazletova was
there with her boyfriend. Tona and Francka Bilkotova came
with their boyfriends. Jože and Francka from Biščevi, Ivan
Bazle, Anna Mae and I went together and we drank paškareto.
We went to Odolina to see the church of St. Peter that was
built in 1630. We went to Fiume [Rijeka] by bus and visited the
Bazletevi boy in the hospital, Karel. I gave him some cakes to
eat and he looked happy to see us.

Materija will have opasilo on the 18 July, then we will go to
Vienna, and then we will make for home if we are able to get
space. We were so comfortable on the French line it matters
little whether we go back to France to take the Champlain, or
we could go through the Adriatic on an Italian steamer.

Nona is a very sweet, cozy, and dear woman. But of the others, I do not like to say much. Enough for today. Goodbye and
don't forget to send money. *Ivanka*

Jane enclosed a letter to her little sister in English much different
from the one her parents received.

Dear Mary Elizabeth,

The ocean trip was marvelous and we had a 100 percent
good time. Povžane and Materija are dead but I enjoy Trieste
and Fiume very much. In this locality there is hardly anyone

of my age we can associate with. There was one opasilo, it was fair, and on the 18th, there will be one here. I know that Jugo-Slavia (sic) will be a swell place. Things are different there. I understand Pepina Jurkotova married quite well. Mr. Kastelic [Božidar] gave me the address of his nephew who is a banker (he is married) who we are to visit in Maribor. Mr. Kastelic taught me some German so when we are in Vienna we will not be completely lost. *Jane*

Latrobe, July 7, 1937
    Dear Jane,
    We were really excited to receive your first letter. Mom read it while all of us kids listened. When Mom read the part where you cried, she laughed, cried, and read it—all at the same time. We were interested in every word. Mom thought it odd you didn't tell us anything about Uncle Pepe.
    Christina of Gabrk and her family were here for three days, July 3, 4, 5. You probably know this by now because she sent you a postcard. Christina liked it here very much and when it was time to go, she would have liked to stay longer. We visited John and Gela Ban and she was very *huda* [angry] because you didn't come over. She baked two *poticas* [traditional rolled sweet bread with nuts] on the day that was circled on her calendar. One potica was to eat that day and then to take home, and the other was to take on your trip. We stopped at the airport and Mr. Carroll [Charlie Carroll, founder of the airport and flying instructor, gave scenic rides for 50 cents] took Sylvia up in the airplane. I did not go up, but the next chance I get, I am going to grab it. *Pa še kako!* [and how!]
    On Sunday, the 4th of July, there were 12 of us for supper including Uncle Rudy Fradel. Johnnie Kobes showed us the pictures of you that were taken at New York. As he helped Sylvia dry the dishes, Christina just about fell in love with him because he is so well built, good looking, and nice.
    Rudy was supposed to come today but he has to play with the Trio seven days out of nine so we decided it was best for

him to rest while he has this chance. Rudy sings, *"Moje Dekle Je Še Mlado"* on the Trio recording. [A popular song that can still be heard on Spotify]. He sounds nice. Now he is coming on July 14th, the day after I'll turn seventeen. We got your postcard from Hrpelje Kozina you sent from Trieste.

Your sister,
Marička [Little Mary]

Their mother was not entirely satisfied with Jane's letters and added a little scolding:

How is it you don't write anything about uncle's cows and sheep, haven't you seen them yet? Do you ever get up in the morning to see when the cattle go to pasture? And in the evening, don't the little bells on the cows and sheep tinkle? It looks like you are really not interested in what happens in Povžane and its surroundings. These quiet little villages have their attractions. You only talk about going other places. Father asks if you have seen his tumbledown house. He asks you to carefully examine everything to see what kind of damage it has.

Povžane No. 4, 13 July 1937
HAPPY BIRTHDAY MARY ELIZABETH! HOW DOES IT FEEL TO BE SEVENTEEN AND NEVER BEEN KISSED?
Dear Little Golden Mother,
Yesterday we were happy to receive the letter which you wrote on 30 June, and Anna Mae got a letter from her sister. Since we have been in Slovenia, we have had a very good time, even on the 4th of July. Yesterday we were at the office of the Italian Line. We will leave on the *Saturnia* on 12 August and arrive between 27 and 30 August. It's a shame it is necessary to go, but when one doesn't have money, one has to go home. I hope to earn enough so that you, Mother, will be able to go to the old place in the springtime. While we were in Trieste, we saw Zora Bazleteva; I have plenty to tell you about her. There are many other things to talk about; when you hear the stories you've been told before, from a different point of view, your

heart will feel better. Anna Mae and I go to Tublje almost every day to walk. One day I raked hay with students at Jurkotevi. Daddy's house has been torn down but it looks more like the wind demolished it. I have plenty to say about this as well.

I will tell your friends again that you greet them. Marija of Gabrk and Pepa Blaževa are great women. I will have plenty to say about Pepa's husband when I come home. He reminisced about how beautiful you were, right in front of Pepa. I am going to visit Daddy's sister Antonija in Artviže one more time. She is a very great and smart woman. Rezina has been very good to me and her daughters are very kind. Frane Bilko, who is in the army, has greeted me many times and we wrote to each other.

On Saturday, Nona will bake a cake for opasilo in Materija on Sunday 18 July. She is a cute little thing. She works a lot in the house and likes to laugh. Every so often I catch her and we dance a little and she laughs so much. She says she is very happy I came, but you know she would really love to see you. Her praise for Naneta is now profuse; I don't know what she said about Dad in 1913. I bought her a cute aluminum canteen to carry water upstairs when she goes to sleep. Our people think I do not eat enough. They enjoy saying that I will be buried in Brezovica, or that I will marry in Brezovica, because one or two boys here think they are in love with me. After opasilo we are going to Ljubljana, Maribor, and Vienna. You don't have to reply to this letter because it will not arrive in Povžane before 12 August when we are going on the steamer.

When we climbed to the top of Slavnik, we took a picture of Anna Mae, August of Drauf, Tonči of Gabrk and me, with the shepherd. I hope the photo will be good.

Goodbye, Golden Mother and the whole family.

Love, *Ivanka*

Maribor, Jugoslavia, Thursday 29 July 1937

My dear Little Golden Mother,

In Jugoslavia everything is very beautiful. We have been with Daddy's sister, Pepina Jurkotova, since Sunday and we will leave on Saturday for Vienna. It would not be possible to find

<u>kinder</u> people. We have clean beds and good food, so it's really
nice to be here. Pepina and I have a good time, we understand
each other, and <u>not once</u> did she speak about the farm.

Karlina, your cousin from Trieste is also here in Maribor.
She said that you and she were great friends. Everyone tells
me what a lively, happy, plucky, and beautiful woman you were.
I tell them that you still are. We were at dinner with Marija
Geist, Daddy's cousin, the sister of Janez Ban from Pittsburgh.
Everyone praised Daddy for being so very hard working. I will
have plenty more to say when I get home! We went to a café
to dance and they enjoy the same music we know. On another
evening we went to a concert given by the Jadran Society, which
is the Primorska choral society in Maribor. They sang *The Last
Supper* very beautifully and I thought of you, little Mommy.

Tomorrow we are going mountain climbing in Pahorje. If
Rudy Fradel comes to visit you, tell him that his sisters send
their best wishes. Until now they thought, for some unknown
reason, that he had lost an eye. They were very happy when I
told them that this was not so.

It is nice here but I am homesick for Materija, Nona, and
<u>somebody else</u>. I enjoyed myself on opasilo. But why wouldn't
little Jennie enjoy herself? I sent cards to Nona from Ljubljana
and Maribor just so they will know that I am alive.

Goodbye and Best wishes, *Ivanka*

Jane wrote home upon their return to Povžane after their 16-day
tour of Ljubljana, Maribor, and Vienna. The long train ride from
Vienna to Trieste gave them the opportunity to appreciate the land-
scape of snowcapped mountains, lakes, stone train bridges over
sparkling rivers, charming villages, and castles. After the scolding
from her mother, Jane reported Uncle had three cows, two calves,
three pigs, and three sheep. She rose at least once to see the cattle
going to the pasture and in the evening, she heard the bells on the
cows and sheep tinkling. She and Uncle Jožef planned to walk the
whole Jurkotevi farm before her departure.

On the steamship M/N SATURNIA, *Thursday, 12 August 1937*

Dear Little Golden Mother and the whole family,

I am on the steamship on my way back to America. My cabin is nice and I am sitting in bed as I write this letter. The Adriatic Sea is beautiful, but when you said the sun shines most beautifully in Povžane and the moon is most beautiful in Povžane, you spoke the truth.

Before we left, we danced at the opasilo in Tublje, I saw all of Daddy's farm, and I visited your Aunt Terezija in Trieste on Sunday. I cried when I had to leave such good people and such a lovely place. Someday I will go back to see your old homeland and Mother, you will go with me. I have plenty to tell you—I believe I will be able to talk for a whole month and still not say everything. We could have stayed longer but we have to go home so we can earn money again. Thank you for the money you sent. Now I owe you $120.

Anna Mae and I danced tonight on the ship. It was strange to hear American "latest hits" that are new to me, but I'm sure Mary Elizabeth will teach me and I will teach her to dance the tango when I come home. Tomorrow the steamship will stop in Dubrovnik. On 14 August, we will stop in Greece, and on 15 August we will go to Naples to see Vesuvius and Pompei. I will mail this from Naples and hopefully it will arrive before I do. Then we are going to Palermo, Sicily, where they grow lemons. It is nice on the steamship. I hope you are all as happy and healthy as I am. Enough for tonight. See you soon. *Ivanka*

The *Saturnia* arrived ahead of schedule at Ellis Island on 26 August 1937 and Jane and Anna Mae headed home. The "someone else" that Jane missed while they traveled to Maribor and Vienna was Tonči Jaksetič, one of the boys who had serenaded them on those first few evenings in Povžane. Romance had blossomed at the opasilo in Materija. Tonči was the younger brother of Kristina of Gabrk who had spent the fourth of July with the Fradels in Latrobe. Tonči's twin was Mija, and their mother was Marija of Gabrk, all part of the network that held my grandmother's life together, and now her daughter and the son of Marija of Gabrk thought they were in love! A month after her return, Jane received these letters.

Materija, September 1937

Dear heart, I'm writing to you from my heart, a few words to your heart. I hope you will write back. Dear Jane, when you left Materija on the bus and when we hugged for the last time, I started to cry. I was not at peace until I could see you once more. So, at two-thirty in the afternoon, I went to Trieste so I could see you for the last time on the steamship. I hope you saw me, too. My heart was breaking seeing you on the ocean and I was on the land. When the steamship left, I was still waving but you didn't see me at all.

Dear heart, when I went home to Materija, I reminisced about our lovely time together. Oh, how short a time! Since you left, my heart hasn't had any peace and it will never have peace again, my dear heart, Jane. My sister, Mija, is also sad you are gone. It reminds her of how sad it was when Kristina left.

Dear, unforgettable, loved one, I am sending you my picture so you have a remembrance of me and will think of those hours we were together, happy, and satisfied. With this I will finish. Hugs and love, *Tonči*

Materija, 5 October 1937

Dear Ivanka,

I was really satisfied and happy to receive your letter on 30th September. Dear One, are you still considering returning to our place next summer as you talked about? Dear One, (valuable, golden one) what are you doing that is interesting in America? I think it is better there than here... right? If possible, I would love to have a copy of the picture we took together up on Slavnik.

Dear One, do you remember the evening when you mentioned the way the moon was shining? I will not forget this. Oh,

how we had a good time and how we willingly liked each other ...
and God willing, we still will. Jane, I wish that it would be so.

With this I conclude and I send with happiness and kisses,
yours (you know) and I am always thinking of you. *Tonči*

*

Jane took classes at the University of Pittsburgh and worked at Montefiore Hospital. She remained active in socialist politics and S.N.P.J., and was a big supporter of President Franklin Delano Roosevelt. In 1938 she wrote an article about her trip published in two-parts in *Prosveta,* the S.N.P.J. bi-monthly newspaper.

A regular contributor to *Prosveta* was Louis Adamic, a Slovenian immigrant who became a successful American writer. A Guggenheim Fellowship enabled him to travel to Yugoslavia and write his 1934 book, *The Native's Return.* His descriptions of life in Montenegro, Croatia and Serbia tell of dire poverty, backwardness, and political repression, yet in describing life around his former home in Blato in Yugoslavian Slovenia, he paints a rosy picture of folksy, happy prosperity. In her *Prosveta* articles, Jane gave a romanticized picture of Primorskan farm life that was derivative of Adamic's writing style and his stereotyped depiction of the happy Slovene who always had time to sing, dance, play the accordian, and eat potica, despite his hard life.

She acknowledged irredentismo but emphasized that the stubborn cheerful spirit of Slovenes could not be repressed. She praised the accomplishments of Mussolini: tree lined highways, the clean canals, and sparkling white buildings of Trieste, the friendly, broadminded carabinieri stationed in Materija who spoke to her in Slovene. She commended the lovely modern market of Trieste, but neglected to say anything about the taxation on agricultural products that were sold there—a taxation so severe that Slovene peasants were forced to sell their farms at auction and flee to Maribor.

At age 24, Jane might be accused of political naiveté, or conversely, be credited with embracing the world with an open mind and kind heart. She did not see life in Povžane through her Uncle Jožef's eyes. Her positive views on the accomplishments of Mussolini and fascism were not hers alone. In 1937, many in the U.S. and Britain still admired him for his economic achievements and governments sought to make deals with him and steer him away from an alliance with Hitler.

*

Tonči was five years younger than Jane. When he turned 21 in 1939, he was conscripted into the Italian army. Italy was already at war in North Africa and Albania. In 1942, his troop transport ship was hit and he was killed. Jane did not return to Slovenia the next summer, nor ever again.

CHAPTER EIGHTEEN

1938: Nieces and Nephews

When I was 24, the same age that Jane had been on her visit, I also visited Povžane. My arrival in May 1977 was one month short of 40 years since Jane's arrival in June 1937, and no one else from the family in America had visited in that period. May was indeed a beautiful month, just as Jožef had suggested to Jane.

Before I left for my world travels I visited my grandmother in 1975 to tell her about my intentions and say goodbye, and she urged me to visit her village. I had only a vague notion that I would ever get to Yugoslavia. In fact, my geography was pretty bad and most of the time I had no idea where I was going. My plan was to spend some time in Australia with a boyfriend, and then go with the flow. Grandma let Maria Basioli know that I might call on her in Sydney, and when I did, I was welcomed as a long lost cousin. I visited with her family twice and told her of my plans to travel overland through Asia back to the U.S., which could include stopping in Povžane. She wrote to her parents Marija and Miha Fabjančič at Maharinčevi to introduce me.

I left Istanbul at the end of April 1977 on the Orient Express—a train that fell very short of the expectations of grandeur the name might invoke. The toilet was a hole in the floor and there was no food or water available to purchase. If it had not been for the generosity of

the Turkish families traveling to work in Europe who shared their
baskets of food with me, it would have been a hungry three days
on that slow-moving train. Sometimes it did not move at all and
just sat in the fields of Bulgaria for hours at a time. I couldn't even
purchase a cup of tea from the vendors in the stations because I had
no Bulgarian coins and nowhere to change money. I happily got off
the Orient Express in Trieste and walked several miles north from
the city center to a youth hostel, which was once a grand house overlooking the Adriatic Sea. I toured another well-preserved palace in
the same neighborhood, with ornate, gilded walls and ceilings, tall
windows admitting lots of light, and views of the Adriatic; sometimes I wonder if Zora worked in such a place. I stayed in Trieste
only two days, just enough time to rest up, do some laundry, and find
the bus station. Getting to Povžane required a bus ride to the border
of Yugoslavia, leaving the bus to pass customs, then waiting by the
side of a rural road for another bus. I could have sat there for hours
or days, not knowing if or when a bus would come—so I started
hitchhiking. Within a few minutes, a border guard getting off work
picked me up. He knew a little English. When I told him where I
was going, he said he knew those people and would take me there.

When we arrived, he knocked on the door of Povžane #4. Janez
Fabjančič, the younger son of our letter writer, Jožef, opened the door.
Yes, they knew who I was, and they led me and the border guard into
a formal room set with a big table, and offered us food and drink.
Then they called for their daughter, a university student who spoke
some English. The atmosphere was stiff, if not unfriendly, and I had
a sinking feeling that my unannounced arrival, perhaps my whole
visit, was a mistake. After what seemed like a very long time, the
border guard left, and the mood suddenly lightened. An animated
conversation ensued with my cousin struggling to translate, and a lot
of hand gestures. I asked her what was going on when I first arrived.

"Oh, we do not like him. He is Serbian." This was communist
Yugoslavia, and Tito's system of surveillance of one ethnic group by
another was still in force.

I spent just the weekend there, relying totally on my cousin's translations, and she was only home for the May Day weekend, so I went back to Ljubljana with her. But we packed a lot into those few days. I had the village tour including the church and the cemetery and made the rounds to meet every living relative. We went to Trieste and other places that I could not name, enjoyed an evening out at a seaside town, and stopped in to a village opasilo for a couple of polkas. Some of the older people, ones who had been young in 1937 when Jane was there, remarked: "Isn't she just like Ivanka?"

*

When Jane arrived in Povžane in June 1937, the marriage had already taken place. Cousin Marija Biščeva did not have to change her name when she married Miha Grgur because Fabjančič is not an uncommon name and they were only remotely related. The newlyweds did not go far. Maharinčevi is next door to Biščevi, her parents' home, and across the street from Grgurjevi, his parents' home. Mekovka had formerly lived there. Marica, my cousin now in Australia, was born in October, less than nine months after the wedding, and a son, Josef, who still lives there, was born three years later.

As soon as the whirlwind of Jane's visit was over, the new bride Marija wrote to her aunt on 18 August.

> Dearest Aunt, Please do not be upset because I did not write sooner. As you well know, there is always so much work to do, especially in the summer. Our farm is not large, but we help out with work for the others.
> Dear Aunt, thank You for the gift You sent through Ivanka. I am happy to have this memory of You. Here, such a fabric is hard to find and very expensive. I am doing well, Miha is good, and works hard to earn money. He is caring, not an alcoholic, and does not use tobacco. If it stays like this, our life will not be bad.

Since our marriage we have little to do with Miha's family at Grgurjevi. He went there once so they could prepare a payment from the dowry. His oldest brother, Drej, argued with Miha. Drej and Grgurjova do not understand why Miha is willing to pay out thousands for a farm rather than just working for someone else. Drej does not understand that if land ownership is good for him, it is also good for us. We do not want anything from them. So, You see, Aunt, it was not enough for them to destroy life for Jože Grgur and Marija Rejčeva, for whom they still wish only bad. Ivanka will tell You that Marija asked her one day if she knew anything more about Jože. She complained about him and cursed him; he is to blame she is still here rather than in America, if he had invited her, she would have gone. She would, at least, like to have his address in Cleveland so she could write to him once more. Ivanka said she really felt sorry for her. Grgurjevi cut Frane out of their will and forced him to move to Bač, and then he was killed. If it had been different, he might still be alive today. Drej and Grgurjova want to do the same to Miha because he does not want to listen to them, and they want to take the dowry away from him. You can understand why there is such anger. Z Bogom, *Marija Fabjančič*

Mary cared a lot about her nieces and nephews and had she stayed in Povžane, she fantasized they would have been the best of friends to her children. Jane was like a ribbon that tied them all together, and after her visit, they stayed in contact with each other. In a world that was rapidly getting darker, they always shared a memory of a golden peaceful time from that summer of 1937.

Jane's experience in Slovenia made her even more invaluable to her parents. Her mother could talk about home, and Jane understood. Jožef's daughters: Marija, Milka and Pepca, initially connected to their Aunt Mary as scribes for their Nona, and later as independent correspondents. Fani Colja wrote like a little sister would write to a big sister. Zora and Ivan Godina thought of her as their maternal substitute and benefactress. Marija Bilkotova, Rezina's oldest daughter wrote to her Aunt Mary, but because of Rezina's coldness, the younger ones missed out.

Zora Godina, the younger daughter of Tona, worked in many fine homes in Trieste and spoke Italian well. She appeared a modern, sophisticated woman—attractive, with dark hair, an angular face, and a nice figure. Zora had an eye for boys, and a reputation for being "loose" and "headstrong." Her mother feared that Zora would do things she would regret, like consorting with Italian men. Zora changed jobs frequently and seemed to be unwell a lot—perhaps some of it was induced by the stress she experienced as she bounced between city and village culture. When feeling poorly, she took refuge with her mother to buffer the ups and downs of her life. Zora was 27 when her mother died. Estranged from her father, separated from her more traditional sister, Fani, and judged poorly by people from her village, she felt alone. She wrote to her Aunt Mary from her place of employment in Trieste at the time of Jane's visit. She obviously had not been at the wedding of Miha and Marija, nor been in touch with anyone in the village, because she did not know Jane had already arrived as she wrote.

> *27 June 1937*
> Dear Aunt!!!
> I know that You will be surprised I am writing to You. I did not need to write to You when my Mama was alive, but now, dear God, unfortunately she is not anymore, and I feel her presence in many places.
> Dear Aunt, I can tell You that I am planning to get married. I've known this young man for a long time, he is a good boy and likes to work, but what good does it do when there is no work, the pay is poor and everything is so expensive? It is hard to start a family in such times. I have a job and I like to work, but the pay is low. I spent whatever savings I had when my deceased mother was sick. I have written three letters to my brother, Jože, and received no reply. Dear Aunt, I am asking You from my heart to ask him why he does not write to me. I

do not have a single soul to turn to when I need help, and that is why I asked my older brother to kindly send me some lire.

Dear Aunt, I hear that You will come this year. When will that be? Write to me so I can welcome You, I would love to see You. I feel that I will see my poor Mama in You, as I cannot forget her. She was the only one I had in this world, the only one I could talk to. Now I have no desire to go home because she is not there.

Your devoted niece, *Zora*

Jane did not form a positive view of Zora after they spent time together in Trieste, she planned to discuss her impressions with her mother in person, rather than leave it for posterity in a written letter. Zora's excessive use of "Moja draga teta" (my dear aunt) sounds like a manipulation for sympathy and favoritism that reflects the friction amongst the Biščevi, Bilkotevi, and Bazletevi branches of the family. The occasional dollar Teta Marija enclosed in a letter, worth about 20 lire, was an incentive for Zora to keep up the correspondence. Mary may have felt the manipulation from Zora but more importantly, she appreciated the frankness and honesty of Zora's letters, and recognized how emotionally close Zora had been to her dear sister, Tona. It was something they could authentically share.

Trieste 1938

Moja draga teta, I thank You for being so kind to me, it feels like my Mama. My Aunt, I can tell you how many nights and days I dream about her, she is always with me, and she always reminds me to write to You. One night I was talking to her in my dreams, and I told her my aunt wrote to me, and she answered she also needs to write to You. Dear Aunt, You can see that she loves us. Dear Aunt, it has been two years and I am still missing her.

My Aunt, Mama had written to me at work that she was very sick and I took her to the hospital, but it was too late to help her. All her body was yellow; the hospital told me they

could only give her a little more time. She did not have anyone
except my wicked father who treated her badly, just as he was
treating me badly. He was always shouting at us and telling
Mother she has never been any good. Aunt, when my Mama
was in the hospital, she cried that her sister and brother did
not visit and said if it were not for me, she would die. She cried
because I am a poor girl and soon, I would not have anyone.

Dear Aunt, let me tell You why we were angry at Biščevi.
The day I came home from Trieste to take my mother to the
hospital, little Pepka Biščeva came to the house. She was just
eight years old. She liked me a lot. I brought some sweet ver-
mouth for my Mama, and Pepka said she liked it, too. I poured
some for my mother into a white cup, together with sugar and
eggs, and Pepka was watching and waiting for me to give her
some. I gave her a little from another cup. But Pepka's mother
claimed my mother gave her the same cup to drink from. It was
a hot summer day and the air was bad, and later Pepka was not
feeling well. The next day, when I was taking my mother to the
hospital, Biščeva told everyone my mother was purposely giving tuberculosis to children by sharing the same cup. She said
my mother should be ashamed and everyone who was with
her should go to the hospital because they had tuberculosis,
too. But my Aunt, I have been sleeping with my Mama for two
days before she died and I did not get anything from her, My
dear Aunt, I can also tell you I lent Biščevi money when they
needed it, but they returned me half of it as manure they said
was worth 15 lire. When my mother was sick, they came to my
door, and said we owed them 10 lire for drying our pork meat
for us. My dear Aunt, when my Mama was dying at home, I did
not want to see them because they were not treating us in a way
that was fitting. We lost her when she closed her bright eyes
and she died after midnight, at three o'clock. And I remember
how she held hands with everyone; I still have her in front of
my eyes. Dear Aunt, Please remind my brother Jože to write to
me; he has not replied to any of my letters. Ivanka and I got
along well and I hope she will continue to write to me. I send

regards to Your entire family and I kiss You all. I also send You
regards from my boyfriend. Regards, *Zora*

Pepka Biščeva eventually had tuberculosis, but she had ample exposure to her sister, Francka, who had been frail and sick with it most
of her life. After Tona's death, Marija Fabjančič, the new bride, took
on the role of chief scribe for her Nona, Mary's mother. Her letters
were typical and repetitive.

> My dear Daughter! You had not written in such a long time I
> was afraid that you were very sick. Thank you so much for the
> two dollars. That God would repay it to you a thousand times,
> that you still remember your mother; because Rezina does not
> know me, or that I am her mother. Once again, I am sending
> best regards to all and wish you all good health. *Your Mama*
>   Beloved Aunt, I am also sending best regards to You, broth-
> er-in-law and to my lovely cousins. Z Bogom *Fabjančič Marija*

*

On 12 March 1938, in a move called Anschluss (Union), Germany
peacefully annexed Austria. This demonstration of German power
had long been dreaded by both Italy and Yugoslavia. During a
country-wide referendum held in Austria, 99 percent of the voters
supported Anschluss. The events in Austria were not discussed in
letters between members of the family and it was all too obvious to
everyone on both sides of the Atlantic where this was going. In fact,
the tension in Europe may have been a factor in Jane's decision not
to return to Povžane in 1938.

*

Zora was lonely and wrote every month to her Teta Marija. She
talked about her boyfriend, the difficulties of earning enough

money, missing her mother, and her brother Ivan. Fani in Yugoslavia did not write to Zora. Joe Godina had stopped writing to everybody in Europe after his mother's death, and his brother and sisters felt that he was dead to them. By September, Zora made the decision to move in with her boyfriend, and before long they married. It was not destined to last, however the details of this are lost.

Zora felt closest to Ivan, who turned 16 the month their mother died, and quickly found work away from home to escape from his father. On his days off, he saw Zora in Trieste and visited Karel at the hospital in Rijeka. When he turned 18 on 1 January 1938, he enlisted in the Italian Army and was stationed in Pola. Zora and Ivan wrote frequently and encouraged each other. Ivan was embarrassed to write to his aunt because of his poorly written Slovene, so Zora sent Ivan's address to Teta Marija and asked her to write to him. Mary reached out to Ivan—their relationship would grow stronger over the years—and Ivan's response was a technological breakthrough in the annals of the family correspondence: it was typewritten! He was proud of himself, yet shy about showing off.

On the other side of the stationary was a handwritten note:

> My Dear Aunt,
>
> You should not resent me for writing on the typewriter; I only wanted to show You that I have learned to type since I am with the Navy. If my sister Zora told You that I do not know how to write in Slovene that, of course, is not true. I just wanted her to write to You because she writes more nicely than I do, doesn't she? Everything that I know about writing Slovene is what my deceased Mama taught me when I was a small boy. She loved me so much. I am sorry I could not help her. I was still a small boy and we had to suffer together at home. This should be enough of these writings of mine for now; I will continue next time. I am sending my best regards and kisses to the entire family,
>
> *Ivan Godina*

5 Nov 1938

My dear aunt,

I send You best regards from my heart. I received Your precious letter a few days ago, one that I never expected. You wrote that my brother Jože and You talked about sending me tickets to come to America. I would love to go, but it is too late; America will not let me come anymore. How are Jože and his wife? Is there love between them, or is it like it was with my deceased Mama? I am surprised that they are still without a baby.

Dear aunt, today I did well on my final exams. The top 30 students have been chosen to learn to use typewriters so this is how I am writing to You. Now I will do practical work in the hospital here in Pola. On 14 December I go on vacation for 15 days, but I have nowhere to go since my father is at home alone and that will be no fun.

I send my best regards to Ivanka. I am sorry that she left without coming to see me. In the first days, we spent a lot of time together. She said that she had things that You asked her to tell me, but unfortunately, she never told me anything. I would love to have the photograph that she, Jože Biščev, and I took together on the street in Povžane. Could You send me that picture and one of Your entire family? Since I do not know my cousins, I would at least like to have a photograph of them. I will also send You a nicer photograph of me; the last one was taken before I knew how to wear the Navy uniform.

Dear aunt, I will leave school now that exams are over. Other students are glad to finish, but I would prefer to stay here. I have learned a lot these nine months in the Navy, including Italian, geography, arithmetic, human health, and diseases. I am pleased to be living here, every day I get meat, wine, fruits, and a stew. Please reply and send me the address of my brother Jože.

Ivan Godina

The letters Jane wrote home during her sojourn in Slovenia were filled with a sweetness, joy, and excitement that cast a different light on the people that, thus far, have been described only by Jožef and Tona. Mama was known to be cranky, Pepa Blaževa was less than noble, Rezina was distant and self-centered, and Antonija and Pepina Fradel were alternately angry or pathetic. Jane, however, saw them all as lovely, strong women. She was well-schooled by her mother about what she put in writing, never knowing what other eyes might see the letter. She adhered to the norm for ladies that *if you cannot say something good about a person, don't say anything at all*, but Jane was not always sweet, and she did have opinions. She often wrote that she would tell all when she got home, and among those singled out were Jožef, his family, and Zora. What Jane said to her parents about them is not recorded, but nuances conveyed in oral history suggest that it was not positive.

Jane's opinions did not change her mother's affection for her brother nor his for her, but life was passing by, and the facts were all too apparent. John was never coming home, not even to make one small visit to relieve Jožef of his responsibility for the four acres under Slavnik. All talk of summer visits stopped as Europe braced for war. Without his previous hopes, and in the pits of local economic and political despair, Jožef had less and less to say and little motivation to write. His letters became sparse.

5 September 1938

Dear Sister and Janez!!! I wrote to you in the beginning of July, but I have not received your answer. Mama received the money that you sent and we could see that the bank ate a lot of it. You wrote that you sent five dollars [100 lire], but what we got was 75 lire, which means that the bank took almost one dollar. We had to go to Trst to get the money because they only sent us a check. Mama was very pleased and she thanks you from her heart. You know, Marija, she does not request any treats except coffee now and then, and she drinks wine twice a day. She would drink as much as she had, but I cannot afford that much. We often do not even have enough to have salt at home. Therefore, she is extremely pleased when you send her a dollar or two so that she can afford a liter of wine.

Dear Sister, I do not know if you have read about what is going on here in Italy. Last year we got a notice from the State that everyone whose land tax is more than 130 lire, must also lend money to the State. First, the loan was to be 800 lire and then it increased to 2,358 lire, and it was even more for the rich ones. Last year they said that the cooperative must also lend money to the State. We complained that there is nowhere to take this money from and so it got delayed until this year. Now a note came that we need to lend the State 11,150. I am telling you, 11,150 lire! Additionally, there are 850 lire of taxes and also 3,000 lire more to pay. This is almost 16,000 lire [$800]. This is hanging above our heads. Even if we were to give them this money, we would still have to pay 425 lire per year in taxes for the next 25 years. They say that in 25 years the State will return the money. But this is very hard to do here. Even if half of us make the effort to contribute, what do you do with the other half? How do you collect money from them? The entire sum needs to be paid in six parts. If we do not pay, then some bank will pay for us, but all this needs to be formulated and we will lose our land. Now they say that this will also come upon the smaller land owners, and we cannot protect ourselves. In these times nobody will buy your farm, because people are as scared as a sparrow when a cat jumps on it.

Dear Sister, everything moves slowly here. There is enough hay if we can keep the livestock. We will have some potatoes; it looks that they will not rot away. I was well over the summer, but now I've been weak in my legs for a month and I get tired fast. I've been in bed twice, each time for four days. I haven't been this weak since the operation. How are you? Do Ivanka or Marija plan to marry soon? What are Janezek and Jože doing?

Joe and Mary graduated from Latrobe High School in June 1938. Joe, my father, went straight to work for McKenna Metal. Phillip

McKenna had recently patented a new technology, a tungsten tita-
nium carbide alloy, that when used in machining steel could rapidly
produce tools that cut faster and lasted longer. The plant in Latrobe
opened that year with 12 employees and Joe was among the first.
McKenna Metal became Kennametal in 1941, flourished during the
war years, and today produces tools in 60 countries and is the
second largest metal company in the world. My father would work
there until he enlisted in the U.S. Army in 1942. Meanwhile, his
real interests were cars and his brother's airplane. Mary's part-time
secretarial job at the Mahady and Mahady Law Firm became full
time after her graduation and she worked there until her marriage
on 7 August 1941 to Matt Hrebar.

*

On 30 September 1938 Italy, France and Britain signed the Munich
Agreement, which allowed Nazi Germany to annex the Sudetenland,
a region of Czechoslovakia with a German majority population.
Hitler promised that it would be the last territory he would claim,
and the Agreement was seen as the only alternative to war.

*

Viktor Colja's family lived in the Italian-occupied city of Gorica,
and while he was working at the gostilna at Gabrk, where he met
Fani, his parents fled to Ljubljana. Viktor was also forced out of
Primorska for political reasons and Fani and Viktor moved in with
his parents. After six years of marriage, they looked to Maribor to
find their own place. Fani kept her aunt in America updated on her
activities with regular letters. Without giving any reason, her Aunt
Mary specifically asked her to check in on Fani's Uncle Milan, her
father's younger brother, when she visited Maribor.

Milan Godina had been in Maribor since before the Great War
and did policework, as so many Primorskans did. He married Marija

Nedoj from Pajserevi, the Povžane neighbors that Jožef Fabjančič
mentioned—often in admiration or envy. During Fani's visit, her
Uncle Milan revealed that his wife had mental illness. Their eldest
daughter, Milena Godina, was a rising actress in Maribor and they
had a son, Albin, and another daughter, Marija.

Here is Fani's reply to her aunt's query about Milan Godina.

October 1938
My Beloved Aunt!
A few days ago, I received Your dear little letter with two
photographs. We congratulate You from our hearts for Your
25th wedding anniversary. Aunt, You say that in these years
You have experienced everything, good and bad. Even though
we have been together for only six years we have also experienced so much happiness and so much loss. Aunt, You do
not look like You have been married for 25 years. In the photograph You look like an 18-year-old girl. You are really cute,
and Uncle is so strong; there is nothing wrong with him either.

Aunt, You asked me about my uncle. On September 15th we
were in Maribor and I went to see them. The boy [Albin] was
the friendliest of all and Uncle [Milan Godina] talked to us a
little bit, but Aunt [Marija Nedoj] and the girls [Milenka and
Marija] did not have much time for us, though it is true that
we left rather early because we had other errands. I teased the
uncle a little bit, by saying that the aunt is fat. He said that she
is fat, but that she is not very healthy. He said that she was in a
very poor condition when she came from the hospital. When I
asked him what happened to her, he said that she had nervous
breakdowns, was completely crazy and that now she cannot
work or think much, that her nerves are not good. When I was
in Ljubljana, I had heard that she was sick, but I could never
find out what was wrong with her. In Maribor there are many
natives of Primorska; I know some of the younger ones, but I
do not know many people that are her age that would give me
news about her. The distance from Ljubljana to Maribor is the

same as the distance from Ljubljana to Trieste and sometimes people lose interest in things that happen so far away.

We are healthy and I wish the same for You and Your entire family, precious health. Aunt, I still remember the mlinček, and the wooden doll that You bought when You went to Trieste to sell the peas. I remember that You sewed clothes at home for the little doll. My beloved aunty, when I think of Your departure and our last farewell, tears start flowing down my cheeks. That one needs to go so far away, to be so far from each other, is so sad. Greetings and kisses, Your *Fani*

A *mlinček* is a coffee grinder. Trieste used to be famous for good coffee and related supplies.

*

When I talked to my grandmother in her last years, as we sat at her kitchen table with the soft light coming in the windows, she alluded to having beaus before my grandfather. Though she enjoyed telling stories, she was not good at answering questions, so I did not push her. Decades later, after I started reading her letters, I imagined that Božidar Kastelic might have been a beau, and then, elsewhere, she mentioned how well she and Josef Ban danced together. Sometime around 1978, my father, Joe, asked her to write about her family, and she made a list of her siblings and a few aunts and uncles. While she spoke, my father grabbed a little notepad and scribbled down what she said. He never transcribed his scribblings to make sense and the spelling was atrocious. When I found these messy scraps of paper, I learned such trivia as what she put in her travel trunk, which train she took from New York to West Virginia and the like. But one intriguing note was about Milan Godina. My grandmother revealed to my father that she and Milan Godina had wanted to be married. He had given her a missal as a present, but her parents were opposed to the marriage and she was forced to return the gift.

She had no choice; it was the father who ultimately decided who the daughter would marry. My father's note adds that Milan Godina was Grandma's "most serious suitor" and I had not realized that her sister, Tona, was already married to Milan's older brother, until I read this letter.

This romance took place when my grandmother was about 20 and John Fradel was away in West Virginia. The note, and the little pebbles of truth she dropped here and there about other men, lead me to the realization that my sweet old grandmother had actually been a beautiful and vivacious heartbreaker. Milan Godina, the spurned suitor, turned to Marija Nedoj from Pajserevi and like my grandmother, she was pregnant before she was married. One can just imagine the women *educating themselves* at the expense of the reputations of my grandmother and Marija Nedoj.

CHAPTER NINETEEN

1939: Dark Skies

The Great Depression hit the agrarian countries of southeast Europe later than the industrial nations, but it hit harder and lasted longer because it intensified all pre-existing economic problems. In Yugoslavia it bottomed out in 1934, where the average peasant's income had fallen by two-thirds and bank loans were the only means of survival. Slovenia fared better than Serbia and Croatia, and they were better off than the more southern regions of Yugoslavia. Destitute people crowded into cities and the government was forced to hand out food and other relief. By the start of the Second World War in 1939, the standard of living had not even returned to its 1920 level.

Contrary to expectations, Yugoslavia did not fall apart after the assassination of King Alexander in 1934, during the worst of the economic depression. Regent Prince Paul was a strong Anglophile, educated in England, and counted many in the British aristocracy and government as personal friends. He was intelligent, mild mannered, and cultured, and in his private life enjoyed collecting fine paintings. His goal was to maintain the integrity and neutrality of the kingdom until his nephew turned 18 in September 1941. But the problems of Yugoslavia could not wait.

In addition to the kingdom's internal strife, the ascendency of Italy and Germany proved ominous. In 1935 Italy sought to add Abyssinia to its colonial empire. Britain offered to assist the invasion and split Abyssinia with Mussolini in a secret deal called the Hoare-Laval Pact. The plot was revealed, the British public was outraged, and the Pact never went into effect. Mussolini conquered Abyssinia alone, attacking the civilian population with horrendous mustard gas sprayed from airplanes. Britain quietly made other agreements with Mussolini, which were intended to keep Italy from aligning with Hitler.

After World War I, lands that once belonged to the Kingdom of Hungary were awarded to the newly created nations of Yugoslavia, Czechoslovakia, and Romania. To resist efforts Hungary might make to reclaim territory, they formed an alliance called the Little Entente, with backing from France. At their conference in June 1936, members of the alliance acknowledged that France's offer of protection had become useless when Germany sent its military into the Rhineland, breaking its post-World War One agreement that this region of Germany that borders France, would remain a demilitarized buffer between the two nations. The Little Entente reached the gloomy conclusion that the Soviet Union and Germany were the only great powers in Eastern Europe, and the victory of either one in another war would end independence for all members of the alliance.

Prince Peter tried to steer a course of neutrality through this international morass. Internally, the path was equally convoluted. The Kingdom of Yugoslavia was torn by differences in ethnicity, language, religion, and political ideology. Upon declaring the dictatorship in 1929, King Alexander had banned Croatian separatist parties, yet their continued demand for autonomy was the greatest threat to the kingdom's stability. To put a damper on divisions, he reorganized the country into nine *banovinas* (government departments), disregarding previous borders and ethnicities, and named them after rivers. Serbs were the majority in six of the banovinas.

In his message to his subjects, King Alexander presented "Yugoslav nationalism versus tribalism" as the only choice, and propaganda was delivered in schools, newsprint, radio, and cinema. Backing it all up was a ruthless squashing of dissent through arrest, imprisonment, torture, and disappearance.

The banned separatist Croatian parties moved abroad and started a fascist organization called *Ustaša* (Insurgents). The movement depended on charismatic leaders and paramilitary groups that trained in Italy and Hungary—the primary adversaries of the Yugoslav state. Ustaša made claim to a Croatian racial pureness, looking back to a time before the Turkish conquests, to claim historic rights to an independent ethnically homogenous Croatian state. Although many Croatians sympathized with Ustaša ideology, its actual membership was perhaps not more than 4,000.*

For centuries, Serbian nationalism centered on a romanticized view of the Battle of Kosovo between the Serbs and the Turks in 1389, which they felt entitled them to a large and prosperous kingdom that included territories now populated by other people. A new Serbian fascist movement combined theories about race, blood and soil, anti-Semitism, and Orthodox mysticism. As in Croatia, it appealed to a conservative population, but its membership was not more than 5,000 to 6,000 (Calic).

Communists supported the idea of a unified Yugoslavia and aimed to improve the lives of all its people by the elimination of class differences in a new egalitarian global order, a message that had an increasing appeal to broad elements throughout the country. As the boogeyman of all European leaders and churches, communism was outlawed in the Kingdom, but many saw it as the only resolute opposition to Franco, Mussolini, and Hitler. Early members were skilled laborers, artisans, and students. Village teachers and worker-peasants, those who moved back and forth between village and city, disseminated communist ideas to rural areas. We have seen how these ideas germinated in the mind of Jožef Fabjančič.

*Calic, Marie-Janine, 2019, *A History of Yugoslavia,* p. 112.

In June 1935, Prince Paul appointed a new prime minister. Milan Stojadinović had the big jobs of pulling Yugoslavia out of the Depression, keeping it neutral, and solving the Croatian separatist crisis. His party's platform was: "One King, one nation, one state, prosperity at home, peace on the borders." Among his first acts was to loosen censorship and free 10,000 political prisoners. He personally adopted the style and semantics of fascists hoping to inspire unity in a way Mussolini had done for post war Italy or Hitler had done for an ailing Germany, but he never adopted fascist ideology.

An upswing in the economy resulted from his promotion of exports of food, agricultural products, iron ore, and copper to Germany in exchange for manufactured goods. He promoted state subsidies for heavy industry and arms, the liquidation of farmers' debt, and the stabilization of prices. He supported increased trade with Germany despite the political perils of being drawn into its sphere. Stojadinović tried to correct the balance by promoting trade with England and France without great success. In 1938, in preparation for war, Germany unilaterally declared Yugoslavia would be part of its Greater German Economic Sphere. Yugoslavia was told to provide raw materials for armament exclusively to Germany, and in return receive weapons and airplane technology.

In 1938 Germany occupied Austria and the Sudetenland. Meanwhile, Britain and France failed to act, convincing Prince Paul that those he called friends were prepared to sacrifice Yugoslavia for the sake of improved Anglo-Italian relations. Prince Paul feared how easily the Germans or Italians could establish an independent puppet state for his rebellious Croats if given the chance. Stojadinović believed any successful solution for Croatian demands was a long-term proposition. He deftly handled relationships in Italy and Germany to ensure that Croatian separatists would not find sympathy and support in Rome or Berlin for assisting independence.*

*Bakič, Dragan. 2018. Milan Stojadinović, "The Croat Question and the International Position of Yugoslavia 1935-1939"

   With these successes to his credit, Stojadinović called for a state election with confidence that his party would prevail against the opposing party calling for Croatian autonomy. His party did win the general election of December 1938 but the margin of victory was so slim that Prince Paul decided to dismiss Stojadinović and change course on the Croatian question.

*

In November 1938, Fani and Viktor Colja moved to Slovenska Bistrica, which is not far from Maribor, where they earned money doing farm work for others. Fani mentioned the state election of December 1938 in a letter to Mary. The results were unsettling even for simple people like the Coljas, and brought fears of foreign intervention, economic downturns, political oppression, and civil war. Fani was a hopeful person, and in her own life she tried to see the best in people, with perhaps the exception of her old friend Gela Skominčič, and avoided family conflicts.

> *Nova Gora 104, Slovenska Bistrica*
> *14 December 1938*
>   Dear Aunt!
>   I received Your dear letter, thank You very much. Here things are as usual, the winter has not arrived and we have not yet had any snow, but the harvest work is done. We just had the State elections and this is why everything is even more wrong. As You wrote, right after the war You were thinking of returning to Your home. You can only thank God that You stayed there. I believe that Francka from Gabrk [Francka Ban] regrets that she returned so soon. She has two beautiful daughters and they were thinking of getting the younger one married to a member of the armed police force. Everything was ready, but he was Italian and he said that he would first like to go home to see his parents, but he never returned. Now the girl is left here in shame.

When I was in Maribor recently, I did not visit Pepina Jurkotova [John's sister]. I am afraid that she would only vaguely
remember me. I am not sure that she would like my uninvited
visit, people these days prefer to keep to themselves. We saw my
Uncle Milan. My mother had told me that in the past my uncle
came home drunk, and smashed things. Now he seems to be
more subdued. And how is Skominčič from Bač doing, and that
filthy Gela? They had one truly bratty son; do You know anything about them? Do You ever get letters from home? Nobody
ever writes to me. I occasionally hear things from others and
learn something new. *Fani*

Mary sent money to her mother for Christmas 1938 and Jožef wrote
a short note of thanks. Despite his regular complaints about her, he
had extraordinary patience with his grumpy mother.

Many thanks for those lire that you've sent to Mama. She
could not be more pleased; she acted as if she were holding
100,000 lire. She brought home both of your letters, gave them
to me, and I gave her one back, saying that it was addressed
to her and that she can have it read by anyone she chooses.
She gave it to my wife and said that she trusts her more than
anyone else.

Marija Fabjančič, now 23 years old, recruited 15-year-old Milka to
write the thank you note to give her Slovene writing practice. Mama
had the usual complaints.

I'm the same as always; my feet hurt and my days are passing,
my hours are nearing the end. I'm a poor woman, all alone, I
have nobody but you and my son. If I ever wanted to pass my
time, as other mothers do with their children, I have nobody.
Rezina Bilkotova is the same as always when I meet her, she
does not even look at me.

Ivan Godina was transferred from Pola to Venice and wrote his aunt
on 4 February 1939.

> Dear Aunt,
>   I regret that my Mama had to leave me all alone so soon. I
> would not have willingly joined the navy if she were still alive.
> I regret that I am so remote from every one of my own, and I do
> not have any news of them, not even about my sister Fani, who
> never writes to me, or my brother Jože. I often visit with my
> brother Karel in Fiume but You know that there is nothing to
> talk to him about, he is such a poor wretch. Today I also wrote
> to my brother Jože, and I sent him a photograph, the same one
> that I am sending to You. Thank You for sending me the dollar,
> it always comes in handy, I usually run out of lire at the end of
> the month. *I. Godina*

The Godina were scattered around the world. Joe was in Sharon,
Pennsylvania; Fani Colja lived in Slovenska Bistrica, Yugoslavia;
Zora lived in Trieste, Karel was in an asylum in Rijeka, and Ivan was
stationed at a naval hospital in Venice. Mary Fradel wrote to each of
them, relayed news between them and encouraged them to stay in
touch with each other. There was a flurry of letters in the spring of
1939, and Mary sent a dollar in each. Fani wrote in February 1939:

> I've mentioned in my letter that nobody ever writes to me. I
> have written to my brother Jože but he does not answer. I won-
> der if his wife also prefers to be left alone, or if it is only him? I
> do not know anything about my brother Ivan. I am happy that
> You have been corresponding with him. There are five of us
> scattered all over the world, like we almost do not know each
> other, and father is alone at home. He used to say, "Go and earn
> your own living, do you think that I will take care of you?" Now
> in his old days, he finally is a poor man himself. But he was ill
> tempered and bad, and he almost deserves a bit of punishment.

We would invite him to live with us, but I remember how mean he was when I was still at home and I am afraid that he would act the same way here, that he would fight here, too. We are living in peace like birds; we are poor, but we do not say one bad word to each other. But father is the complete opposite and of that, I am really afraid. But now I decided that after a long time, I will at least write to him for his Name Day [Feast of St. Joseph, 19 March].

We are holding on to the few dinars that we saved during the summer; we keep them like we never had them to spend, so that we can buy some land where we can build our own little house. If earnings are good, maybe we can add something to our savings this summer. I will finish now and send my best regards to You and to the entire family. Also sending regards are Viktor and Slavko, who is already learning how to write and read. *Fani*

*

15 March 1939. Germany's invasion of Czechoslovakia was a clear violation of the Munich Agreement, in which Hitler had agreed to forego invading additional territory after the Sudetenland. The establishment of a separate puppet state in Slovakia confirmed Prince Paul's fears for Croatia. He had just installed a new prime minister, Dragiša Cvetković, who would support limited Croatian autonomy within Yugoslavia to prevent it from becoming a pretext for foreign intervention.

*

Fani wrote a few days after this event:

18 March 1939
   My dear Aunt!!
   Yesterday I received Your dear letter, thank You so much for it and also for the dollar that was inside. You write that

You received a letter and photo from our Ivan; he indeed is a very beautiful boy. It is true that we are all missing our deceased mother and it is true that Ivan misses her a lot; he always listened to her and never treated her with scorn. Zora was the stubborn one; she angered Mama the most. Perhaps Your brother already told You how badly Zora treated Mama when she was sick. She did not tend her the way she should have and she chased other people away. You tell me that she is planning to have a wedding; I would also like to see her get married, but maybe You have heard that she has a very bad reputation because she has a different boyfriend every day and a different job every month. But she is a beautiful girl that only few can match, and when it comes to working and keeping things clean, she is very diligent. Our deceased mother was always beefing about Zora's future because she cannot be told anything. Mama told Zora to go to school and father said, "Why should she go to school, she knows everything." He was making fun of her, of course, but Zora took it seriously. Ivan went only to Italian school, but Mama taught him at home how to write and read Slovene.

I did not know that Francka, our Biščev cousin, was sick with tuberculosis. I do not write to them and they prefer to be left alone. We, the Bazle children, were never appreciated by Biščevi or Bilkotevi; they always treated us with scorn. Even today nobody cares about us. And regarding my uncle Milan Godina and Marija Pajserova; You know them better than I do. It might be best that You do not tell me anything more or I will form an even worse opinion about them than what the reality is. It is only Your poor mother, our Nona, that loves us all. The younger ones care only about their own families.

Regarding my own condition, I can tell you that I've been feeling weak for two months because I am pregnant. I did not expect that I would be so miserable but there is nothing I can do to prevent this from happening, as Viktor does not let me and I would like to have a little girl.

Special kisses for my dear aunt, *Fani*

Ivan Godina wrote from Venice on the 20 March 1939:

> Thank you so much for the photographs of my cousins, and the
> dollar. I am still waiting for a letter from my brother Jože after
> I sent him my photo. I am also curious about any news from
> my sister, Fani, because I heard that she asked about me. Zora
> stays in touch with me; it's been 14 days since she last wrote.
> My father has enough to get by because he is renting out the
> fields and he always earns something on the side. Tenel fam-
> ily does his laundry and he is still involved with that broad.
> I think that she will leave him once she devours everything.
> But it does not matter to me. He will get his misery. I will tell
> You more after I go there on vacation for the Easter holidays. I
> need to thank You for your lesson and I can promise You that
> I am not, and will never be, like my father. I know well how it
> is when the drunkards come home.
>   Always Yours, *I. Godina*

*

7 April 1939. Italy invaded Albania, which cut off Yugoslavia's
access to the Mediterranean Sea. Prince Paul had made it clear to
Mussolini that he opposed Italy's proposed annexation of Albania, but when it actually happened, he took no action, not even
to denounce it. This inaction strained Yugoslavia's relationship
with Turkey, who had an interest in Albania because of its Muslim
population and ties to the former Ottoman Empire. Turkey and
Britain formed an alliance to protest further Italian aggression
in the Balkans, but Prince Paul called the alliance "ill-timed" and
declined to join them.

*

A week after the invasion of Albania, Ivan Godina wrote. His leave
had been cancelled, the Italian draft had been expanded to older
people and the Germans were arriving.

16 April 1939

You asked about my vacation. They did not let anyone go home because of different things that are going on here now. You may know that they are drafting older people, those that are between 30 and 38 years old. I stayed and had fun here in Venezia—this was the first opportunity I have had to go around and meet people. I can inform you that I do not have a girlfriend. It is fashionable these days for girls to have many boys. Here in Venezia, girls are not worth much and almost all of them are ill. I am afraid to catch something. The girls at home are not faithful; they have fun with other boys and then they laugh at you. I expect some news from you, Ivanka, if you still remember me. Will you, please?

There is nothing else for me to report as things here in Venezia are the same except that the Germans have started to arrive now that the weather is nice.

Yours, *I. Godina.*

I wonder if the "Germans" were just tourists coming for fine weather, or whether "fine weather" was a code word for the invasion, with the Germans there for military reasons.

A rare letter from Antonija Fradel in Artviže, was saved (I suspect that John Fradel was never happy to see her letters and usually tossed them in the trash). Antonija still wanted Jurkotevi, but John never responded to her, leaving matters to be handled by Jožef Biščev. Despite the expected formal pleasantries in the opening and closing of the letter, it conveys anger and desperation.

6 March 1939

Dear Brother,

Before I write you more, I first send you my best regards. I am writing to tell you that I've written multiple times. What have I done that you are so angry with me? Please write to me, tell me how you are doing, if you are healthy. How is Ivanka doing? Our children are worried about her. When I saw her, I felt like the heaven opened. What did I do to her that you resent

me so much? You do not write to me. I strongly urged Ivanka
to tell you exactly how it is here. What are you thinking? To
get rich there? As you know I would have stayed in Polžane if
things were divided differently. Pepina wanted me to be there.
I thought that you would come home, but now I see that you
will not. Times are different now and we are not twenty years
old anymore. I am poor, Ivanka should tell you.

It would be better if we could talk like brother and sister. If
you come home, I will leave everything to you. I would help
you in any way I can. Please do something. Come home. I will
not let things get this way again. Now I am sending you best
regards from all of us to your entire family, especially to Ivanka,
Rudolf and Marija. Please reply. Z Bogom, *Antonija*

The nineteenth of March is the Feast of St. Joseph and the name day
for Jožef and his son, Jože. It was a big day for them in 1939. Jože
turned 20 and was an adult, ready to help carry the workload at
Biščevi, but Mussolini had a different plan for him. Jožef's words of
grief were subdued but the paper was smudged from tears.

19 March, 1939

Dear Sister and Janez!!! Two months have passed without
a letter from you. We got the photographs and we thought
that a letter would follow, but there has been nothing. The
photographs are truly beautiful; all of you are beautiful, tall,
and fat. One can see that you do not live in poverty. Because
we cannot see each other in person, we can at least know each
other in photographs.

Things here are as usual. We had a mild winter and February
was just like spring. But now in March it is cold and yesterday
it snowed all day, as if it were Christmas. Today is the feast of
St. Josef and there is snow everywhere. Well, if things want to
go wrong, then this is exactly how they need to do it.

Yesterday, on the 18th, our Jože was drafted and is already
confirmed as a soldier. (photo 16) That's how it is. I've been
waiting and raising him to help me with work, so that it should

be easier for me now. But he will have to go; we do not know for how long. I made a request to shorten his service. If there were peace that might mean something, but if the army ignites, there is no request that would be valid. I'm getting old and instead of getting some rest I'll have to work just like I always have. Janez is learning to be a blacksmith. He is not interested in working on the farm. Pepka is still too young, so only Milka is here to help. Mama cannot work anymore, she can barely walk, but she still does some things by force of will; she is used to doing that.

Everything else is as usual. Ivan Ban, who had gone to live with his daughter [Marija of Gabrk], died on the Shrovetide [28 Feb 1939]. Things on Gabrk are bad. In November they had the first forced sale, it was valuated at 80,000; nobody came. On 1st March there was the second forced sale, and they lowered to 47,000. Again, there were no buyers. Now in the first days of May there will be the third forced sale and everything will be offered for 37,000 lire. Kastelic is also in extremely bad shape. This winter his children are going around homes to beg for a few potatoes. He does not have anything to eat and nothing to wear. If one told him five years ago that he would be begging, what would he say? But as long as a man is alive, anything can happen.

I will end now because I have nothing good to write; you read about bad things every day anyway. Bazle visited today and he is also sending you regards.

*

26 August 1939. Prince Paul agreed to a semi-autonomous Croatian province led by the Croatian Peasant Party. Hitler encouraged Mussolini to annex all of Croatia because he was preparing to invade Poland and he thought Italian action in the south would distract his adversaries.

1 September 1939. Hitler invaded Poland with little resistance. Britain and France declared war on Germany two days later. They

could do very little for Poland's defense, without direct military action. This next period of inaction in Eastern Europe was called the "Phoney War," but real war was waged in Africa between the declared adversaries.

*

How does a mail service stop? Did Italy make an announcement that the mail was suspended? Did the mail just pile up somewhere and never get delivered? Mary would not receive another letter from her brother for six years. A single letter from Fani Colja in Yugoslavia arrived in October 1939. Fani tried to sound normal, to express the usual sentiments, and to share news as if wishing to be normal would simply make it so, but at the end of each paragraph her fear crept in.

8 Oct 1939

I do not know how things are with You, my dear Aunt, because I have not received any letters. The latest one was mailed on 6 April and I received it on 20 April. In June I received Your package and I was also expecting a letter, but it never came. I wrote to thank You just like I am thanking You again today. It is true that many things in Yugoslavia are wrong and mixed up, such as the mail, because many employees are attending military exercises.

On 20 September we got a girl, and we are all happy and pleased. Her name is Dragica. We are both healthy and I hope that nothing bad comes our way. Viktor is still at home, but we are most afraid that his invitation to join the military will arrive any day. One should always think about good things; bad things come on their own. Otherwise, everything is as usual and the days are getting colder. Masonry work will soon be retired until spring. I ask God that the war does not come here, and that we'll get through everything else ourselves.

I hope that the times are not as tense at Your place as they are here in Europe, ready for the war.

Please write to me about my brother Jože. I wrote to my father and he replied once, but then nothing more. I was in Maribor in August and my Uncle Milan showed me a photograph of Ivan. He is a very handsome boy; he is big and strong and one can see that nothing bad is happening to him. How is Your Ivanka, is she already married? Milena, our uncle's oldest one, has married a journalist. [Milena Godina, actress, lost her job in the Maribor theater because of her communist activities and took refuge in Skopje, Macedonia. There she married Viktor Acimovic, a Macedonian photographer, journalist, and revolutionary.] Forgive me, but today I am not capable of thinking or writing any more. Once again, Viktor and I send You and Your entire family our best regards. *Fani.*

... And that was the last that Mary knew of her home and family until September 1945.

CHAPTER TWENTY

1939–1945: *World War Two*

Dread of another war weighed heavily on Jožef and his neighbors. Italy's military threat was evident to them via the widened roads, new water resources, army barracks, and military drills in their fields. The economic and cultural oppression was unbearable. Even without knowledge of outside events, war seemed inevitable. This war was going to be different from Jožef's war. In his war, soldiers moved slowly on wagons and horses, then trains. Battles began on fields and were reduced to men cowering in trenches with advances and retreats measured in yards for months at a time. The average soldier did not know what that war was about other than their kaisers and kings fought to keep their empires and if they deserted, they would be shot.

The second world war was fast. Invasions happened quickly. Armies moved by train, trucks, tanks, and ships. It was not just about taking territory; it was about changing populations. Airplanes rained bombs on cities, armies took over villages, and executed the residents. Undesirables were packed into railcars to be interned in work camps and factories, or prisons, or marked for extermination. Unlike the first war, this one was driven by political ideology and unfettered ethnic hatreds.

ONSET OF THE EUROPEAN WAR

On 23 August 1939, Hitler and Stalin signed the "Molotov-Rib-bentrop Pact," pledging non-aggression, with a secret agreement to divide Eastern Europe between them. Germany's invasion of Poland a week later was the last straw for Britain and France. They declared war on Germany, although there was nothing that they could actually do to help Poland. The Soviets occupied the rest of Poland weeks later.

In the 22 May 1939 "Pact of Steel," Mussolini and Hitler pledged mutual support, but Mussolini was caught off guard by how quickly Hitler moved, and did not rush to join the war. Italy was handi-capped by outdated equipment and his advisors told him the man-ufacturing sector could not be fully prepared for war before the end of 1942, and the economy was not healthy. Great chunks of the national budget had been used for Italy's military ventures in Abys-sinia and assistance to Franco in the Spanish Civil War. The occupa-tion of Albania, while relatively easy, further strained the country's resources. Italy relied on coal imported from Germany through the port of Rotterdam to power its industries. One of Britain's first acts of war was to blockade the transport of coal from Rotterdam, and attempt to entice Italy away from Germany with offers of armaments and concessions in Africa. While Mussolini thought about it, Hitler began sending coal to Italy by train over the Alps.

On 26 August 1939, Yugoslavia's attempt to satisfy Croatian desires for independence with the creation of a semi-autonomous banovina was a gamble to prevent foreign interference. The Croa-tian banovina included parts of Montenegro, Macedonia, and Bos-nia that angry Serbs considered their own, and they had concern for the safety of Serbs in the new Croatia. Muslims were especially bitter that their homes in Bosnia and Herzegovina were divided between the Serbs and the Croats as if Muslims did not exist at all.

Vladko Maček, head of the Croatian Peasant Party, was appointed deputy prime minister of the Croatian banovina. His rival was Ante Pavelić, the leader of the fascist Ustaša who lived in exile in Italy.

Pavelič had been sentenced to death in absentia by Yugoslavian courts for his role in the death of King Alexander. The Italians also distrusted him, fearing he could incite Croatian nationalist sentiments in Istria, so when he was not in an Italian prison he was closely monitored by police. That winter, Pavelič made a proposal to Mussolini that he could instigate trouble in the banovina of Croatia that would require Italian intervention, and provide the opportunity to establish an independent Croatian state aligned with Italian fascism. Mussolini agreed to the scheme, with the stipulation that a strip of the Dalmatian Coast would be given to Italy. Just when they were ready to go into action, Hitler nixed the plan. An invasion of Croatia would have been a useful distraction when Germany was about to invade Poland, but now that the deed was done, the risk of Soviet or British intervention in Croatia might interfere with his next phase. He preferred things to be quiet in Yugoslavia, and Mussolini agreed.

In that winter of 1939–1940, General Archibald Wavell, the British commander of Operations in the Middle East, compared Mussolini's inaction to that of someone standing at the top of a diving board: "I think he must do something. If he cannot make a graceful dive, he will at least have to jump in somehow. He can hardly put on his dressing gown and walk down the stairs again." On 10 May 1940, the *blitzkrieg* on Western Europe began, and Mussolini got ready to jump in. Even though Italy was not ready, he wagered that the war would be short. He said to his army chief-of-staff: "I only need a few thousand dead so that I can sit at the peace conference as a man who has fought." Just days before German troops took Paris, Mussolini declared war on Britain and France, and occupied a small area of southern France. On 21 June 1940, the French signed an armistice with Germany, and three days later they signed another with Italy.

Many men Mary and John knew were spared the Italian draft because they had already done their time. The younger Frane Košanc, Drej and Miha Grgur did peacetime service. Frane Bilko went during the Abyssinia campaign. Ivan Godina was now voluntarily in the navy. In 1939, in addition to Jože Fabjančič, other draftees included Tonči Jaksetič (Jane's sweetheart) and Zlato Kastelic, (Boži-dar's eldest son).

MUSSOLINI IN AFRICA AND GREECE

Mussolini saw Italy's control of the Mediterranean and its posses-sions in the Horn of Africa as advantages to his regime at sea. With the occupation of Albania, Italy effectively enclosed the Adriatic Sea, turning it into an Italian pond. The recent armistice with France had given Italy control of Corsica and Tunisia, further solidifying its control of the Mediterranean all the way to the Straits of Gibraltar and the Atlantic. Mussolini saw the friendly regime of Franco in Spain as an advantage, despite the British control of Gibraltar. The fly in Mussolini's ointment was the British Protectorate in Egypt.

While Mussolini was savoring his triumph and territorial gains after a two week war with France, the British seized Fort Capuzzo in Italian Libya. The Italians retook it and Mussolini ordered the occupation of the Suez Canal despite the fact his forces could not possibly succeed. In mid-September 1940 the Italians crossed the border into Egypt and advanced about 60 miles, where they stopped and established a series of fortified camps setting the stage for des-ert campaigns between the Allies and the Axis armies. Six weeks later, Mussolini used Albania as a jump-off point to invade Greece. The Italians were met by fierce opposition and entrenched warfare ensued along the Greek-Albanian border.

Hitler wanted Russia for its rich resources and as space for the German people. He also wanted the destruction of Bolshevism and the Jewish people, and Russia was full of them. To invade, Hitler had to disable any threat from Western Europe and, if he could not occupy Britain, he needed to be able to fend off their attacks. Fear-ing that the British might strategically occupy Norway, Germany took control of Denmark and Norway. Hitler knew from Napo-leon's infamous experience in the harsh Russian winter, that he needed an early spring start and a strong army to ensure victory.

Sending troops into North Africa or Greece was not his preferred course of action, but the Italian Army's failure to hand the British a decisive defeat in North Africa was a great problem for him and the arrival of Australian and New Zealand forces in Egypt made it worse. Mussolini's foray into Greece was Hitler's nightmare. The British arrived to defend Greece, bringing Allied forces far too close to Hitler's southern flank as he marched to Russia. To stave off this danger, Hitler deployed an army through a complicit Bulgaria in the direction of Greece in March 1941.

HITLER AND PRINCE PAUL COLLIDE

Prince Paul had made every effort to protect the territorial integrity of Yugoslavia and steer a neutral course. Under intense economic and political pressure, he had resisted agreements with Hitler and done his best to solicit British protection. But the German Army's presence in Austria, Hungary, Romania, and Bulgaria encircled Yugoslavia and as the army moved toward Greece, the noose tightened. In negotiations with Germany, Prince Paul was assured that Yugoslavia's borders would remain safe and military assistance in Greece would not be requested. In a final desperate move, on 25 March 1941 Prince Paul signed the Tripartite Pact that aligned Yugoslavia with the Axis powers of Germany, Italy, and Japan.

All hell broke out in Yugoslavia that day. Masses of people took to the streets demanding a return to neutrality. Only 24 years earlier, Germany had decimated Serbia and the survivors wanted no part of an agreement with Hitler. Two days later, Serb generals deposed Prince Paul and put King Peter II on the throne, even though he was not quite 18. Hitler took the coup as a personal insult and was furiously determined, he said, to "destroy Yugoslavia militarily and as a state...with pitiless harshness ... and without waiting for possible declarations of loyalty of the new government." "Führer Directive 25" called for Yugoslavia to be treated as a hostile state.

Mussolini and Pavelič pushed forward with their plan for an independent fascist state in Croatia. Ustaša para-military were released from Italian prisons, and from a radio station in Florence, Pavelič made his first late evening broadcast on 1 April calling for the "liberation of Croatia."

THE WAR DESTROYS YUGOSLAVIA

Germany's Operation Retribution began at 7 a.m. on 6 April 1941, without warning. Flying in relays from airfields in Austria and Romania, 300 Nazi aircraft attacked Belgrade. Dive-bombers silenced the Yugoslav anti-aircraft defenses, while medium bombers attacked the city. The 90-minute rain of destruction was carried out at 15-minute intervals in three distinct waves with main efforts directed at the center of the city, where government buildings were located. The bombers continued their attack on the city for several days, while the dive bombers were diverted to destroy Yugoslav airfields. When the attack was over, some 4,000 inhabitants lay dead under the rubble.

The Axis forces—Germany, Hungary, Bulgaria, and Italy—invaded Yugoslavia from multiple directions, rapidly overwhelming the Royal Yugoslav Army. Eleven days after the bombing started, Yugoslavia surrendered and ceased to exist. The invaders picked the corpse apart, beginning with Croatia. The Nazis preferred a puppet government that would allow them to control and exploit the region's resources without having to commit significant military forces. Vladko Maček, the existing deputy prime minister of the banovina of Croatia, was a perfect choice. He was popular among Croats, supported Prince Paul's signing of the Tripartite Pact, and had his own paramilitary force. Twice, the Germans asked Maček to proclaim an independent Croatian client state, and he refused. Although the Germans had doubts that Mussolini's puppet, Ante Pavelič, would govern as they wished, they saw no other option. On 16 April 1941, Pavelič signed a decree appointing the new Government of the Independent State of Croatia which quickly became a fascist regime. A month later he visited Rome to present the Dalmatian Coast to Mussolini.

In the broken Yugoslavian kingdom, all the hurts and outrages that had accumulated over centuries of Roman, Ottoman, Austrian, and Hungarian conquests, and occupations, as well as divisions in language, religion, and ethnicity, were laid bare. The Yugoslavia hastily cobbled together just two decades earlier was a manifestation of Serbian dominance that angered others. The surrounding countries wanted to reclaim territory that they felt rightfully belonged to them. Ethnic and religious divisions further complicated matters, as different groups vied for power and influence. In this chaotic and tumultuous environment, collaborators with the occupying powers were everywhere.

The royal government took refuge in Greece, then Egypt, with British assistance. Along with other deposed European rulers, King Peter II set up a Yugoslav government in exile from London, but his struggle to recruit ministers other than Serbs, made his government open to accusations that it did not represent Croatia, Slovenia, or the other provinces. Young King Peter was a target of scorn as he finished his studies at Cambridge University, and celebrated his marriage to Princess Alexandra of Greece in 1944, while his countrymen suffered from war and deprivation.

In the independent state of Croatia, Pavlič declared himself *Poglavnik,* the equivalent of Fuhrer or Duce. He was a true fascist, determined to create a pure Croat nation, even though only half of the 6.3 million residents were Croatian. His Ustaša paramilitary took up the mission with zeal. Serbs looked like Croats and spoke the same language but used a different alphabet. Their other identifying attribute was Orthodox Christianity, and the rough plan was to forcibly convert a third to Catholicism, drive another third out of the country, and kill the rest. Within days, Pavelič banned the Cyrillic alphabet, annulled mixed marriages, and prohibited Serbs from using public transportation. Within weeks, families were deported to Serbia, Orthodox churches and monasteries were destroyed, and forced conversions to Catholicism took place. The Vatican said nothing and local Catholic leaders publicly supported the Ustaša. The new Croatian state participated in the Holocaust, with the regime actively supporting genocide. They established concentration camps and carried out brutal massacres, including the notorious Jasenovac camp where tens of thousands of Serbs were murdered. The Ustaša did not have modern, clean ways of murder, like gas chambers, and they did not want to waste bullets. Serbs were hacked to death, or herded into barns that were set on fire, or loaded into trucks driven into the mountains and pushed into gorges. Pavelič and the Ustaša murdered about 30,000 Jews, 29,000 Roma, and somewhere between 300,000 and 400,000 Serbs. Even the Germans said, "The Ustaša have gone raving mad." The regime's crimes against humanity continue to be remembered and mourned to this day.

By the end of 1941 most Croats had turned their backs to the regime as a result of the terror perpetrated and pro-Yugoslav sentiment began to re-emerge, along with pro-communist feelings. Croats who wanted to fight their fascist government had only one place to go: the Communist Partisan resistance, organized by Josip Broz Tito. Croatian on his father's side, Slovene on his mother's, his name was Josip Broz, and later he added his *nom de guerre*: Tito (Titus).

Albania, an Italian puppet state, and Bulgaria, a German puppet state, pinched off the southern tip of Yugoslavia. Albania claimed Kosovo and Western Macedonia, and Bulgaria claimed Eastern Macedonia. On both sides, Serbs were murdered and deported, and schools, churches, and cemeteries were destroyed to eliminate anything Serbian or Macedonian. The famous actress Milena Godina, daughter of Milan Godina, (my grandmother's former flame), previously arrested for communist activities in Maribor, had found refuge in Skopje before the war started. She married a Macedonian, kept a low profile, and halted her theater work, declining offers to work in Nazi Bulgaria.

Under the direction of General Milan Nedić, Serbia also became a German puppet state. Yugoslav gold and securities made their way to German banks. Infrastructure, mining, armament factories and

agriculture were aligned to the needs of the Reich. Serbs numbering in the hundreds of thousands, were deported to work in German factories, and the Nedić government introduced compulsory
labor duty for everyone aged 17-45 remaining in Serbia. The cinema,
theater, concerts, sports events, radio, and printed material were
censored to conform to the Nazi agenda. The streets were empty
and people in the poorer districts were starving by the first winter.

Serbian resistance to the Nazi occupation was composed of Chetnik fighters directed by General Draža Mihailovič who also served
as the exiled King Peter's minister of war. Chetniks were fierce,
independent fighters and did their best to defend Serbian villages
under attack by Ustaša, while carrying out ethnic cleansing of their
own through the deportation of Croats and the murder of Muslims
living in Serbia. They assisted downed Allied airmen and received
support from the Allies in the first years of the war.

SLOVENIA DIVIDED THREE WAYS

Slovenia was initially divided into three sectors: Hungarian, Italian,
and German, which reflected the historical and ethnic relationships
of each region. For the conquering forces the split provided opportunity to rectify decisions about borders that had been made after
the Great War.

During the first years, in the Hungarian controlled sector of Prekmurje, the government aspired to the *Magyarization* of its mixed
population. They acted on their age-old hatred of Slavs primarily
focusing on the extermination and deportations of Serbians. In
1942, the fascist Independent State of Croatia allowed Hungary
to formally annex Prekmurje. The Volksdeutsche (German settlers from the 18th century known in other parts of Slovenia as
Gottschee) received "special status" and authorities were permissive
towards ethnic Slovenes. By March 1944, Hungary realized that it
was on the wrong side of the war, and tried to join up with Allied
forces, which provoked a complete takeover by the Germans. Before
their retreat in 1945, the Germans completed the extermination

of the Roma and Jews in Prekmurje, just as they did throughout Hungary, and evacuated 60,000–70,000 Volkdeutsche to Austria.

Italy annexed Ljubljana, finally ruling the territories to which they felt entitled after aligning themselves with Britain and France during World War One. Italianization was promoted with even greater rigor than what they had achieved in Primorska, and 300,000 men, women and children were deported to concentration camps. Gonar and the island of Rab were the most infamous sites for these camps. A barbed wire fence with guards around Ljubljana controlled who went in and out, and its men were not drafted to the Italian army because they could not be trusted. Although thoroughly anti-Semitic, Italian fascists were lackadaisical about Jewish extermination, and Jews were relatively safe until Italy capitulated in 1943, and Germans assumed control.

Germany annexed northern Slovenia and Maribor, where the economy was restructured to suit the needs of the Reich. To restore the dominant German culture that existed before 1919, Primorskan immigrants, intellectuals, and "politically tainted" Slovenes were the first to be deported. Some 220,000 Slovenes were forced to labor in factories in Austria and Germany, and others were placed into German army units to dig trenches and labor on the Eastern Front. Within a few months, faced with labor shortages and insufficient numbers of Gottschee to take their places, Slovenes who worked in industries that aided the war effort, as well as those considered to have desirable racial characteristics, were allowed to remain, and be "Germanized" through education and cultural organizations. These deportations outraged Slovenians and nobody felt safe.

Among my people from the valley under Slavnik in Maribor, Pepina Fradel was deported to Austria to a factory work camp, and it's unknown where her husband went. They lost their home in Studenci. Their son, Jože Babič, was politically tainted by his participation in communist activities, and was sent to Auschwitz. He managed to escape and joined the Polish Resistance. His younger brother, Lada, joined the Partisans. Frane Fradel, the municipal policeman, was arrested and sent to Maulthausen, where he died in 1945. His wife and daughter, Mary, were deported. After the war, Mary filed for reparations for the loss of her home, and may have returned to Primorska.

TITO AND STALIN

On the same day Germans bombarded Belgrade, they invaded Greece from their position in Bulgaria. Greek forces, along with their allies from the British, New Zealand and Australian armies, were pressed from both the east by the Germans and the northwest by the Italians. Despite their valiant efforts, the Allied forces were eventually overwhelmed, and the Germans and Italians captured Athens, occupying the entire country. By the end of April 1941, around 7,000 Allied soldiers had been taken as prisoners. Hitler had intended for the German Army to invade the Soviet Union earlier, but it was not until 12 June 1941 that they finally launched the invasion.

Tito awaited military direction from Stalin, the head of the Communist Party. Only after the Germans invaded the Soviet Union, did Stalin deem that a Yugoslav resistance effort would be a useful distraction of German resources from the Russian front. Consequently, it was not until 4 July 1941, three months after Operation Retribution, that Tito declared that armed Partisan brigades would liberate Yugoslavia from its German and Italian oppressors.

In the Slovenian sectors, Germans were more effective than the Italians in squashing resistance by their employment of spies, policing, and cultural organizations to monitor everyone, and their merciless reprisals. In late 1942, Italy launched an offensive against the Partisans around Ljubljana and Lada Babič, 22, (photo 17) son of Pepina Fradel, and member of the Partisan Tomsič Brigade, died in combat on 24 February 1943. The Italian offensive though effective, failed to eradicate Partisan resistance, and instead, it grew stronger. In the Italian sectors, the Partisans established a robust infrastructure, including printshops and hospitals. One notable woman, Dr. Franja Bidovec, established a Partisan hospital well-hidden in the forest. In 1944, Dr. Franja visited Britain and met my aunt, Lt. Jane Fradel, a registered nurse in the 74th General Hospital stationed in England, with whom she had some photographs taken. After returning to the Partisan hospital, Dr. Franja continued her work until the end of the war and was later recognized as a national hero.

THE YUGOSLAVIAN CIVIL WAR

The Partisans were not the only resistance force. Chetnik fighters were present throughout the former kingdom, but they lacked the leadership, discipline, and the unifying perspective that made the Partisans so effective. Although loyal to the monarchy, the Chetniks were not above forming alliances with the occupying forces to achieve their local aims, such as ethnic cleansing or eliminating communists. The Chetnik strategy was to stay alive and prepare to support the Allies when they arrived to liberate Yugoslavia. They generally employed only defensive tactics to avoid vicious German reprisals, which were more brutal in Slavic countries than in Western Europe. In France, for every German soldier killed, ten civilians were ordered to be shot and hung: in Eastern Europe, the order was to shoot and hang one hundred civilians. The hanging of that many corpses became time-consuming, so hostages were executed in groups of 30 to 50 and their bodies dumped in mass graves.

In contrast to the defensive strategies of the Chetniks, Partisans sought open warfare, and let the locals suffer the reprisals. Tensions mounted between Chetniks and Partisans, and often they were fighting each other as much as they were fighting the occupation forces. In Slovenia, many Chetniks were motivated by their Catholicism, and accused Partisans of staging attacks in proximity to villages that supported them, to selectively bring reprisals on Catholics.

Both Chetniks and Partisans aided Allied pilots shot down over their territories and, initially, the British and Americans assisted both resistance groups. The Allies later decided the Partisans were more effective in fighting Germans and gave them all their support. Fighting between the various factions in Yugoslavia devolved into a brutal civil war, with control of any given area constantly changing hands. Loyalties, and ideology stood for very little and no one felt safe. Day to day, people made major decisions based solely on how best to survive.

Tonči Jaksetič died in 1942 when his troop carrier on its way to Tunisia was torpedoed. Zlato Kastelic died at sea in 1943. In March 1943, Janez Fabjančič, the younger son of our Jožef, was drafted into the Italian Army and sent to fight in Greece.

ITALIAN CAPITULATION

As battles between Italian and the British forces dragged on in North Africa, the Germans were forced to get involved. Operations expanded as both sides received reinforcements, with Americans joining the action in May 1942. Stalin asked his British and American allies to extend the battles in Africa to divert German resources away from the Soviet Front. The final North African campaign took place in Tunisia and the Allies emerged victorious on 13 May 1943. They turned their attention to Italy, with invasions of Sicily beginning on 10 July. Two weeks later, King Victor Emmanuel deposed Mussolini and had him imprisoned in a hotel on the Island of Ponza until he was sprung from jail by German paratroopers and installed as head of a Nazi puppet government in northern Italy.

Italy surrendered on 8 September, and for a few days the Partisans controlled the entire Italian sector of Slovenia, but the Germans soon sent forces to secure the area. On 14 September 1943, they arrived at Jožef Fabjančič's dooryard in Povžane.

THE EUROPEAN WAR'S END

Tito's Partisan units had been stuck in south Serbia for a long time suffering major losses, but finally they were able to break out into Croatia and Serbia, gathering new recruits. The people who joined them were not always ideologically communist, but they saw Yugoslavian unity as the only way forward to end foreign occupation and the brutal war.

In the Soviet Union, Russian forces were pushing back the faltering Nazi troops while two million Americans readied themselves in Britain. On 6 June 1944, the D-Day invasion took place, with Allied troops pressing forward from the beaches of Normandy to liberate France. In Slovenia, the Germans couldn't keep enough soldiers to maintain their grip on the region so they organized the *Domobranci* (Slovene Home Guard) to help them fight the Partisans. In its ranks were former Chetniks and right-wing militias, some of whom still believed in the Nazi cause. Many Catholics joined the Home Guard to protect themselves against the Partisans, whom they viewed as "Godless." They accepted German arms and uniforms on a temporary basis, ultimately expecting that the Allies would occupy Slovenia and after ousting the Germans, the Partisans would be defeated, and the monarchy restored. But in fact, controversies continue to this day about whether the Domobranci took an oath of allegiance to Hitler and fought the Partisans alongside German troops.

The tides of war in Yugoslavia turned in the fall of 1944, after the Partisans took Belgrade. As each area was liberated, all men from the ages of 17 to 50 were mobilized, while enemy soldiers were urged to defect and granted amnesty unless they had the blood of atrocities on their hands. German troops evacuated Greece, Albania, Macedonia, Bosnia-Herzegovina, and Serbia. An estimated 170,000 Croatian Domobranci and Ustaša, 36,000 Chetniks, 18,000 Slovene Domobranci and 7,000 of Nedič's Serbian soldiers were still fighting both the Germans and the Partisans in March 1945.*

The Soviet Army surrounded Berlin on 25 April. Three days later the Germans withdrew from Italy. Mussolini, disguised as a German soldier, was caught as he tried to slip out with them. He was shot, and his body put on public display, along with that of his lover, who tried to shield him. On 30 April, Hitler and his wife took cyanide in his bunker. On 4 May, the last Germans, and the surviving leadership of the Croatian Ustaša, withdrew from Slovenia, and the

*Calic. *A History of Yugoslavia*, p. 160

Partisans were left in control. On 7 May the German armed forces surrendered unconditionally in the West.

PARTISANS WIN THE CIVIL WAR

Estimates vary, but in the days following the German withdrawal, fearing Partisan retribution, at least 25,000 and possibly up to 200,000 Domobranci, Ustaša, and Chetniks, and their families, formed a 38-mile-long chain of political refugees attempting to flee to safety in British-occupied Austria. Some 20,000 made it to refugee camps before the British stopped any more potential German collaborators from entering Austria. The Partisans issued an ultimatum to those fighters hemmed in near the Austrian border to surrender, and when they did not, they were attacked. The fighters and refugees fled into the woods, died in rearguard battles, were taken prisoner, or executed.

Those who made it to the refugee camps in Austria were deluded in their belief that it would be a matter of weeks before the Allies would establish control of Slovenia. Britain had already pressed King Peter to allow Tito to form a government, and the British policy throughout Europe was to hand collaborators over to the victors. Starting on 13 May, and for the next two to three weeks, the British led the waiting Domobranci to believe that they would be transported by train to Italy to join forces with other exiles, with the goal of organizing an invasion to oust the Partisans. In truth, the trains delivered them to the Slovene border where they were handed over to the Partisans. Some 16,000 of these individuals were bound with wire and marched to limestone pits, where they were shot and killed.*

*Corsellis and Ferrar. *Slovenia 1945.*

CHAPTER TWENTY-ONE

Artviže

The story of World War Two in Brkini, and its outcome, can be heard in the stories of Antonija Fradel and her family from Artviže. Part of the story is that my family in America lost all contact and knew almost nothing about my grandfather's Fradel family. How we found each other is an interesting prelude. In 1977 I wrote to my father from Australia about my plan to visit Povžane on my overland trip home, and he asked me to be sure to find out more about the Fradels. I was in Povžane in May that year, and just by coincidence, my Aunt Mary and Uncle Matt came to Slovenia a few months later to visit the Hrebar family in Borovnica and Cerknica, and then came to Povžane. They had long warm conversations because my aunt and uncle were fluent in Slovene, and my aunt took photographs, one shows my paternal great aunt Antonija Fradel—a wizened old woman in a black scarf and dress—seated in a chair with her blonde daughter, Slavica, standing beside her at her home in Izola on the Adriatic coast. My aunt and uncle were on a two week tour, and they ran out of time to learn more about the remnants of the Fradel family. Decades later, when the bundles of letters my grandmother had saved came into my possession, I first learned that Antonija had lived in the village of Artviže, at #4 in a house named Cesarevi.

In Slovenia for opasilo in 2014, after Sunday Mass at St. George in Tublje, I asked Alojz, who is my cousin Milenka's husband, and his daughter, Ana, who speaks English well, to explore Artviže with me. We strolled through the small village to St. Servulus Church, built in 1634 atop the crest of Brkini ridge, which gave us an expansive view of the valley, and the Julian Alps. The church is not in use though the bell remains in the steeple, and I could not resist the urge to ring it. We made a few inquiries and found where Antonija had lived—house #4 was the one closest to the church. A new home occupies the site, and while I was snapping pictures, the owners came out and invited us in. On their wall, was a framed picture of the original two-story stone Cesarevi.

The owners, Ivan and Mojca, are a middle-aged couple from the Golenska region and the happiest people I have ever met. Ivan proudly proclaims Artviže is the best spot in all Slovenia. When they purchased Cesarevi, it was no longer structurally sound, so they built a modern house on the footprint of the old one. Of particular delight was a Russian stove just like the one in the home of Franc Prešeren, the great Slovenian poet. A Russian stove is a wood stove, the heat is generated into an immense masonry structure covered with tiles, before entering the chimney. A bench where people can sit or sleep with their backs pressed against the warm tiles on wintry nights surrounds the masonry. Ivan showed off his modern heating and cooling systems, the home's appliances, and a basement with cool, thick walls to store vegetables, home canned goods, smoked meats, wines, schnapps, and vinegar, as well as a bed to sleep in on unbearably hot summer nights. Ivan gardens, cuts wood, and maintains livestock while Mojca works in Koper. As we were leaving, from the upstairs balcony of the house next door, an elderly woman waved and called to us as if she had something to tell us, but we had to be on time for the opasilo feast in Povžane.

The following summer my husband and I spent a sweltering day with my young cousin, Barbara, and her partner, Samo, at a beach on the Slovenian coast. Our plan to visit the salt pans off the city of Piran in the blistering heat was no longer appealing, and I was itching to find the old woman in Artviže who waved to us. Hopefully, she could tell us something about Antonija Fradel, and Artviže would be ten degrees cooler. We rang the church bell, strolled past Ivan and Mojca's house, and sure enough, our happy couple was outside, and just a "hello" brought us an offer of home-made dandelion wine, another tour of their well-stocked basement, and directions for drying, roasting, and grinding dandelion roots for coffee. We learned the chatty neighbor had dementia and was moved to a rest home. I asked our hosts if they knew anything of the former residents of Cesarevi and Mojca recalled that a man she worked with in Koper told her that his mother once lived in the house. Mojca called her co-worker for the contact information of his mother, and by the following day intrepid sleuth Alojz turned up not just one, but three living daughters of Antonija Fradel. One lived near Koper and two near Maribor, and we had an invitation for lunch in Maribor on Saturday.

We visited Ema, the oldest daughter, and Slavica, the blonde, blue-eyed girl whom Jane had admired as a toddler, and who appeared in Aunt Mary's photo of Great Aunt Antonija. Later, we would meet Amelja on the coast—it was her son that Mojca worked with. We learned that Antonija had five children, but the other two were deceased. The three women each told the same story, almost word for word. People don't care to talk much about the past and when they do finally open up, they choose their words carefully. Retelling their personal accounts offers a narrative of the war in Brkini as ordinary people had experienced it: the Italian occupation, fol-lowed by the German invasion, and a civil war that resulted in the triumph of Tito, communism, and the unification of most of Pri-morska to a new Yugoslavia.

*

Antonija's husband, Stefan Godina, (not closely related to Josef or
Milan Godina from Bač) died at home in September 1942 from
tuberculosis. Frane, their 16-year-old son, was too young to be
drafted into the Italian Army, and joined the Partisans. In the spring
of 1943, Antonija stuffed dried wild mushrooms into a stocking
and smuggled them into Trieste to sell. A slightly different version
claims that she was selling butter. The family said that she was
raising money for the Partisans, though it seems more probable
she needed money to feed herself and her four fatherless daughters.
Antonija, then 45, was accused of being a Partisan supporter and
sentenced to two years in an Italian prison. The family did not say
where she was sent, but Italy operated several large concentration
camps full of "disloyal" Slovenes and Croatians. One of the most
notorious was located on the island of Rab, off the southern coast of
Istria, where people lived in tents or were exposed to the elements,
eventually dying of starvation or dysentery. Antonija was lucky. In
September 1943, Italy capitulated and she was released after two
months in prison. Ema, then only 12, cared for her three sisters, aged
nine, seven and four, in her mother's absence.

After the Nazis replaced the Italians, a German soldier was killed
near Artviže and the Germans retaliated against the village. Antonija's family's version recalls the Germans attacked the village because
the Partisans were encamped at St. Servulus Church—that quaint
stone church at the crest of the Brkini ridge with the magnificent,
and militarily advantageous, view. The facts are that on 21 July 1944
in Artviže, the Germans randomly chose 20 men and shot them.
Children were taken from school and lined up against the wall
to be shot, the family said, but a German officer spared their lives.
The Godina daughters were not there that day as they were already
hiding in the fields. With a son fighting among the Partisans and
her prison record for collaboration, perhaps Antonija had received
a warning to lay low and told her girls to flee for their lives. Her
house was among those destroyed and her three cows were killed
as the Nazis firebombed the village. Slavica says she tried to save

one cow from the fire but was prevented from doing so by fellow villagers who refused to help her. For six days, the children were separated from their mother as they concealed themselves in the forest. When things quieted down, the villagers took refuge in the school, and the Godinas were safely reunited. The two younger girls were taken in by relatives in nearby Gradišica, and the two older girls were employed in other homes as servants. War reparations enabled Antonija to rebuild her house and her son and daughters came home. She eventually married Josef Stančič, also a widower, and after his house was rebuilt with reparations, they were able to sell it at a profit. Josef died in 1952.

A third of Brkini was destroyed during the war, and post-war Brkini—in fact all of Primorska—did not have much to offer young people. Ema moved to Maribor in 1947 when she was 16, and stayed with her Aunt Pepina, who had returned from her wartime deportation to Austria. Ema worked in a kindergarten and later at a textile factory. Her uncle Jože Babič had a job in a kitchen cabinet factory, where every few months there was a party. It was at one of these gatherings Ema met Miha Šoštarič. She and Miha loved to dance. Ema had been courted by many men, including a Yugoslav army officer, but her uncle preferred Miha because "he knew how to do things." He came from Croatia where he had been a baker, then a carpenter, before the Germans deported him to Mauthausen, at Velz near Innsbruck, a German concentration camp where he spent 18 months. Trains would arrive from the Russian front carrying dead animals and he would collect their blood to drink, such was the level of deprivation in the camp. He said he lost 40 kg in weight, and described a life of hard labor, mining coal, and removing live bombs from homes. His freedom came when Americans liberated the camp in May 1945.

During our 2015 trip to Slovenia, my husband and I had lunch with Ema and Miha under their grape arbor in the backyard of their home in Maribor. They lived in a comfortable, modern house, with their two adult children and grandchildren close by. Miha died later that year. On another visit we made in 2019, eighty-eight year old Ema was watching a Slovenian polka band on television and she commanded my husband to dance with her. It was a moment to be treasured.

After Cesarevi was destroyed, Slavica worked locally as a servant, and went to school in Kozina for a year, before following sister Ema to Maribor in 1950. Soon after her arrival, Slavica met her husband, Ludwig Brandstetter, at another party at the kitchen cabinet factory. Danica was next to go to Maribor where she married, and had a child. For unknown reasons, in 1956, when she was only 20 years old, and Danilo was a toddler, she killed herself in the city's Drava River. Slavica took Danilo and raised him with her own son, Vladimir.

After ten years in Maribor at the kitchen cabinet factory, Slavica and Ludwig moved to Koper in 1960 to work at the Tomas motorcycle factory. For at least the last few years of her life her mother came to live with them, and it was there that Aunt Mary visited them in 1977. Great Aunt Antonija, died in 1982 and was buried in Brezovica, above her parents Ivana and Valentin Fradel, as is the custom in crowded European cemeteries. In 1983, Slavica and Ludwig retired to Ludwig's family home in Selce, a village about 15 miles from Maribor. Their house was an ancient stone one, covered with stucco, and remodeled in a way typical of rural communist Slovenia. Ludwig died in 2007. When we visited Slavica in 2015, she admitted that she was lonely there but she felt she couldn't leave Selce because she needed to take care of the gardens. She was, at heart, a daughter of the soil with deep respect for the land.

Amelja, the youngest child, stayed at home with her mother in Artviže long after her sisters left, and married Marjan Ivančič whose father was among the hostages executed by the Germans in Artviže on that fateful day. Amelja and Marjan dreamed of going to Australia with his brother. They waited until the brother was discharged from the Yugoslav army in 1960, and the three of them made their way to a displaced persons camp in Italy. However, faced with the prospect of months or even years of uncertainty while waiting for resettlement, although his brother chose to stay, Marjan and Amelja returned to Artviže. In 1966 the couple was hired at Tomas, the motorcycle company in Koper where Slavica and Ludwig worked, and they built the lovely home where they remain today, high up in Hrvatini with a great view of Koper, and their enviable vine-yards and gardens gracefully lining the hillside. Although Ema and Slavica had not expressed political views on our visits, Marjan was loud and boastful in proclaiming to us how the Partisans had set them free, and how much he hated the Domobranci. I imagined how he had been repeating these sentiments for seven decades. Tito's portrait still hung on their wall, 25 years after the establishment of the Republic of Slovenia.

Antonija's only son, Frane, the 16-year-old Partisan soldier, also went to Maribor. He died from cancer at age 59, and was buried at St. Stephen's Church in Brezovica with his mother, Antonija, his grandparents Valentin and Ivana Fradel, Marija and Stefanija who died from the Spanish flu, and the half dozen little ones who did not see their third birthday.

CHAPTER TWENTY-TWO

Jane and Joe in Europe

When the war began, Mary and John would sit in their living room to listen to the radio, read the newspapers, and imagine what the family might be experiencing in Italy and Maribor. They held their breaths when the Germans took Poland, and when Britain and France declared war in September 1939, when Belgrade was bombed, and when the Axis forces overran Yugoslavia.

On 16 September 1941, the U.S. government instituted draft registration, stipulating that it was only for service in the Western Hemisphere. But when Pearl Harbor was attacked on 7 December 1941, America declared war on Japan, and four days later, on Germany and Italy. The children of John and Mary Fradel would do a lot of growing up in the next few years.

Joe was still working at Kennametal when America joined the war and he was the first in his family to enlist. He was assigned to the 526th Ordnance Tank Maintenance Company—a good fit for a man interested in cars and engines. His job was the operation and maintenance of a mobile machine shop for tank and vehicle repairs, all loaded inside a 22-foot truck, along with his bunk. After one year of training, his unit with all their trucks and equipment, embarked on the *Queen Mary* on 2 December 1943 and disembarked nine days later at the Firth of Clyde in Scotland. Their first stop was a small town called Letcombe Regis in central England, where they set up camp in some horse stables. They moved to Grimsditch near Salisbury to work on developing new, experimental ordnances. In May 1944, they moved again to Widdecombe House, a beautiful mansion near Torquay in Devon, overlooking the English Channel. It was here that they first learned their unit would partake in the actual invasion of Europe.

Sergeant Joe Fradel, my father, was not much of a writer. While in England he wrote to his parents about every six weeks, and after D-Day he did not write at all. His mother worried endlessly, while Jane, who wrote to her every day, reassured her that Joe was busy, he was a "Real Soldier," and that no news was good news. (photo 18) At the end of the war, he typed out one long letter to describe everything that happened.

In preparation for the Normandy invasion, Joe was selected for Detachment A, which consisted of two officers, 100 men and equipment that would land in the third wave on D-Day. Detachment B was loaded onto two transports. During the crossing, one transport was torpedoed with the loss of 27 lives, and the rescue of eleven. Joe's detachment arrived on Omaha Beach on 7 June. He wrote, "We landed at nite (sic) and it was the most exciting moment of my life I assure you. Jerrys (Germans) were all out with Luftwaffe and raised hell. A bomb landed very close to our landing craft." He described the tearful or stoney faces of the women they passed in France, the destruction of villages and the roads lined with dead bodies. They picked up parts and engines from already destroyed ordnances and stuffed them into their trucks to replenish their stores since so much had been lost when Detachment B sank.

"The people of Paris were simply crazy with happiness," Joe wrote about their arrival in Paris on 28 August, three days after its liberation. For the next eight months they worked their way across France, Luxembourg, Belgium, Holland, and Germany, all the while mercilessly dogged by the Luftwaffe, buzz bombs, long range artillery, the threat of parachutists, and the German Army itself, sometimes only ten miles down the road. The 526th was a supply unit servicing the 38th Calvary, not a fighting unit, yet Joe wrote, "Our company has lost 31 men killed, approximately 60 or more wounded with about 10 or so crippled some way or another for life. I haven't fired a shot out of my carbine, except five rounds on New Year's night at Verviers, Belgium."

They arrived in Czechoslovakia in May, a few days after the Germans' surrender. In Holysov, they encamped at a former German ammunition factory for two and a half months, where Joe enjoyed his own room, a nice bed, a big sink with running water, a desk, and a lamp. From there he wrote home, describing his experiences in the kind of detail that had not been permitted until censorship was lifted. He had fun in Holysov with a Czech girlfriend named Hana, singing songs, drinking, and smoking plenty of cigars that Jane sent to him. He was welcomed into the homes of several expatriate Slovene families, and described one elderly woman: "She is sort of the way I thought my grandma would be. She was so glad to hear me talk Slovene that she cried. She was dressed in traditional black (for old age) stood very straight and held her hands in prayer and said "Hvala bogu do ste prisele" (*Thank God you come*) over and over again."

His detachment moved to Nuremburg on 22 July and then on to Marseilles for the voyage home. In France, dozens of staging camps, or tent cities, where units stayed for one or two weeks, were named after American cities and cigarettes. At the end of September, Joe and Jane met up at a Paris club that allowed officers and enlisted men to eat together, and they celebrated and talked until he had to catch the truck back to Camp Baltimore at midnight. He was stateside in October and discharged from Fort Dix on 8 November 1945.

*

After her return from Europe in 1937, Jane was active in politics, worked in Pittsburgh, and dated interesting young men. Among her boyfriends, her family favored Tony Laurich, a tall, good-looking Slovene. She was serious about Al Ferraro, but her parents would not even agree to meet him because of his Italian heritage. At the onset of the war, she was working at Latrobe Hospital, 30 years old, single, and eager to join the war effort, but was rejected by the Army because of her mild asthma. She pestered them with letters until they granted her an exemption. On 11 October 1943, she was posted to the hospital at Aberdeen Proving Grounds in Maryland, assigned to the 74th General Hospital. In February, the 74th gathered in Fort Dix, New Jersey, and followed the same route overseas that Joe Fradel had taken. The hospital unit was transported by rail to its staging area at Holyoke near Liverpool, and Jane was sent to work in a hospital just outside London amidst bombings and air raids. In early May 1944, the 74th moved to Tyntesfield, seven miles from Bristol, and Jane was recalled to the main unit. The 74th was the largest American hospital in the European Theater of Operations. Before D-Day, it provided routine care to the 1.5 million American servicemen in England.

Jane wrote to her parents every day using V-mail, short for Victory Mail, which provided a quick service to and from soldiers overseas. A standardized stationery combined the letter and address into one piece of paper. The letter was reviewed by censors, sorted by state, then photographed in microfilm before the spools were flown to the U.S., printed at one quarter the original size, and delivered by the postal service for free. Frequent use of V-mail was considered a patriotic act because messages helped build morale amongst service men and women and saved on shipping and airplane space. Each person got two free sheets per day. Jane's daily letters were brief and airy, full of questions about the family, and reassurances to her mother about herself and Joe. She gave no details of her work, or her patients, and the places where she was stationed were not revealed until the war was over.

The nurses of the 74th were warmly greeted in Britain. In Holyoke and in London, Lieutenant Jane Fradel stayed with families, and was invited to luncheons and teas by local folk. She also found connections among Slovene expatriates in London and enjoyed dinner and conversation with Dr. Drago Marusič several times during her stay in England. Dr. Marusič was in London to serve the Yugoslavian Royalist government in exile. She described him as an old and dear friend whom she had met through family connections in Yugoslavia in 1937, when he had been a member of the National Assembly. She wrote home so enthusiastically about him that her sisters teased her about a possible romance until Jane set the record straight. He was about 60 years old, a widower from the Trieste area. He had two brothers with whom he had lost contact since the war began in 1941, and had been in Primorska as recently as January 1944. Jane's acquaintance with Dr. Marusič gave her a peek inside the Yugoslavian government.

As the war came to a close, the British pressured King Peter to establish a government with Tito. His prime minister, Ivan Šubašić, was given this assignment and Dr. Marusič was his Minister of Justice and Traffic. When King Peter yielded to Tito, Dr. Marusič served in the transitional government until 1948, then became head of the Yugoslavian Red Cross.

Dr. Marusič introduced Jane to other Slovenes from Trieste and Primorska at the Jugo-slav (sic) House in London. Dr. Vladimir Rybár—undersecretary for foreign affairs at the embassy in Washington D.C. before the war who had married an American opera singer—was personally acquainted with John and Mary Fradel through social and political events sponsored by S.N.P.J., the Slovene National Benefit Society. When Jane met Dr. Rybár in London he was Minister of Foreign Affairs in the Šubašić administration. He represented Yugoslavia at the Bretton Woods Conference that determined monetary policy for the post-war era, and established the International Monetary Fund and the International Bank for Reconstruction and Development. He was instrumental in securing post-war relief for Yugoslavia, with special attention to Primorska. He served in the transitional government, and became ambassador to Norway in 1946.

Jane wrote home about meeting Mr. and Mrs. Boris Furlan, and
their daughter. Boris Furlan was also a member of the Šubašić
administration and the official Slovene speaker for Radio London.
Dr. Lambert Mermolja was a dentist who had spent time in detention
under the fascists and the Nazis. Slavo Klemenčič, a Partisan journalist, who worked for the BBC and other news organizations had
lunch with Jane on two occasions and took her to the BBC to watch
a broadcast. Her mother was pleased with Jane: "You meet more
Slovenes in London than you did at home." She asked her to use her
connections to get news of her family in Povžane, without any success.

Another acquaintance was Dr. Franja Bidovec, the Slovene doctor
who managed a Partisan hospital hidden in the forest that received
aid from the Americans and British. During this time, Dr. Franja
faced opposition from male colleagues and was ousted briefly. Two
family photos show Dr. Franja with Jane. In one my aunt is wearing
her uniform at the 74th General Hospital. (photo 19) The other is a
small personal photo signed by Dr. Franja. I imagine that they met
through Dr. Marusič, and that Jane acted in an official capacity as a
translator when Dr. Franja visited the hospital.

Some of the nurses were invited to coffee with Lady Astor, the
American-born wife of Lord Astor and famously the first woman
elected to and seated in Parliament in Britain. She was a Conservative politician who held a seat in the House of Commons from
1919 to 1945 and was known for her wit and intelligence. Jane
describes her as having "plenty of vitality and the ability to speak
well." Jane and her roommate, Jane Heimbecker, thoroughly enjoyed
Lady Astor's company and spent another day with her, then she
invited them to visit her in London and to see Parliament in session,
although I believe they were not able to get leave.

The Officers Club in Bristol offered Jane plenty of opportunities for entertainment, music, dances, and to fraternize with other
officers. The Red Cross ran a club in Bristol that afforded her a
homey place to hang out. Jane Heimbecker was a great roommate,

she good-naturedly did all Jane's sewing, and they took holidays together in Scotland and Plymouth, by the sea.

The first trainload of wounded patients arrived six days after D-Day, on 12 June 1944. Subsequent hospital trains arrived steadily through November. After the period of acute care was relieved, the focus moved to rehabilitation. Almost none of the patients returned to active duty. The story that her siblings tell, one that is probably derived from what Jane told Joe that evening in Paris, is that she fell in love with a R.A.F. pilot, but he was killed over France on 17 July 1944 during his 50th bombing raid. After reading all her letters, I can only add that his name was Geoffrey, he had a sister named Lucille in Liverpool, he was born in Australia, grew up in India, and from his photo I can see that he was a paratrooper, not a pilot. The effect of his death on Jane, just judging from her letters, was devastating but brief. Other nurses suffered the loss of brothers and sweethearts, but despite their pain, they continued to perform their duties caring for the dying, the wounded, those on their way to recovery, and those who were disabled.

On 27 June 1945, a year after D-Day, the 74th hospital in England closed and moved to St. Quentin, north of Reims in France. They prepared for transfer to the Pacific theater, but after Hiroshima was bombed the war ended, and some personnel prepared to go home. Jane was transferred to the 191st General Hospital. She sometimes lived in a home, or in a hotel with other nurses. She moved between hospitals in and around Paris, taking care of all sorts of patients— sick nurses, psychiatric patients, American soldiers, even German POWs. Other nurses were sent to hospitals in Germany and Vienna.

In love with Paris, Jane had her portrait done, got her hair permed, took buggy rides, visited the Louvre, and all the sites. The city was bustling with Americans at the end of the war and she and brother Joe had the chance to spend the day together on 28 September. The U.S. Army took over certain hotels and chateaus for "Rest and Recreation," some were just for nurses so Jane had weeklong breaks in

Switzerland, Cannes on the Riviera, and at a chateau in the river-front city of Nancy.

She seriously considered volunteering for the Army of Occupation, the military force that would remain in Europe for several more years. She thought of requesting an assignment in Trieste and getting in touch with family in Slovenia. Tonči may have written to Jane in 1939 to let her know that he had been drafted, but Jane wouldn't have known until after the war that he was dead. But as the months went on, she got less busy, a little bored, a little homesick, and a little edgy to claim her old job at Latrobe Hospital where she would not have to do night duty, her least favorite. She left Paris on 13 December for Camp Phillip Morris at Le Havre to await her transport home and worked stateside until her discharge on 17 March 1946.

The other three Fradel children were stateside during the war. John Fradel, my uncle, was a commercial pilot employed in 1940 at Daitz Flying corps at Roosevelt field in Nassau, New York. (photo 20) There he met a beautiful dark-haired woman, Maria Di Geronimo, but marriage to an Italian did not please his parents, especially his mother, and they did not attend his wedding. John and Maria had their first child just a few months before John enlisted in the Army Air Corps on 17 September 1943 and underwent training to teach recruits the basics of aviation. Despite my grandparents' disapproval of the marriage, Maria and the baby stayed with them for some months until John was settled at his postings. He was assigned to Bowman Field, Kentucky, known as "Air Base City," the place where recruits underwent basic training to become pilots in bomber squadrons.

Mary worked as a secretary before her marriage in 1941. Her husband Matt Hrebar, son of Slovene immigrants, had a degree in mining engineering and taught at Pennsylvania State College. He was called up to serve in the U.S. Naval Reserves in February 1944, while Mary was due to give birth to a son that July. It was a hard and lonely time for her and it sounds like she suffered from postpartum depression, something that did not garner much sympathy in the old days. Her sister, Jane, the army nurse tending to wounded men, certainly had no sympathy, and sent scolding V-mails telling her to pull herself together, count her blessings, and write to her husband every day.

Sylvia lived at home during the war and worked as a secretary. She immersed herself in volunteer activities to help the war effort. She organized blood drives and was a leader in the Latrobe Home Service Club, putting on programs and dances for servicemen and cadets at St. Vincent College. There she met Duncan Woodward, a Marine from New Hampshire who had been selected for Officer Candidate School. Duncan was madly in love and wanted to marry right away but Sylvia insisted on waiting until the war was over. When he left for active duty, they wrote to each other every day. Very soon after the war's end, on 25 July 1945, they married; Jane and Joe were disappointed not to be present because they were still in Europe.

John and Mary Fradel were proud of their children's contributions to the war effort and felt blessed that they were alive and coming home to Latrobe. The S.N.P.J. played an important role in organizing relief activities for Slovenia, including gathering thousands of pounds of clothes to ship as soon as it was permitted. Slovenes in America anxiously waited for the outcome of negotiations amongst the Allied victors that would determine who would govern Istria, Trieste, and Gorica—the entire north Adriatic coast that had been occupied since 1918 by the now-defeated Italy. My grandmother wrote to Povžane and waited impatiently and hopefully for news that her brother and loved ones had survived the war.

The first thing Joe Fradel did upon reaching home was to buy a watch and a car. He met Dorothy Glasstetter from nearby Greensburg at a summer party and they married 31 October 1946. He used his G.I. benefits to go to California State Teacher's College in Pennsylvania for a degree in teaching industrial arts. After graduation in 1950, he taught at a high school in Maryland, then moved on to a job at Aberdeen Proving Ground, home of the Army Ordnance School, where he taught what he had learned as a soldier. He was a specialist in tank maintenance and worked there until retirement. He and Dorothy, my parents, had seven children and lived in Aberdeen, Maryland.

After military service, my uncle John Fradel settled in Latrobe and worked for Carborundum Corp., a company that made precision ceramic parts and insulators. John and Maria added another daughter and two sons to their family. My grandmother gradually let go of her resentment of Maria's Italian heritage, and Maria became her friend and support in her later years.

Sylvia moved with Duncan while he finished his degree and earned a masters in poultry science at Penn State. They had one child. They divorced in 1957 and Sylvia married William J. Walker. Despite frequent relocations, Sylvia always found work because of her excellent secretarial skills.

Matt and Mary built a new stone home in Beaverdale near Johnstown. Matt, the son of a immigrant miner, now owned a mining company, the Mary Elizabeth Coal Company, where Mary worked as secretary. He also served as the mining engineering consultant for the Commonwealth of Pennsylvania. Their only son also became a mining engineer.

Jane got her job back at the Latrobe Hospital. Jane was an independent-minded woman ahead of her times in many ways. Her early political activity, involvement in S.N.P.J., her ability to speak her mind in person and in writing, brought great admiration from her Slovenian community. She had the personality of a nurse able to take charge in times of trouble and tell people what to do—her family leaned on her for this. Others, such as my mother who was a meek 20-year-old when she married my 29-year-old father, were intimidated by her forcefulness. When my mother's first child was born with spina-bifida, Jane took charge. It all came from a place of love and tenderness. During the war she wrote reassuring letters to her parents every day, she wrote to Joe "The Real Soldier" every three to four days, and to her brother John and sisters to keep their spirits up while she cared for the wounded soldiers from Europe and hid her own frailties. Her trip to Slovenia in 1937 and acquaintances with prominent Slovenes in London strengthened the family's link to their homeland. They all believed that Jane was the best in the world and could do no wrong.

After ten years of far-flung romances, Jane yearned for normalcy. She was 34 when she married Frank Drasler, a 37-year-old Slovene from Forest City, Pennsylvania in 1947. The family was disappointed in her choice. Weighing just 150 pounds on a six-foot frame, they made fun of his appearance, his apparent lack of ambition, and his work. In 1941, he had been too old for the draft, but he worked at Crucible Steel Company in Harrison, New Jersey, a major producer of weapons and ammunition. He returned to Latrobe after the war to work at Kennametal. My father said with scorn, "He was just a screw salesman." The family did not like Frank, but the only reason given was a vague: "She could have done better." Not until I read the private messages to and from Jane did I realize that the family, in the old village tradition of meddling in marriage making, had decided that she should marry Tony Laurich. Her mother nagged Jane about him and Jane replied sharply that she didn't want to hear any more about him. As a young woman, my father, recognizing my similarities to Jane and clumsily attempting to advise me on my choice in men, told me what a mistake Jane had made when she spurned Tony Laurich. Tony had what the family admired. He was a graduate of California State Teachers College and an industrial arts teacher in a Pittsburgh high school before the war. He joined the Navy and made it his career, rising to the rank of commander, but never married. Among the family photos is a good-looking American sailor in post-war Trieste, standing between Pepca Fabjančič and another woman. (photo 21) On the back Tony Laurich had written: "Here are the two girls I looked up for Jane Fradel."

CHAPTER TWENTY-THREE

1945–1948: The New Yugoslavia

From the beginning, the communists envisioned that war would provide an opportunity to establish an egalitarian society in the form of a federation of states, similar to the Soviet Union. The People's Liberation Army, better known as the Partisans, was meant to be a model for this future society. It was multinational and women had full rights, serving as soldiers, combat medics, and doctors. Soldiers were taught to read and write, and indoctrinated into Marxism and socialist values. They read poems by national writers and sang battle songs. The Partisans promised to end foreign exploitation and rule, find solutions for social problems, and spread peace and reconciliation through brotherhood and unity. Their plan was attractive and their numbers grew.

The German retreat began after Tito's Partisans took Belgrade in the fall of 1944, and by December, Montenegro, Macedonia, and Kosovo were liberated. As each area was liberated, People's committees promptly set up local bureaucracies to organize food, supplies, land, and possessions, as well as deal with spies, traitors, and collaborators. They instituted newspapers, postal delivery, telephone service, theaters, and music. By mid-May 1945, the Partisans controlled all of the former Yugoslavia, Istria, and Primorska.

Partisan and Allied forces converged on Trieste almost simulta-
neously in May. The Allies wanted to give Trieste to Italy as a reward
for its 1943 defection to their side, while the Partisans wanted to
reclaim territory wrongly occupied by the Italians since 1918. On
a larger scale, Stalin's plans to extend the Soviet Union's sphere of
influence conflicted with Tito's plans for the Balkan region. Demon-
strations of military strength took place and ultimately Stalin sided
with the Allies. The Partisans pulled out of Trieste in June and
the area was provisionally divided. The area surrounding Trieste
and northwards to Gorica, known as "Zone A," was controlled by
a joint British and American military government. "Zone B" to the
south, which included Koper and Istria, was controlled by the Partisans. This arrangement may have suited international geopolitical
strategies, but it was devastating for Primorskan farmers like Jožef
Fabjančič who could not enter Trieste or Zone A. Jožef depended on
Trieste to sell his surplus goods, to shop for essentials, to bank and
obtain medical care, as well as stay in touch with his family. Zone
A would be permanently awarded to Italy in 1954.

The Partisans were thoroughly prepared to seize absolute
power when the moment arrived, and much of it was not pretty.
In May 1944, Tito created *Odsjek za zaštitu Naroda* or OZNA, the
secret police. As the Partisans advanced, the liberated areas were
cleansed of anyone who had supported the bureaucracy of the
occupiers, or enemy troops. In the fall of 1944, an American liaison
officer reported from Dubrovnik that the inhabitants were living
in a state of mortal terror. The Partisan attitude was that anyone
who had stayed in Dubrovnik during the occupation, and didn't
work in the Partisan underground, was a collaborator. Every day,
the dreaded secret police took people from their homes to the old
castle to be shot. OZNA kept files with the names of collaborators
and war criminals. So-called courts of honor were created to pros-
ecute war crimes.

From a sense of political conviction, or embitterment and revenge,
between 1943 and 1948 the Partisans systematically eliminated

their opponents, whom they called "the quislings," in reference to the infamous Norwegian politician who collaborated with the Nazis. Right after Italy's surrender in 1943, an estimated 500 to 700 representatives of the Italian fascist regime were executed, their bodies dumped in the sinkholes of the karst. In the spring of 1945, hundreds, perhaps thousands, more victims followed. These atrocities became known as *foibe,* the word for these limestone sinkholes. Hundreds of thousands of Italians fled, and the half million Gottschee, German settlers from the 18th century, who were given favor by the Nazis, were also targeted for Partisan retribution. Then, in early July 1945, Tito gave the order to free all imprisoned quislings over the age of 35, who had not committed an atrocity. However, this order was slow to be implemented and the rampage didn't end until the year's close.

The new Yugoslavia was organized as a federation of six co-equal republics: Slovenia, Croatia, Bosnia-Herzegovina, Serbia, Montenegro, and Macedonia. Within Serbia, two autonomous regions existed: Vojvodina and Kosovo. Minorities that were given an official status were the few remaining Germans, Italians, Muslims, Jews, Roma, Vlachs, Magyars and Albanians.

Throughout its 46 years of existence, the communist state never acknowledged the injustices done in its name. The violence provided grounds to question the legitimacy of the new system. In Slovenia and Croatia, where the re-establishment of Yugoslavia itself was not universally approved, the rift running through society was particularly deep.

*

Mary and John Fradel settled into a personal, post-war contentment. Jane and Joe were safe in Europe, Sylvia had a beautiful wedding, John returned to Latrobe with his wife and little daughter, and Matt came home to his wife, Mary Elizabeth, and his son. They wrote to Povžane several times before they finally got news from Jožef. With trembling and tears and joy, Mary opened the first letter from her brother in six years.

23 September 1945

Dear Sister and Janez!!! Today I received the letter that you wrote on 16 August. We are glad to hear that you are all alive. This is not the case with us, and you will cry when you read this letter. On 18 October it will be two years since we've buried Mama. Dear Sister, I know that you want to know how it was with Mama at the end. The last days were sad, we brought her to the kitchen, and she sat next to the stove for the entire day. For 20 days she could not sit anymore, but she did not suffer. Only in the last three days she hurt everywhere and we moved her around and carried her so that she felt better. I sat with her for four days before her death. She worried about what would happen to her. I told her that she should thank God that she will die soon and that she will be buried as a Christian, the rest of us did not know where we would be killed and buried. After that she was much more patient. She had a clear mind until the end. Let her rest in peace.

Over the next six months their letters crisscrossed and the events of the war years came out in bits and pieces because they had no way of knowing when or which letters reached their destination. This is a composite of Jožef's letters from September 1945 to February 1946:

My daughter Franca went to the hospital in Trst in May of 1943 with tuberculosis. (photo 22) She stayed until the collapse of Italy in September 1943, and then she came home. On the 14 September 1943, there was much fear when the Germans came to Materija. They burned down Zupančičevi and people fled in all directions. People from Polžane ran up into the hills. I could not carry Mama, and I could not leave her home alone, so I decided to stay; if they were to kill us, it was better to die at home, rather than somewhere in the woods. But the Germans came, I greeted them, and they did not do me any harm on that day.

Franca suffered a lot at home, particularly during the last three months. She was also talking until the last minute. She died late in the evening on 27 April and we buried her on 29 April. If she had lived another 30 hours, we would have been unable to bury her because on 30 April the Germans had to run and the Partisans arrived. The war started around here and for eight days nobody could go to Trst. The Partisans took the boys and young men on the first day and put them under arms.

We do not know anything about our son, Jože. On 17 December, it will be three years since he last wrote to us from the Russian Front. We do not know if he is a prisoner, or if he is dead. We have been looking for his cross, but so far, we haven't found it.

Jožef had last heard from his son on 17 December 1942, reportedly from the River Elan, a tributary of the Prut in Romania. In late summer of 1941, Mussolini sent the Italian 8th Army to aid in the invasion of Russia. In December 1942, the month of Jože's disappearance, 130,000 Italian troops were strung out along the River Don facing the Soviets who launched Operation Saturn—an initiative aimed at annihilating their foes. According to Italian sources, about 20,000 soldiers died in the fighting, 64,000 were captured and 45,000 were able to withdraw. By the end of February 1943, the rout of the 8th Army was complete and Mussolini withdrew what remained of his army from Russian soil. The failed leader tried to hide the survivors from public view, so appalling was their appearance after enduring the Russian Front.

Survivors blamed Fascist politicians and generals for sending a poorly prepared and ill-equipped force to the Russian Front. Hand grenades rarely went off, and rifles and machine guns had to be warmed on a fire to work properly in the cold, thus they often failed to discharge in the midst of battle. German commanders were accused of delaying the withdrawal of the Italian divisions after the Soviet breakthrough, in order to rescue their own troops. That is what 23-year-old Jože Fabjančič, a boy from Povžane, endured in his fourth year of service in the Italian army.

Jožef's younger son, Janez (photo 23) was drafted into the Italian Army in March 1943. He was in Greece when Italy collapsed and the Germans captured him and sent him to a labor camp in Upper Silesia. He wrote home multiple times from there. When the Russians took command of his camp, communications went silent, but in October he arrived home unharmed.

The youngest daughter, Pepka, was admitted to the hospital with tuberculosis in May 1945, just as the war was ending. Her five-month stay recovering from pneumonia cost 150 lire a day and the family had to bring her packages of food every week. Jožef continued:

> Therefore, it's been only three of us at home for the last year; I and my wife and daughter, Milka. While the German was here, Milka worked for the military for seven months. If he had not escaped, I would also be dead. They've already taken me to Kozina and from there I managed to escape.

Jožef and Milka (photo 24) were involved in some activity for which they feared retribution from the Partisan government. Milka's son told me that everyone in the village was required to work for the Germans and that his mother was sent to Črni Kal to sew German uniforms. He explained that she also worked for the Partisans. The villagers also had no choice in providing the Partisans with provisions. What people did was based less on ideology than survival.

Who "the German" was, where he escaped from, or why his escape saved Jožef from execution lacks explanation. My theory is that Milka was also doing some work for a German, perhaps cooking or washing, and Jožef had been taken prisoner by the Partisans to Kozina. His fate was in question, but he got away. Timing may have been on his side. Tito's July 1945 decision to dismiss charges against those over 35 who had not committed atrocities, worked in his favor. Jožef continued:

> Dear Sister, imagine how much we had to endure, just how much fear there was. It is true that we have not been hungry,

but everything else was suffering. There was illness and death in the house. For 18 months, Fascists were on Gabrk, Germans were in the village, and in between were the Partisans, whom we had to support. You can imagine how lucky we are to be alive. The bodies of Slovenian boys are scattered throughout Europe. We still haven't heard anything from our Jože, every day there is less and less hope that he is alive.

Antonija, sister of John Fradel, decided to test the new government's land policies and made claim to the unused four acres of Jurkotevi. The Partisan government tried various strategies to redistribute land—everything from the confiscation of large estates, to collectivization, to limiting ownership to the acreage a family could till on their own without hired labor. Briefly, a policy was implemented that allowed claims on land with absentee owners simply by cultivating it, and it may have been at that point that Antonija thought she could win in court. Jožef wrote on February 1946:

Dear Sister and Janez,
Antonija has been a widow for two years. You know that the Germans burned Artviže down. Now she is thinking of getting married. He is also widowed. Her children are not happy about this, and she came up with the idea that she would come to Polžane. Under the Italian Fascists, she and her husband tried to take control of your farm, but they were not successful. Now Antonija thinks that the Partisans will give the farm to her. She has already filed a lawsuit against me. I gave them proof that she already acknowledged that she had received her inheritance from Number 11, but the courthouse in Kozina agrees with her. I have already filed an appeal at a higher court.
I would in fact be pleased for her to have the farm, but without Janez's permission, no one will take your farm. I will protect your rights until the end. I will write to the highest entity so that she will only get her way when they destroy every contract and agreement that was made under the former Austria and Italy. Now I am awaiting your reply so that I can represent you.

You will receive a letter from her, so you do whatever you see
fit. Antonija says that she has often written to America but that
you, Marija, threw her letters into the fire so that Janez would
not see them. You know for yourself if there is any truth in this.

By early 1947, news of the war years had been exchanged and pro-
cessed, and interest turned toward catching up with old friends and
neighbors. Packages with used clothing and photographs were sent.
The price of new clothing was exorbitant, and most folk were walking around in castoff German and Italian uniforms. When I was
in Povžane in 2014, I was shown some old photos my grandmother
sent to her brother after the war—pictures of Mary Elizabeth and
Sylvia dressed in coats with luxurious fur collars, laughing as they
slid into big American cars. I just cannot fathom my grandmother's
insensitivity in flaunting the prosperity of her family in America to
her brother in war-ravaged communist Slovenia. I was embarrassed.

Miha Fabjančič, husband of Marija at Maharinčevi, had already
done his time in the Italian Army and while in Povžane, he spied
for the Partisans, according to his son. He was required to report
on fascist and Nazi movements as well as disloyal neighbors, to
Partisan command in Kozjane. Evading detection was dangerous,
and oftentimes Miha could not come home. After the war, he could
at last sleep at Maharinčevi with Marija and their small children.
Frane Bilko was released from the Partisan army after serving 28
months. As the only son of Bilkotevi he was sorely needed. Zora
Bazleteva left her husband in Trieste and was looking around at
new prospects. At Bazletevi, young Ivan Godina was the new master.

Božidar Kastelic lived in the old school. He had a job weighing
wagons, but did not earn much and relied on what his friends and
neighbors could share. His misfortunes had aged his appearance to
that of a shriveled, bent man much older than his 59 years. Marija
from Gabrk was doing well, still wearing her double aprons, and
preparing tasty meals out of almost nothing. She lived at Drauftevi
where her daughter, Mija, was now the bride. Mija had married

her twin brother's best friend. Her twin, Tonči and August Drauf had teamed up to serenade Jane and Anna Mae during that golden, peaceful summer in 1937. Tonči was now just a bittersweet memory to many, his body trapped in the wreckage of a ship in the Mediterranean.

Under the motto *Nema odmora dok traje obnova!* (No rest while we're rebuilding!) Yugoslavia undertook the great task of clearing the wreckage and starting anew. At war's end, more than a million people were dead and 3.5 million had no roof over their heads. Large sections of the country had no running water. The retreating Germans destroyed factories, mines, businesses, roads, railway tracks, and bridges. Cheerful brigades of young people were sent out to start the work. Individual landowners were compensated through the war reparations program.

The process of redevelopment in rural communities was hindered by severe droughts that affected central Europe in both 1947 and 1949, and Yugoslavia was unable to feed itself. This was most demoralizing for Jožef Fabjančič, who had lived through two wars, lost his son and heir, and struggled every day of his life to coax food for his family out of soil hampered by weeds, unfavorable weather, and the burja. His lifetime of ceaseless work was reduced, in his last days, to depending on meager government handouts. Aid came from the Soviet Union and the United Nations Program for Reconstruction and Development (the program that Dr. Rybár, Jane's acquaintance in London, had helped institute) which provided $419 million in aid, the highest amount awarded to any European recipient. Most of this was used to purchase food, clothing, and medicine. As the rift between Stalin and Tito escalated, the American perspective portrayed Stalin as the "bad communist" while Tito was seen as the "good communist." This political dynamic led the United States to contribute millions of dollars to support Yugoslav development.

Property belonging to banks, companies, churches, monasteries, large landowners, and ethnic Germans had been confiscated by the early Partisan government, even before the war was over. In August

1945, the new communist government legalized these confiscations and limited peasant farms to roughly 62 to 86 acres. No one in the valley under Slavnik was in danger of losing their meager acres. What remained in private hands were homes, peasant farms, and artisan workshops that employed no more than four people. A second major reform in 1953 reduced individual ownership to 25 acres for peasants, and to 7.5 acres for people who farmed on the side. These limits were still not a big deal for the people under Slavnik.

What did bother them was a centralized purchasing system for agricultural products called *otkup* that required farmers sell surplus production (including firewood) to state agencies at low fixed prices and purchase industrial goods at high market prices. Many farmers circumvented *otkup* by selling on the black market. Already hardened by years of terror, threats of arrest and severe sentences did not discourage them, and the black market flourished, to the frustration of both authorities and the general population. The new government was forced to issue an amnesty in the summer of 1946.

The cornerstone of the new communist economic plan was rapid industrialization as directed by the state to meet the country's needs: heavy industry and electrification, a demand for consumer goods, and self-sustaining economic growth—one that could absorb all those younger sons and low producing farmers in rural areas. Additionally, a socialist transformation of village life was sought through education, diversification, modern agricultural technology, and ultimately, an increase in productivity.

A campaign to convince the youth of the village to leave rural areas for industrial work began. Contrary to the methods of the Soviet Union, the peasantry was not terrorized into entering this new age, but rather persuaded of the benefits. This cannot have been difficult in Primorska since the younger generation had been aching to get away to new opportunities in America, Argentina, Trieste, or Maribor for the previous half century. Between 1945 and 1953, 1.5 million people throughout Yugoslavia left their villages and moved permanently to the cities, just as Antonija Cesareva's children went to Maribor and

Koper, and Rezina's daughter moved to Postojna. Another 800,000 became part-time industrial laborers and commuters.

21 October 1947

Dear Sister, You read in your newspapers that there was a drought here. It lasted the entire year, twice we got soaked a little, so that the drought was separated into three parts. We had less than a third of our usual wheat, very few potatoes, and only a fourth of our usual hay in the fall. Livestock has nothing to eat and we had to pick the leaves from the cherry trees to feed the pigs. Now there is nothing to make them fat. It seems that one misery leads to another. The drought is so bad that people in the villages have no water for livestock, or themselves. People from Skadanščina walk to get water from Markovščina, from Male Loče they go to Obrov, even in Hotična they have no water. We in Polžane have the water distribution system that the Italians built. We improved it so that in the middle of the village we have a well and a drinking trough for the livestock. This year we were fortunate to have adequate water.

As you know from the newspapers, the economy here is bad. Lire have been replaced with the dinar, but we have very few of them, and will have even less in the future. The hardest thing is that we are not allowed to go to Trst. Without Trst we cannot survive. My daughter needs to go there for tuberculosis treatment; twice we applied for permission to go to Trst, but so far, we have not received anything.

You write that Skominčič is planning to come home to sell his farm, and that you have similar intentions. Honestly, this is not the time to think about selling. Nobody has any money to buy land. The laws are changing all the time and it is becoming apparent that our country will not allow us to sell our land. You will have to educate yourself about the new laws, or I can attempt to tell you. We fought for freedom from Italy and Germany, and now we are taking orders from our own.

You ask if we've put up a tombstone for Mama for Remembrance Day. We have not gotten one because we cannot go to

Trst with the cart, so the only option is the black market. We nicely prepared the grave, poured cement the entire length and planted flowers inside. When things go back to normal, I plan to purchase a plaque with inscriptions and mount it on the wall.

11 January 1948

Two months have passed since I last received your letter. I expected to receive one around the holidays, but the holidays have passed, and still no letter. So, today I decided to write to update you about our life. We haven't had any winter; we had sunshine for the holidays, it felt like spring for the New Year, and the pleasant weather continues. I wrote last year that we cannot get dried fish for Christmas Eve soup, and soon we will not know what bread is. We get four kilograms [8.8 pounds] of corn flour per month on our food stamps. During the war, when the times were hardest, we never had less than one kvintal [220 pounds] of flour at home. There have been times in the past when we did not have much, but we could do something about it, but now we cannot help ourselves, we cannot go to Trst and we cannot earn anything at home. Here at home, we are of fragile health, particularly my wife and I. Daughter Pepka is doing much better, although she still needs tuberculosis treatments in Ajdovščina every 15 days. It is free, all she has to pay for is transportation. Son Janez is still at home, but now we hear that everyone who has not yet served in our military will have to join the army.

You mention that you do not get much news about Yugoslavia. In some newspaper articles that you sent, there is a lot of praise for our country, when in reality this is not true. Let me tell you something that should concern all of you in America who have farms here. An announcement was made that you retain ownership, just as you did under Italian rule. You can sell it as before, but it is not a favorable time because people do not have the courage to buy land as long as things stay like they are. Can you imagine that they pay only 63 dinars for a kvintal of firewood? One liter of wine is 55 dinars!

Dear Sister, you've written many times already that you will at some point come to see us. Do you think that you could help our daughter Milka get to America? There is nothing for her here.

Exclamation points, or lack thereof, reflected Jožef's mood, but nothing explains why Jožef used question marks in the greeting of the following letter. Strangely, eerily, this was to be the last one of his letters that Mary tucked away.

22 February 1948

Dear Sister and Janez?? Last week I received your letter from 7 November and I replied to that. A few days later I received the one that you wrote on 15 November, then yesterday I received one from 14 January. Dear Sister, you said that you sent us a package, but I have yet to receive it. I remain hopeful that it will arrive and I thank you for it in advance. We did not have any winter until 17 February; now it turned cold and has been snowing for two days. We already have more than enough snow and it continues to fall.

You wrote that it would be good if we started a market in Kozina since we cannot go to Trst anymore. There is a market in Kozina, but it does not work. We have to sell at the same price as markets that are many kilometers away. For example, they pay 63 dinars for a kvintal of firewood whether it is in Kozina where wood is scarce, or in Snežnik where wood is abundant, but in Trst they pay 800 to 1,000 lire per kvintal. What a difference that is! It is like this for everything. Everything is organized as cooperatives; you have a cooperative for food, a cooperative for livestock farming, a cooperative for rebuilding, an agricultural cooperative. Craftsmen each have their own cooperatives. I am not registered in any of them, and I will not, until they force me to.

You wrote that I do not mention my son Janez. He is a good blacksmith, but he does not have tools. He works hard on the farm, and listens to everything. He still has no interest in getting married. He has the courage and desire to see the world. He wishes that Jože would come home so that he could leave, but Jože has not returned.

Tito's economic plan transformed the nation and the economy grew sufficiently diversified so the newest generation could either find work in rural areas or choose to commute. In the 1950s a toy factory opened on Gabrk, where the gostilna used to be. Janez worked there, and farmed part time. His daughters chose professions and moved to the cities. His son trained as a mechanic and started a business that today has expanded to employ both his son and daughter, and others in the villages under Slavnik.

CHAPTER TWENTY-FOUR

1949: The End of a Hard Life

Jožef Fabjančič died at home on 5 May 1949 at the age of 62. He had a happy youth, enjoying the company of his siblings, sharing a special confidence with his younger sister, planting, harvesting, storing food, and tending livestock, foraging, visiting the city, happily learning to read and write, and being part of an ancient village of unbroken traditions that extended back five hundred years or more. All that changed on 27 July 1914 when he climbed onto the wagon that would transport him into the thick of the Austrian Empire's last war. He once said he lived "In a way that I would not wish on my enemy." Jožef was blessed with a good wife and their six children survived the usual plagues of childhood that robbed so many families of their joy. He should have had a good life. Instead, the old gratitude of Austria was replaced by Italian fascism, intent upon the destruction of his language and his culture, and on siphoning away whatever meager wealth he possessed in his few acres, the fruits of his labor, and his children. The ensuing economic and social destruction precluded the return of his sister and others who had gone to work in North and South America, and to Maribor, and the ancient rhythm of life under Slavnik was broken.

Jožef's illness was protracted. My aunt said that it was kidney failure. Although Mary did not save his last letters, they stayed in touch to the end. She felt adrift without her brother, and she reached out to others in her old world to maintain a sense of connection. Weeks after Jožef's death, on 26 May, his daughter, Pepka, wrote:

> Dear Aunt! Yesterday we received the letter that you wrote on 22 April. Your previous letter written on 8 April came on 5 May. If the letter had arrived just a day earlier, our beloved Dad would have been able to read your letter and look at the photographs that you sent, but on that last day he was no longer aware of anything. Just a few days earlier he wanted to write a letter to you, but he just could not lift the pen. Dear Aunt, he had the will to send you his last greetings, but not the strength.
>
> We thank you greatly for your photographs. We liked Ivanka's husband as soon as we saw his picture; he looks very tall and gentle. You are all very good-looking, and nicely dressed. You look as young as if you were still a girl. If you lived here, you would surely look like we do, as black as dirt. Only state employees get stamps for food and clothing that permits one suit, one shirt and one pair of shoes. To those of us who are living on the farms, they give nothing. We are not alone; it is the same everywhere in the cities and the countryside of Yugoslavia. They say that we should give our farms to the state, and work for the local commune and then we would get stamps as well. So instead, I went to Rijeka to buy a little bit of black color to dye some clothes. We received the package that you sent on 12 February, we already wrote to you about it, and I think that by now you should have received that letter. Again, we thank you for everything.
>
> *Pepka Fabjančič*

Then Milka wrote on 24 July:

> Dear Aunt!! A week ago, I received the letter that you wrote on 7 June, and yesterday I received the one from 22 June, thank you very much. I apologize for not responding to your first one, but these are the months when we have the most work to do

and now it is only three of us. [Milka, Janez and Pepka]. Even if we wanted to hire a worker, we are not allowed to do so. If the Committee learned about it, they would fine the worker 10,000 dinars, and the landowner who hired him would have to give a piece of land to the community, since he has shown that he is unable to cultivate it on his own.

You mentioned in your letter that you were planning to visit us this summer, but since Dad has died, you will not come. I understand how hard it is for you to lose your dear mother and father, and your beloved brother, but my dear Aunt, we really long to see you. You know that we, too, have just lost our dear father, our Nona, our sister, and our brother, and have nobody but you, dear Aunt. It does not matter to us if Godmother Bilkotova is alive or not. Dad had been sick for a long time and she did not come to see or comfort him. We cannot understand why they are so angry with us or with you. I met her on my way from the post office, and she stopped for a while. I told her that I received a letter from Aunt in America and she said: "So you did, what do I care?"

Antonija Cesareva went to the Committee five days after Dad died. She told them that the caretaker of the land did not exist anymore and that the farm should be given to her, as well as a piece to each of the others, and that in the case that the Committee did not want to do this, then the land should be nationalized. Therefore, my dear Aunt, we ask you to come back, at least to take care of things related to your farm. The Committee does not care about what the family needs, but only how much of the total usable land we have. They do not measure how things are produced now, but what used to be produced on the land when it was worked on. Depending on how much land we have, that much we must give to the state. In the spring we had to give them an ox that weighed five kvintals. They haven't paid for it yet, and the same goes for the entire harvest.

You are writing that my brother, Janezek, should be a diligent and attentive landowner, just like our beloved Dad. Janez

is diligent and attentive and we will continue to work hard
and follow the path that he has set. But unless things get better, we will not be landowners anymore. They will take away
everything and make it communal. Dear Aunt, Dad wanted
to write to you about all of this, but death was faster and he
will never write to you again. We thought that he would be
better by spring. When he was feeling worse, he said that he
was not afraid of death, but that he would like to live for a
few more years so that he could help us. We always asked him
for advice and we told him everything. Now there is nobody
to ask or talk to. It is so sad. Wherever we turn we can see
him in everything. Even when he was sick, he was still working; he could not be without work and this is why he died;
because he worked too much and because he suffered through
so much sorrow.

He is buried right on top of your father. On one side is your
mother, and on the other side is my sister, Francka. Now all four
of them are together. The wreath was made from dry flowers
that we bought in Rijeka. We kept two flowers from the bou-
quet; I am sending you one of them so that you can have this
sad memory of our beloved Daddy, your brother.

Dear Aunt, we have not yet received the package that you
sent, but we hope that we will soon. We thank you from our
hearts. We send you many greetings, to all of you, but especially
to you, my dear Aunt, from me, from Pepka, from my Mommy,
and from Janezek.

Milka Fabjančič

Between the pages of the letter an impression remains of a red
carnation, the national flower of Slovenia. The impression is there,
but the flower is gone. "Janezek should be a diligent and attentive
landowner, just like his beloved Dad" sounds like a warm-up to
the topic of who would become the caretaker for Jurkotevi. Jožef's
persistence and devotion to his sister's interests would be a hard
act for anyone to follow.

For 37 years Rezina had not written to Mary and now they were the only siblings left. Mary sent a generous package, knowing that Rezina would feel obliged to write a letter of thanks. Rezina's poor penmanship, spelling, and odd grammar made her letters barely decipherable and what she had to say was simple and halting. She wrote in 1950:

Dear Sister, After so many years you are hearing from me again. I received the unexpected package from you with things that are so essential for everything. You have really pleased me. So, from my heart, I thank you.

We have not been writing like sisters, but that is not my fault. I only felt that I should write and explain the wrongs which have happened to me.

I write very slowly, because I have weak eyes. I would have to go to Koper or Sežana to get glasses, however I do not have the nerve to do this because of the long bus ride. I also have a heart problem and varicose veins. I need medicine that cannot be found here, but my daughter, Marija, was able to send it from Trst.

I am alone with my husband, Jože, and our son, Frane. Jože has a leg that has been hurting him from the beginning of the year. He has two big sores on it which require bandages. He is able to use his cane to walk to the Co-operative.

This is how it is with my children: Marija lives in Trst, and lives like a lady. Her older daughter is married and has one boy who is 12 years old. Tončka works in a hospital in Postojna as a midwife. Francka is married into the Skalon family in Markovščina which is rather difficult for her, but her daughter is very diligent and the best student at the school in Hrpelje. Her little boy has not yet started school. Frane is at home with me; he works like a beast and is diligent. He is a careful master but unfortunately, he is still alone. My dear sister, things are slow here. Conditions are really bad here with us, and still worse is that they are skinning us, so that soon we will not be able to maintain our household.

Your sister, *Rezina*

I was disappointed that Rezina did not give an explanation for her failure to write. I suspect that it was a matter of personalities as well as deep-seated sibling rivalries, and had something to do with the fact that she was the oldest child. Rezina hung onto small slights from the days of their youth. She mentions them, but they are hard to understand. One time, they were all employed for a job cutting grass and a mean comment was made, but this is hardly a reason to not write for 40 years. Additionally, Rezina didn't talk to her mother, brother, or other sister. She seems to have married a good man and had been a loving, successful mother, but she just did not like her family. Rezina's husband died soon after this letter in 1950 and Mary and Rezina continued exchanging letters over the next decade or so.

The eldest daughter, Marija, who was married and living in Trieste, died in 1958. She had been held up by many as a paragon of Slovene womanhood: beautiful, modest, hardworking, kind, and a help and consolation to her widowed mother. When she died at the early age of 53, it broke her mother's heart. Rezina wrote, "Many thanks for your condolences on the death of my daughter, Marija. This loss has affected us all powerfully. We lost her as though someone stole her from us. She was with us on 1st May and we buried her on 29 May. She had poor blood and nerves, which sent her to a premature grave." Rezina died in 1963 at the age of 80. Frane never married. He farmed part-time and worked at the toy factory on Gabrk. I met him in 1977 when he lived alone at Bilkotevi. He was an odd-looking, tall, spindly man in his sixties who did not smile or say much, and at the time I thought he was perhaps a little simple-minded. In retrospect, I was just a young woman who didn't know a word of Slovene, so perhaps my initial impression was unfair and he was just a reticent person.

Mary also reached out to her old friend Božidar Kastelic, whose fortune went from inherited wealth to complete impoverishment in the mid-1930s. He married Karlina, the family's maid, after they had their first son out of wedlock. She died giving birth to their third child in 1930. Their first son, Zlatozar, was 21 years old when he died in an Italian submarine wartime disaster. The youngest child, Božidar, studied at the University of Ljubljana and became a civil engineer. Dana, the middle child was the single mother of young Egon, who was conceived during the war. His father was a soldier who disappeared. The old Božidar lived with Dana and spent his time writing poetry, a venerable Slovenian pastime. He sent some of the poems to Mary. I find it amusing that Božidar mentioned the success of the choral society and the fire department, in which he had a hand. In his very last letter of February 1948, Jožef had said there was no singing society, and that the fire department only organized dances. It makes one imagine that Jožef was a complete curmudgeon and Božidar a useless dreamer, but the truth was, no doubt, somewhere in the middle. His penmanship had become only slightly less ostentatious than it was 20 years earlier. Again, I suggest that his letter be read out loud so that you will hear the poet.

Materija, Seventh of January 1956
Esteemed friends,
Janez and Marica Fradel!
    On Christmas Eve I came into possession of your much appreciated letter to us.
    On that evening, as so many little lights glowed around the Christmas tree, I was touched not so much by the scene, but by your noble good wishes, which awakened in me unforgettable beautiful memories of our past. Suddenly, as I read, all my sense of humanity brought to memory those flowering times of our never-to-return past together. But feelings for worthy and honest people never pass, and all these feelings serve to shelter and encourage me in these present

*and so difficult times, when because of cruel fate, the paths of our
lives have turned to a narrow, thorny way.*

*I live on the modest earnings of a forestry worker so that I earn a
humble scrap of bread for myself and for my family. I have carried
out this work, which I obtained through the great goodness of your
good-hearted relative, Ivan Godina, for four years now, doing the job
and the battle of the sons of this earth.*

*Here everything is drudgery, and there is no longer that liveliness
in one's glance that there once was.*

Your friend,

Božidar Kastelic

Mary gave Božidar a subscription to *Prosveta* and a Slovenian
American newspaper and occasionally sent him two dollars. In
return he sent her copies of his poems and reminded her of the
grandeur and warmth of their youth. Božidar waxed poetic about
almost everything, including the radio that his son bought for him
in Holland while on an engineering internship. He wrote on 8
December 1956:

Esteemed Friend,

*Let it also be recognized from the depths of my heart that I wish
you all, all the best on your birthday, because you harvested your
noble heart. The years pass quickly.*

*I too will have another year on the 28th of April, 70 years. Looking
only at the number, my whole life seems like a dream.*

*It also awakened for me memories of our never-to-return past
together but we must follow the lead of our times, which pass so
quickly and dictate to us a definite future.*

*I also remember your beautiful "alto" voice because with Maria
Babič you were the best singer in our choir.*

*And still today, while we very rarely sing now, a bitter past
abducts us from the mood of long ago splendid past times.*

*I decided to send you for today, only four of my poems and another
time if you will permit me, please, I will send more from my modest*

scraps. I feel happy that you so good-heartedly consider my little poems such that they love to hurry to you, to you. I repeat, that you are blessed souls and my good sincere friends.

This winter I did not work, as they suspended work for financial considerations. but in the spring, there will be work and I will again embark upon the struggle for existence.

Here we have had, even for winter, extraordinarily beautiful weather. For a couple of days there was almost wintry cold and Slavnik and other Brkini hills were all snow covered.

His death was announced in the newspaper:

BOŽIDAR KASTELIC HAS DIED

The news has suddenly resounded, that on the 13th of February, 1966, the noble heart of comrade Božidar Kastelic, founder, and honorary member of the Fire Department of Materija, ceased beating.

He was born on the 28th of April, 1887, in Povžane at Materija. He was an exemplary father to his family. In the year 1908 he founded and provided for the financial support of the Voluntary Fire Department of Materija. From that time, he selflessly attended every fire and natural disaster, for which he received several awards. Because of exhaustion and insidious illness, the fire department elected him as an honorary member. Despite his great age, until the last two years he took part in the action of extinguishing forest fires. The indefatigable Kastelic was never late for a meeting or parade, where he was always at the head, as the bearer of the department's colors. He was popular with the firefighters and the populace, as was demonstrated in his last journey from the house of bereavement to the cemetery of Brezovica, whence he was escorted by numerous uniformed members of the Fire Departments of Materija and Sežana, and the rest of the population of the local and surrounding villages.

In accordance with his wish, he was carried to his final resting place on the shoulders of firefighters from his local department. In front of the house of bereavement a last salutation was heard from the fire siren.

By the open grave, the president of the fire department, Vidmar, bade farewell to the late Kastelic. His final place of rest was buried under many wreaths. We, the members of the Fire Department of Materija, express our sincere condolences to his relatives.

For the Fire Department A.V.

CHAPTER TWENTY-FIVE

1961: Resolution

Janez Fabjančič did not become the caretaker of Jurkotevi after his father's death. As the younger son, he had planned to leave but his elder brother never came home and his family needed him, so he became the master of Biščevi. Janez was more relaxed than his father, more likely to mind his own business, and avoid trouble. He married Karolina, a girl from Hotična, and worked at the toy factory while farming part-time. They kept some cows, they killed a pig and made pršut, they electrified and improved the house—and essentially lived an easier version of the past. Their four children received good educations in a local school and opportunities for university and technical schools.

His cousin, Ivan Godina, left his unhappy home at 16, trained as a medic in the Italian navy, and learned to speak and write Italian. After Italy's surrender, he was imprisoned in a factory work camp in Germany. He returned home to become the master at Bazletevi, with a bride named Danila and a job as a forestor. (photo 25) He used his position to help the ailing, impoverished Božidar Kastelic get a little work in forestry, and, as head of the Fire Department, he made sure that Božidar was awarded the honorary membership he deserved as its founder. Ivan was also a member of the local government and headed up the co-operative of local farmers.

When people needed something, they went to Ivan, which explains why every story in Povžane and Bač includes something, good or bad, about him. His military experience, literacy and language abilities, connections through work and committees, and his family ties provided him with plenty of *zrihtač*, a word that means the ability to use one's connections to manipulate people and the system to get things done. It's still an important asset in Slovenia.

*

Opasilo at Biščevi in August 2014 brought many extended family home because it was the first visit from my husband and me, and they were eager to meet us. I brought my grandmother's old photos and we admired our family tree that Lojze displayed on a poster board. After a great feast and a little dancing to accordian tunes provided by a pair of musicians who traveled house to the house, we sat in the shade and the bilingual young adults listened intently and translated as I asked Pepca Fabjančič, the oldest among us, to tell me about her life. She told me her pivotal story, one that included Ivan Godina. After the war she was treated for TB, and helped her parents and twin siblings with the work. The family farmed less after her father died, and Milka and her new husband, Marjan Mezgec from Hotična, moved near Koper. The importance of farming in Brkini and the valley was declining in accordance with Tito's industrialization plan. As such, Pepca's prospects for marrying a man with land and earning a living through farming were dim. In the old days she might have found domestic work in Trieste, but now she could not even go there. Other people in her position, like her cousins from Artviže, gained work in Maribor or Koper, or made their way to displaced persons camps in Italy for the chance to go to Australia. The camps were full of political refugees such as Goettschee, collaborators, Domobranci, and Ustaša, but these economic refugees joined them. Pepca, too, wanted to go to Australia. She applied for a visa to see her aunt in Trieste with a plan to enter a camp, but her application was denied.

To cross illegally to Trieste required getting through a heavily guarded barbed wire fence. In 1951, Pepca and three others attempted this at night. Two of them were shot and killed. Pepca and Ema, a woman from Gradišica, were given two-year prison sentences. Pepca served four months in the Sežana prison then transferred to Ljubljana, but the prison there was overcrowded, so she was sent to one outside Zagreb, where she shared a room with 60 others. She described her sentence as "light punishment," which required that she farm, sew, and knit. On her release in 1953, she returned to Biščevi to live with her mother, brother Janez, his wife Karolina, and their children.

Around January 1954, Ivan Godina used his *zrihtač* to obtain a visa for Pepca to visit Trieste, and she left promptly. The next day the police were there to interrogate and harass her family. The family said then, and for many years afterwards, that they did not know how she got a visa, but in recent years they admitted that they always knew it was Ivan. Pepca was still staying with her great aunt on 24 October 1954, when Trieste and Zone A officially became part of Italy. Pepca was counted as an Italian citizen when the census was taken and she married Mario Pangos, an Italian, on 3 August 1955.

In 1956, Pepca's niece, 19-year-old Marica from Maharinčevi, decided to make her break from Yugoslavia and the plan was that Pepca and Mario would join Marica in a camp and together they would leave for Australia. Pepca told me that they met up with Marica just for a day in Udine but Pepca could not leave Italy because she had to have surgery to remove a tubercular kidney. She was 27. Marica spent six months in camps before she was permitted to go to Sydney on her own, and there she met and married Vladimir Basioli, a Croatian immigrant.

In 1960, when Pepca dared to return to visit her mother, she was arrested in Koper. Because her Italian passport predated her marriage, she was given 24 hours to leave the country, and the police came to Povžane to make sure that she was gone. If her passport had been based on her marriage to an Italian, she would have faced more severe consequences. Pepca and Mario had one child, Fabio, who was born in 1964, and spent much of his youth with his cousins in Povžane because Pepca remained in poor health. Finally, in the 1970s, the border sufficiently relaxed so that Pepca could visit her family.

I met Pepca, Mario, and Fabio in 1977 in their apartment in Trieste. I remember she said I was just like Jane, and I marveled she remembered Jane from her visit in 1937. Around 1980 they moved to a house on the main road in Pesek, Italy, just 100 yards from the Slovenian border. Nowadays, the wires and passport control are gone and the sign reads: "Welcome to Italy."

At opasilo Pepca's memory was good. She finished her story with: "There was so much suffering... it was all so unnecessary... What was it all about? ... now we drive back and forth to Italy and it is all so easy." At the end of that day, her Italian husband Mario, and Emmanuele, the Italian husband of her grandniece Martina, helped her into the car, and drove the 12 miles to her home in Italy. She died two weeks later, at the age of 89.

*

Even after the war and the death of Jožef Fabjančič, my grandparents still fostered some dream of returning to Povžane in their retirement, and Jane encouraged that dream. She was still working at Latrobe Hospital and Frank was at Kennametal and they had daily contact with her parents. In early 1951 Jane was pregnant with her first child at 37 years old. The child was stillborn at six months, and it was discovered that Jane had metastatic colon cancer. She died within weeks of her diagnosis. Her parents were devastated. Her siblings were grief stricken and their loss increased the rift with Frank Drasler.

My aunt Jane had been the magnet that held her family together, she strengthened her parents connection to Slovenia, and with her

gone, returning to the four acres under Slavnik lost its importance.
At the same time, my grandparents grappled with the news that
Pepca Fabjančič was starting her prison sentence. Thinking about
their remaining children—John, Joe, Mary Elizabeth and Sylvia—
and their grandchildren, they began to consider the meaning of
family connections, the feasibility of maintaining them, the wisdom
of ever returning to live in a communist country, and the decision to
liquidate their assets there. My grandparents asked Ivan Godina to
manage the sale of Jurkotevi and its four acres under Slavnik, which
included the remnants of a dwelling and 13 different plots of land.

The individual parcels were offered to people they knew. The parents of Ivan Godina's wife purchased one field. Joe Godina agreed to
purchase Veliki njevo (Big Field) and the house. He paid John Fradel
$1,100 directly for the field, but never paid for the house. At auction
on 22 April 1956, Ivan sold the house and the remaining plots to
a variety of individuals. He collected 300,000 dinars. The dinar
was unstable, and sadly, this was the equivalent of 350 U.S. dollars
in 1956 and the rate was falling.* After the sales were completed,
Ivan sent this letter. In May 1957, he provided John and Mary with
a copy of the document he sent to Belgrade to initiate the transfer
of the proceeds to the U.S.

> *Bač, 14 December 1956*
> Dear Aunt and Brother-in-law!
> The remainder of Your estate was sold on 22 April 1956. You
> are writing that my brother, Jože, will keep his promise and
> pay You directly for the Veliko Njevo. Regarding matters with
> the father of my wife, I agree that we should leave things as
> they are. In my last letter, I forgot to ask You what You want me
> to do with Your money. Do You want me to send Your savings
> book to America, or will You leave the money here, should You
> come to visit us? Your visit would really make us happy. I have
> not received the permit yet, and I do not know how to send the
> money in dollars. **But, do not worry about the transfer of the
> property, we will take care of everything.**

*Stojanović. Exchange Rate Regimes of the Dinar. 2008.

*

In the era before television, we kids had time to mull over the complexities of the universe we gleaned from listening to our parents' conversations. This particular memory must have started around 1956, when I was four years old. I know that I was not yet in school, and my sister, who arrived in 1957, had not yet been born because I was home alone with my mother all day.

Listening to my parents talk, I thought that my family had some dark secret, that we were not really Americans, and that my father had a problem because of it. In the evenings my parents fretted, filled out papers, and talked a lot about Jane. I heard words like Slovenes and SNPJ, and I knew we feared the Russians, who were from somewhere else, like Japanese and Germans were from somewhere else. My brothers were not worried so I decided that I was the problem, believing I was really an alien that no one knew about. My theory surmised I was really a Russian. One evening, two men in suits came to the house, which made my parents really nervous. I was sent to my room. No one knew I was Russian, not even my parents, it seemed, but soon after the visit from the men in suits, things got better.

Now as an adult I understand that my father had taken a job in the U.S. Army Ordnance School in 1952, just a few months before I was born, and around 1956 he was ready to be promoted but needed a higher-level security clearance. It was the McCarthy era and the government was aggressively seeking and weeding out communists. Ethel and Julius Rosenberg had been executed for spying. My grandparents still owned land in communist Yugoslavia, they made donations to the Yugoslav Socialist Party before the war, were active in S.N.P.J., and my father still belonged to it. He paid his subscription for life insurance, and occasionally went to one of their social functions. Jane had been a Socialist Party member, although her devotion to it diminished after the New Deal fulfilled many of the goals workers had sought and her participation in World War Two changed her world views.

Despite the questioning of past affiliations, my father did get his clearance and promotion, and continued to belong to S.N.P.J., which consisted mainly of attending its annual picnic in Pennsylvania. I was surprised (as a child might be when she realizes her parents are real people who exist independent of her needs) to see my parents having a good time dancing to the bands that played Slovenian polkas and waltzes in the wooden pavilion. My father even took me for a spin around the dance floor. His family usually spoke Slovene among themselves, so he spoke Slovene to the people he met at the picnic. Once, an older man wearing a brimmed hat, stopped to speak to my father. He smiled at me and teased me. I tried hard to be a good girl, even though I was irritated, but when he put his hat on my head, I was so infuriated that I took it off and threw it on the ground. My father was embarrassed, and tried to laugh it off, but it brought an end to the conversation, then my father bought me pink cotton candy. I now know that man was Joe Godina because years later I saw a picture of him wearing that same hat.

There were further talks between my parents about the farm in Slovenia and I never understood what these conversations were about until all of the letters received from Europe over decades were translated to English. I also discovered in my father's scrapbook a small paper that looked like a bank deposit receipt. On it was written J. Godina, $1,100, and a date in the 1950s. It was an eye-opening moment for me—the receipt for Veliki njevo.

Looking back to the 1970s, when I asked my grandmother about her life, and listened to what my father had to say and what my mother overheard, I was never given an honest story about what happened to the family property in Povžane. I was told that my grandparents sent money back to buy a farm which perhaps they would go back to, or it would be an investment, but the Italian occupation, the Second World War, and communism had prevented their return. An inheritance was never mentioned. My grandmother told me that she thought John had some sisters, but she knew nothing about them. With this background in mind, let us continue with Ivan Godina's correspondence.

*

At the same time that Jurkotevi was being sold off in pieces, Ivan Godina needed the cooperation of his brother in America to register his inheritance of Bazletevi, but Joe had not responded to any letters from Slovenia since the death of their mother in 1936.

> *10 Dec 1957*
>
> Dear Aunt and Brother-in-law,
>
> In October, we were summoned to the court regarding probate proceedings for the property of my late father and my Nona, since she was the owner of one half of the land at Bazletevi. My sister Zora came with me and said that she does not want the inheritance and Fanika provided a similar written statement to the court. The judge gave me statements for my Uncle Milan in Maribor, and for brother Jože to sign, which I am to mail to each of them. But Jože never returned it to me and without it, I cannot do anything. I therefore ask You to write to Jože, my brother, to sign that statement and to send it back to me as I need it desperately to resolve this family matter.

With prodding from John and Mary Fradel, Joe Godina eventually corresponded with Ivan and settled matters at Bazletevi but disputes about Jurkotevi continued even after the auction in 1956.

> *Bač, 26 Feb. 1958*
>
> Dear Aunt and Brother-in-law!
>
> I apologize that we haven't replied sooner but I was waiting to talk to Janez Biščev [Fabjančič] regarding the matter about the field that You also wrote to him about. He told me that he does not acknowledge Your claim that he is the legal owner of that field, and that he will not accept any monetary obligations

from previous times. Regarding Your curiosity about who was writing in Ivan's name, I can tell You that it was his wife. This makes it awkward for me.

One section of Jurkotevi had taxes or a bank lien owed on it and the amount owed exceeded what the land might have brought at auction. John Fradel claimed that he had long ago given this section to Jožef Biščev [Fabjančič], the caretaker of his farm for 30 years, but his son, Janez Biščev, denied ownership. This was inconvenient for my grandfather. If he paid the monetary obligation and sold it to someone else, he would lose money. He hoped Biščevi would take the section off his hands. Ivan continued with his criticisms of Biščevi:

> But now, I am almost happy that they have shown their true nature. They have a lack of gratefulness for the profits that they made with Your farm and the packages that You sent them. What can we do? These are people who are nice only when there is some benefit for them, and when that is gone, all good manners disappear. If they had a little bit of humility, they should not have forgotten You, if for nothing else, then for the packages that You sent during those times when they were so sorely needed. At that time, they were so pumped about it, that they did not want to talk to us, although we've always been there for them. In particular, I was always helping Pepca, and I intervened on her behalf to get the permit when she wanted to go to Trieste.
>
> In our family everything is as usual, we are working hard to survive. Daughter Mirica is at secondary school in Kozina, and son Radko is in elementary school. School requisites and clothes are expensive, particularly when compared to our salaries. My wife is a seamstress and she makes clothes from old things and from some fabric left from the packages that you've sent to us, but now that is gone.

Ivan Godina and Janez Biščev bickered for years over other pieces of Jurkotevi, despite the fact that neither of them had a significant income from farming. Ivan and Joe Godina also argued about the land despite the fact that they lived on opposite sides of the ocean. In 2012, I sat down for lunch in Pennsylvania with Joe Godina Jr. He told me that after his father bought Veliki njevo, he was furious when his brother Ivan planted potatoes on it. "Why?" I asked, innocently wondering what harm there could be in growing some extra potatoes in his absence. Joe Godina Jr. explained that under Tito's laws (briefly), ownership of unused land could be claimed by assuming cultivation, so Joe Sr. thought that his brother was trying to steal Veliki njevo.

Even for a master *zhritač* like Ivan Godina, it took four years to work through the communist bureaucracy to get the proceeds from the farm transferred to a U.S. Bank. Ivan wrote to Belgrade six times before he got a response. Copies of all the sales contracts, the will, documentation of my grandfather's departure for America, his U.S. citizenship papers, and his original savings account book needed to be sent to Belgrade. Meanwhile Ivan suffered a serious concussion that put him out of work for eight months. Inflation was rampant in the new Yugoslavia and as time passed my grandparents watched their nest egg shrivel.

> *8 May 1958*
> Dear Aunt and Brother-inlaw!
> We received your letter from 30 March. Thank you for the newspaper clipping about the honor that You received on Your retirement, we also congratulate You from our hearts. Regarding Your money from the sale of the farm, I will take care of this and let You know how things are. This delay seems strange to me as well, but what can we do?
> Here everything is as usual and we are all healthy.
> Do You remember Ivan Fradel from Bač? He died in the month of April and soon after, Ana Jurkotova, [John's aunt] who was the oldest woman in our village, died after 88 years.

Ivan Fradel from Bač and my grandfather were first cousins; they were both born in 1889. John remembered him well. Ivan was the eldest son at Fradelevi at Bač #3. A hero in the Great War, he saved his team during an avalanche in the Julian Alps and was awarded the Silver Cross by Emperor Franz Josef. He returned to Fradelevi and married Marija Kljun from Misliče. Their eldest son, called Nane, emigrated to Australia in the 1950s. Their second son, Alojz, never married, became the sole inhabitant of Fradelevi, and the village n'er-do-well, an alcoholic who died in 2008. I went to the home of their daughter, Marija, who had married a Ban in Bač, but her memory had failed her so that she could not even remember that she had been born a Fradel.

Ivan Fradel had a younger brother, Frane, who was another member of the ill-fated 97th Regiment and was permanently disabled after both his legs were broken in battle during the Great War. He lived the rest of his life in the Brkini village of Rodik with his wife, Veronike, and two daughters.

Ivan Fradel was the last one to bear sons with the name Fradel in Brkini and the valley. The Fradel lineage, which can be traced back to the 1600s when church record-keeping started, was notably lacking in male children. In the 20th century, two migrated to America, two to Maribor, and one to Australia. Thus, the name has disappeared in Slovenia and is only a dim memory in the lives of their daughters.

*

John Fradel had worked at Vulcan Mold since it opened in 1923. He was its most senior employee in 1958, when he retired at age 68. (photos 26 and 27) He had much to be proud of: two married sons with large families, two daughters, each married with a child. All were gainfully employed and firmly Americanized. But he had losses too, the most painful of which was the loss of his beloved Jane, and then the loss of all ties to Slovenia. Anyone that he knew, aside from his sisters Antonija and Pepina, was dead, and he severed those ties with the sale of all his holdings. Jurkotevi truly was no more.

The money from the sale of the farm was transferred to the U.S. only shortly before my grandfather's death. John Fradel, known as "Pop" to his children, died from a stroke on 5 January 1961. He was 72 years old. Ivan Godina wrote on 22 February 1961:

> Dear Aunt,
>
> Please accept our apology for our silence, but because of my long illness we could not write to You. I was ill for eight months after I had a concussion. First of all, we are sending You our condolences; we were touched by the news that Your husband passed away.
>
> Dear aunt, it is about Your farm that You sold. The buyers cannot enter the lots that they bought from You into the land register because Rudolf and Pepina, the siblings of Your late husband, are still listed in the cadaster as heirs. The buyers went to the court, and the judge gave them this written statement that You need to give to Rudolf. Pepina, Your husband's sister, will also have to sign a statement that she is giving up the inheritance. Please give this statement to Rudolf. He needs to have it notarized in a court. The buyers say that unless this is resolved, they will demand their money back, along with the expenses incurred so far. I will end for now and I ask You to send it as soon as possible as it is really urgent.

My grandmother's response was curt. The fact that her husband did not have a clear title was a detail that she and my grandfather thought had been forgotten or overlooked. She also knew that Jurkotevi would revert to Rudy upon John's death, and then to Pepina. They had not warned Ivan Godina and he had not done his research. The original letter, in my grandmother's handwriting, was tucked in with the letters she received from Ivan. Was this a copy, or did she never send it?

Latrobe, Pa. 22 March 1961
  Dear Ivan,
  I received your letter, thank you very much for your greetings and for expressing your condolences; I'm glad to hear that

you've recovered from your illness. Regarding the sale of the farm, everything was done officially and legally according to the laws of the Government of Yugoslavia and with this, this matter is now closed—

I'm sending best regards to the entire family and I wish to all of You this precious health.

Your aunt,

M. E. Fradel

*

When Valentin Fradel wrote his last will and testament in 1914, he had six children, and could not have imagined that Stefanija and Marija would precede him to the grave. In keeping with the tradition that the eldest son inherited all, John was to inherit the house and land, with 600 guldinars set aside for each of the other children. Since Janez was in America, he stipulated that he would inherit *only if he came back to Slovenia*, and if he did not return, Rudolf would inherit. In 1920 the probate judge assumed that John's return was imminent. Antonija and Pepina received the 600 guldinar that was due to them, but John could not just buy them out. In case he might have forgotten or misunderstood, Jožef Fabjančič, his cousin, brother-in-law, and caretaker for Jurkotevi, told him over and over again that he had to return to file his claim in court, before he could get sole ownership.

The judge in 1920 ruled that if John and Rudolf were to die first, the land would go to Pepina, not to John's widow or children, a decision that Jožef had challenged unsuccessfully. In the long absence of their brothers, Antonija and Pepina logically believed that ownership defaulted to them. Each time they tried to address this matter in court they failed, because Jožef continued to advocate vigorously for John's right to return and claim his inheritance. When John Fradel died in 1961, technically Rudy was the rightful owner, but he cared nothing for the land. After he left in 1921, he never looked back. If my grandparents had asked Rudy, he might have signed off, but Pepina's co-operation was unlikely without a payout.

Thus, when the sale of the land was completed on 22 April 1956, Ivan collected the money, banked it, and jumped through hoops for four years before the money was sent to John Fradel's American bank account. But when Ivan Godina and the new owners went to the Municipal Office, they could not transfer the titles because John was not the sole owner. In February 1961 my grandmother had no motivation to help Ivan. She already had the money and she wasn't present in Povžane to suffer the wrath of the village. Ivan was stuck with the problem of having stiffed his friends and neighbors with a false deal.

*

In 2014, when I visited Slovenia, I believed the farm had been sold and these details were unknown to me. My husband and I were in Povžane, standing at the site where Jurkotevi once stood. I spread my arms over the green square and playfully fantasized that it was mine. About ten years earlier, Suhečevi had torn down their old home and built a larger one, which crossed three meters onto Jurkotevi land. As they were building, the question of encroachment had been raised. Suhečevi said they had called someone in America, and received permission to build there. Everyone in Povžane believed that they were lying. The family urged me to take action to reclaim the land that they thought still belonged to my grandfather. We joked around, and I imagined what it would be like to own land in Povžane. Biščev went to the town office and printed off the deeds for the 13 parcels of Jurkotevi, and sure enough, there were four still in the name of John Fradel, 1004 Alexandria St., Latrobe, Pennsylvania, USA.

The arguments were impassioned. They urged me to fight for the land. Someone could use the space for a new home and Suhečevi were bad people—communists who had done something illegal, and should be held accountable. As I listened it occurred to me that I did not actually have the authority to claim the land, as I have twelve cousins and siblings to consider as rightful heirs of my grandfather. Further, there was the question of unpaid taxes for close to 60 years, lawyers, and the likelihood that once I claimed the land, it would be contested by dozens of people who considered it their own despite the lack of a deed. My husband alerted me that it was no longer a playful joke. On our next trip we made sure the subject never came up. I talked to all my American relatives and no one ever received the call Suhečevi claimed to have made. Subsequently, I feel confident that Suhečevi and Zvrtevi, the abutters, paid for the land in 1956 and were among those who could not register their titles.

Antonija was the only one who actually wanted to farm the four acres under Slavnik. When her last attempt to claim it in 1949 failed, with Cesarevi rebuilt, and her children in Maribor, she lost the desire to farm there. She and Pepina went to their graves angry with John, since they felt he had not owned Jurkotevi, yet he pocketed the proceeds. When I asked Antonija's elderly daughters about it, I was given this simple understatement: "When the land was sold, she was disappointed that she got nothing."

Epilogue

Brothers Ivan and Joe Godina got past their squabbling about land and developed a genuine relationship. Joe Godina's beloved wife, Jessie, was killed in a car accident in 1958. Sometime in the 1970s, Joe, his partner, Betty, and her son Johnny, traveled to Yugoslavia to meet Ivan. Later, Ivan and Danila returned the visit. Ivan and his sister, Fani, also mended their fences. They often visited each other, and Fani's husband Viktor would come to Bač to help Ivan repair and paint Bazletevi.

Zora remained in Trieste. In 1947 she married a second time, to an Italian, Oreste Calas. They didn't have any children. She and her new husband wrote to Joe in America, but again, he did not respond. By the time Aunt Mary met Zora in 1977, she was a widow. She had been a housekeeper for a wealthy family that had a high regard for their dogs. In their will, they left their apartment and fortune to Zora so that she could take care of them. When those died, she acquired one of her own. The picture of her that stands out in my mind is that of an elderly woman in rhinestone-studded butterfly glasses, holding a little brown dog. We call her "The Dog Lady."

The sons of Biščevi and Maharinčevi continue to reside in Povžane. They and their children operate local businesses or commute to jobs in Koper and Ljubljana.

Jože Fabjančič had been missing in action since December 1942. A few years after the war, a man visited Biščevi. He told them that he had been with Jože during a battle with Russian forces. They were leaping across ditches together and when the man looked back, Jože was gone. That was all they knew for over 40 years. In 1991, when the Republic of Slovenia became independent and war records were no longer suppressed, the family learned that Jože had died in a Russian POW camp on 10 May 1946, a year after the war was over.

The Republic of Slovenia joined the European Union in 2004 and entered the Eurozone (making the euro its official currency) in 2007. It became a NATO member in 2004. Slovenia boasts an excellent education system. English, the official language of the EU, is a requirement of Slovenian education. Slovenians are a people proud of their unique and challenging language, their culture, the achievements of their people in Slovenia and abroad, and their commitment to environmental conservation to preserve the pristine beauty of their nation.

Among the hills of the karst country
there is a beautiful memory of history
the view from Slavnik is famous
it ignites in you feelings to express.
All hurry to that mountain
dreaming there to be amazed
and what is beauty in nature
puts creative power in our hearts.
There our grandfathers sang
they gathered in pleasant company
their voices gave us the memory
that Slavnik is baptized our son.
Ah, Slavnik, accept our greeting
know that kinship selected for you
the most beautiful name among mountains
stay faithful to us until the end.

BOŽIDAR KASTELIC

Acknowledgments

I wish to acknowledge my great uncle Jožef Fabjančič. Through his letters I have come to know him as a man of courage, quietly living his convictions. His eloquent letters and loving devotion to his sister in America, my grandmother, made this story possible. I wish to thank his descendants, the family of Biščevi, for their support. They housed and fed me, searched the church records, helped me to meet relatives, and translated for me. They showed my husband and me "the best" of Slovenia.

A particular gratitude goes to my able and tireless translators: Marinka Fabjančič, Ana Drnovšek, Matej Jerele, and Barbara Babič. A special thank you to Alojz Grahor for his magical powers in getting things done. Thank you to Ivan Fabjančič for his superb local knowledge and again to Marinka for geographic expertise. Who else can show me the line where Brkini begins? Thanks to Nevenka Karba in Maribor who helped me meet the descendants of Jurkotevi who emigrated there. Thanks to everyone in America, Slovenia, and Australia who told a story, recalled a childhood memory, or shared a photograph. Thanks to Jane Withoff and Pat Walker, my American cousins who helped to cover the cost of translating the letters. A special thanks to those who are not just my relatives, but now, my friends.

My husband, Arch Davis, provided endless hours of support. In 2015 Arch decided to learn Slovene, and has translated some of the most difficult to read letters and shared my adventures in Slovenia. Then he edited, proof read, and designed the cover. Grace Davis, our multi-talented, techno-savvy daughter, polished maps and family tree, and bailed me out of technical disasters time after time.

I need to acknowledge David Dolenc for translating nearly 300 letters from an archaic Slovene dialect to English. Although we have lost contact, I hope he will learn his translations have not moldered away in a box. Thank you to Sharon Roznik, my editor. I am so happy she understood the story I was trying to tell. She gently advised me when to let go of stray bits that distracted from the narrative, helped reorganize, and smooth out the flow. She was the medication I needed to restore my confidence that this is a story worth telling. As I wrote sometimes I forgot which century I was living in, as I strongly felt the correlation between 1930s Europe and our lives. Sharon saw this, too. What do ordinary people do when they feel things are going the wrong way? What could Jožef have done differently? I hope this story will inspire its readers to ask themselves this question and seek answers.

Glossary

baul	A wooden suitcase typically used by soldiers, which doubled as a wardrobe when stood on its end.
boršt	Forested land.
brin	Juniper berries used to flavor gin.
burja	The strong winds that funnel south from the Alps through the Vipava valley.
carabinieri	Italian policemen.
čentižim	The Slovenian word for a one-cent Italian coin or centisimo.
Chetniks	Bands of fighters dedicated to nationalism or restoration of the monarchy.
dinar	Currency of Yugoslavia.
dolina	A valley or a bowl like sink hole in the karst.
Domobranci	"Homeguard" were regiments of Slovenes organized by the Germans to protect their homes against Partisan attacks.
Edinost	A newspaper and political society of the Slovenian left, closed by fascists in 1928.
flysch	The nonporous bedrock of the Brkini ridge.

gostilna	An establishment to eat and drink similar to a pub, which sometimes offered rooms.
guldinar	Official currency of the Austro-Hungarian Empire until 1892, but continued to be used concurrently with kroner till both were replaced with Italian lire.
Irredentismo	"Redemption" was the official Italian policy to rid the lands of ancient Rome from the taint of occupying cultures.
Julian March	Italian name for Primorska.
karst	Land with a limestone bedrock.
Kingdom of S.H.S.	Kingdom of Serbia, Hrvaška (Croatia), and Slovenia 1918-1929, which was renamed the Kingdom of Yugoslavia when King Alexander proclaimed a dictatorship.
klobase	Slovenian sausage.
kolina	Place for butchering a pig, typically done in November.
kroner	Official currency of the Austro-Hungarian Empire from 1892 until it was replaced with Italian lire.
kvintal	1,000 kilograms or 2,200 pounds.
lire	Currency of Italy.
Narodni Dom	"People's home" was a multipurpose cultural center for Slovenes in Trieste.
nevesta	The bride of the eldest son.
Nona and nono	Grandmother and grandfather.
opasilo	A summer festival in honor of the patron saint of each village.
Partisans	Bands of communist fighters under the command of Tito.

pršut	Pork that is dry cured and smoked. Called prosciutto in Italy.
Pust	The day before Lent begins, known elsewhere as Fat Tuesday or Mardi Gras.
Risorgimento	"Resurgence" was an Italian political and social movement with the goal to reunite all the states of the Italian peninsula.
šalcerat	A two week training for military reserves of the Austro-Hungarian Empire.
slivje	A plum.
slivovic	A brandy distilled from plums.
stara ata	Old father.
stara tašča	Mother-in-law.
stara tast	Father-in-law.
teta	Aunt.
status animarum	A church record of Baptisms, marriages, and deaths.
tholar	Silver coins of the Austrian Empire from 1741-1856. Long after they were no longer official they retained high value.
TIGR	"Trieste-Istria-Gorica-Rijeka" was an anti-fascist resistance group in Primorska and Istria.
Ustaša	Croatian fascists.
Z bogom	"With God." A phrase usually used to close a letter.
Zbogom	"Goodbye." Also used to close a letter.
zrihtač	The ability to use one's connections to manipulate people and the system to get things done outside the official channels.

Bibliography

BOOKS

Adamic, Louis. 1934. *The Native's Return: An American Immigrant Visits Yugoslavia and Discovers His Old Country*. New York: Harper & Row.

Adamic, Louis. 1943. *My Native Land*. New York: Harper and Brothers.

Calic, Marie-Janine. 2019. *A History of Yugoslavia*. Purdue University Press. (Knowledge Unlatched Open Access Edition.)

Clarkson, Roy B. 1964. *Tumult on the Mountains: Lumbering in West Virginia 1770-1920*. Parsons, West Virginia: McClain.

Clarkson, Roy B. 1990. *On Beyond Leatherbark: The Cass Saga*. Parsons, West Virginia: McClain.

Corsellis, J. and Ferrar, M. 2005. *Slovenia 1945: Memories of Death and Survival After World War II*. London: I.B. Tauris.

Kertzer, David. 2014. *The Pope and Mussolini: The Secret History of Pius XI and the Rise of Fascism in Europe*. New York: Random House.

Kranjc, Gregor Joseph. 2013. *To Walk with the Devil: Slovene Collaboration and Axis Occupation, 1941-1945*. University of Toronto Press.

Milač, Metod. 2002. *Resistance, Imprisonment, & Forced Labor: A Slovene Student in World War II*. New York: Peter Lang.

Prisland, Marie. 1968. *From Slovenia–To America*. Chicago: The Slovenian Women's Union of America.

Roth, Joseph, Translated by Joachim Neugroschel.1932. *The Radetzky March*. New York: Alfred A. Knopf.

Starič, Peter. 2015. *My Life Under Totalitarianism 1941–1991: The Unusual Life of an Electronics Engineer*. Augusta, Missouri: Sotina Publishing.

INTERNET

Bakic, Dragan, "Milan Stojadinović, The Croat Question and the International Position of Yugoslvia, 1935-1939" Acta Histriae Vol.26 No.1 2018 https://doi.org/10.19233/AH.2018.09

Bowen, C. and D. Last updated Oct 9, 2010. "Slovenia's War. Dismemberment, Denationalization, and Resistance". http://travels.bowenplace .com/europe_2008/history_5/

Brecelj, Marijan 2013. "Babič, Jože (1917–1996)" in *Slovenian biography*. Slovenian Academy of Sciences and Arts, Scientific Research Center of the Slovenian Academy of Sciences and Arts, 2013. http:// www.slovenska-biografija.si/oseba/sbi1001340/#primorski-slovenski -biografski-leksikon

Ceferin, Aleksandra. 2010. "TIGR-Slovenian Anti-Fascist Resistance Movement". Institute for Slovenian Studies of Victoria. https://thezaurus .com/tigr_-_anti-fascist_resistance_movement/

Concordat Watch. "How the Lateran Treaty made the Catholic Church into a State". http://www.concordatwatch.eu/topic-841.843

Draščič, M., Mavrinac, N. et al. 2012. "The Memory of War and Violence in the 20th-century Northeastern Adriatic." https://www.uni-regensburg .de/Fakultaeten/phil_Fak_III/Geschichte/istrien/index.html

Encyclopedia.com. "The Catholic Church in Slovenia". Last updated 2020. https://www.encyclopedia.com/religion/encyclopedias-almanacs -transcripts-and-maps/slovenia-catholic-church

Hays, J.B. 1997. "A History of the 526th Ordnance Tank Maintenance Company". https://www.bobbittville.com/526ordnance.htm

Harej, Zorko. 2013. "Godina, Milena (1912–1995)" in *Slovenian biography*. Slovenian Academy of Sciences and Arts, Scientific Research Center of the Slovenian Academy of Sciences and Arts. 2013. http://www.slovenska-biografija.si/oseba/sbi1010120/#primorski-slovenski-biografski-leksikon.

Imperial War Museums Institute. "Yugoslavian Partisans in London, December 1944". https://www.iwm.org.uk/collections/item/object/205039145

International Encyclopedia of the First World War. Last updated 19 October 2018. "Italian Irrredentism." https://encyclopedia.1914-1918-online.net/article/italian_irredentism

Jamsek, Franc. 2019. "TIGR", published in Slovenia in World War II Facebook Group.

Jevnikar, Ivo. 2013. "Marušič, Drago (1884–1964)" in *Slovenian biography*. Slovenian Academy of Sciences and Arts, Scientific Research Center. 2013. http://www.slovenska-biografija.si/oseba/sbi923340/#primorski-slovenski-biografski-leksikon.

Klabjan, Borut. 2018. "Borders in Arms. Political Violence in the North-Eastern Adriatic after the Great War". Acta Histriae Vol 26 no.4 2018. https://zdjp.si/en/p/actahistriae/

Kodrič, Majda. 1988. "Class consciousness Among the Second Generation: Expectations and Responses Within the Slovene National Benefit Society in the 1920s". Trieste: Migration and Ethnic Themes Vol. 4 No. 1–2. https://hrcak.srce.hr/index.php?show=clanak&id_clanak_jezik=189284

Military Museum of the Slovenian Army, 2009. "World War One and the Slovenians 1914–1918" (Video) https://www.total-slovenia-news.com/videos/6814-world-war-i-the-slovenians-1914-1918

New York Times. 27 July 1913. "WHALE HITS LINER AND KILLS ITSELF—Raised and Shook Kaiser Franz Josef, Over Titanic Grave, as if by a Tidal Wave". https://www.nytimes.com/1913/07/27/archives/whale-hits-liner-and-kills-itself-raised-and-shook-kaiser-franz.html

Nations Encyclopedia. Last updated 2021. "Slovenia-history". https://www.nationsencyclopedia.com/Europe/Slovenia-history.html#b

Potočnik, Dragan. 2011. "Primorski Slovenci v Mariboru 1918–1941" (*Primorskan Slovenes in Maribor*) 1 (21). Centro di ricerche scientifiche della Repubblica di Slovenia: 55–70. http://www.dlib.si/details/URN:NBN:SI :DOC-NWHRRNVS.

Sancin, Boris. 2013. "Furlan, Boris (1894–1957)" in *Slovenian biography*. Slovenian Academy of Sciences and Arts, Scientific Research Center. http:// www.slovenska-biografija.si/oseba/sbi1009170/#primorski-slovenski -biografski-leksikon

Sedmak, Drago. "Austro-Hungarian Army 97th Regiment". http:// www.100letprve.si/en/mejniki/to_the_eastern_front/97th_infantry _regiment/index.html

Stojanović, Biljana. 2008. "Exchange Rate Regimes of the Dinar 1945– 1990: An Assessment of Appropriateness and Efficiency." Oesterreichische National Bank. Workshops No.13/2008. https://www.oenb.at >stojanovic_tcm16-80905

Tuta, Slavko. 2013. "Dekleva, Jože (1899–1969)" in *Slovenian Biography*. Slovenian Academy of Sciences and Arts, Scientific Research Center of the Slovenian Academy of Sciences and Arts. http://www .slovenska-biografija.si/oseba/sbi1007190/#primorski-slovenski- biografski-leksikon

Wikipedia, "The Economy of Italy under Fascism". Last modified December 12, 2020. https://en.wikipedia.org/wiki/Economy_of_Italy _under_fascism

Wikipedia, "Italianization." Last modified 15 January 2021. https:// en.wikipedia.org/wiki/Italianization

Wikipedia, "Slavo Klemenčič." Last modified 19 Nov 2019. https:// sl.m.wikipedia.org/wiki/Slavo_Klemenčič

Wikipedia, "TIGR". Last modified 8 January 2021. https://en.wikipedia .org/wiki/TIGR

World War II U.S. Medical Research Center. "74th General Hospital Unit History." https://www.med-dept.com/unit-histories/74th- general-hospital/